ZEN AND THE FINE ARTS

ZEN AND THE FINE ARTS

SHIN'ICHI HISAMATSU

TRANSLATED BY GISHIN TOKIWA

KODANSHA INTERNATIONAL LTD.

Distributed in the United States by Kodansha International/USA Ltd. through Harper & Row, Publishers, Inc., 10 East 53rd Street, New York, New York 10022. Published by Kodansha International Ltd., 12-21, Otowa 2-chome, Bunkyo-ku, Tokyo 112 and Kodansha International/USA Ltd., 10 East 53rd Street, New York, New York 10022 and 44 Montgomery Street, San Francisco, California 94104. Copyright © 1971 by Kodansha International Ltd. All rights reserved. Printed in Japan.

LCC 76-136562

ISBN 0-87011-519-7

ISBN 4-7700-1007-9 (in Japan)

First edition, 1971

First paperback edition, 1982

CONTENTS

PREFACE

In the Orient a unique complex of cultural forms arose at about the beginning of the sixth century (Liang dynasty) and flourished for about nine centuries, from the end of the seventh (early T'ang dynasty) until the beginning of the fifteenth century (early Ming period). During this time—equivalent to the entire span of the European Middle Ages—this complex of expressions was transplanted both to Korea and Japan. In the case of the latter, from their introduction in the thirteenth century these cultural expressions blossomed remarkably through the fifteenth, sixteenth and seventeenth centuries. Though in decline thereafter, the roots of this cultural complex still remain alive today.

In the following pages, I should like to examine this unitary cultural complex, presenting as many examples of its creative expressions as possible in photographs, so that its uniqueness may be grasped easily and concretely. Then I should like, analytically, to explain what the unique features of this culture are; and, finally, to make clear why the source from which these characteristics derive is nothing but Zen.

Kyoto, 1970

H. S. Hisamatsu

ACKNOWLEDGMENTS

The author wishes to express his profound thanks to Professor Gishin Tokiwa for his careful and laborious work of translation of the present English edition of the original Japanese *Zen to Bijutsu*. His thanks also go to Professors Richard DeMartino and Norman A. Waddell, who in the process of translation cooperated with the translator by refining the English and offering valuable suggestions. Professor Masao Abe served as coordinator throughout the entire period of translation and publication of this English edition, and contributed invaluble suggestions for the improvement of translation. Without his help, publication of the present book would not have been possible.

The publishers wish to express their full gratitude to Shiryū Morita for his support and effort in obtaining the photographic material.

ZEN AND THE FINE ARTS

SURVEY OF THE ZEN FINE ARTS

I. CHINA: THE MONASTIC SPIRIT

The complex of cultural forms here being considered, which gradually appeared after Zen emerged in China around the sixth century and began to flourish, arose as manifestations of the pure, religious operation of Zen—i.e., the vital working of Zen itself, what is called, technically, Zen Activity. (This is a rendering of the term *Zen-ki*, which also contains the meanings of well-spring, movement, dynamism, impulse, thrust, spontaneity, immediacy, etc.) This Zen Activity has found expression, for example, in words, such as the Zen dialogues; in movements and gestures; in the use of utensils such as a bamboo spatula, a staff, a whisk, a lantern; in architectural forms such as a weathered pillar, a monastery building, a wall or fence; and even in nature, such as in mountain colors, the sound of water, a tree, a flower, a bird, and so on. Zen Activity may manifest itself at any time, at any place, and through any object. Expressions of Zen Activity became prevalent as Zen developed into its purist form, what is called Patriarchal Zen.

An example of such Zen Activity is the famous story of "The Lantern Extinguished." This is a Zen "case" that relates how the Chinese Zen monk Te-shan Hsüan-chien (782–865), having entered the blind alley of empty and futile scholastic pursuit, attained Awakening when he encountered the Zen Activity of Zen Master Lung-t'an Ch'ung-hsin (dates unknown) in the latter's blowing out of a lantern candle. Te-shan then burned his commentaries on the *Diamond Sutra*, a scholastic achievement of which he had been so proud as to carry it about the country for public display. Since it gives a general idea of the anecdotal type of Zen literature dealing with the "records," or "recorded cases," of Zen masters, this episode is quoted here from the collection known as the *Wu-men-kuan* (*The Gateless Gate*).

Lung-t'an was once visited by Te-shan, who, seeking further and further elucidation, remained until it grew late. Lung-t'an finally said, "The night deepens. Why don't you retire?"

Te-shan, taking his leave, raised the bamboo blind and went out. Seeing the intense darkness without, he returned and said, "It is dark outside."

Lung-t'an then lit a lantern and offered it to Te-shan. Just as Te-shan was about to take it, Lung-t'an abruptly blew it out. With this, Te-shan suddenly attained Awakening, whereupon he bowed.

Lung-t'an said, "What kind of truth did you see?"

Te-shan said, "Never after today shall I doubt the utterances of all the old masters under heaven."

The next day, Lung-t'an went before the disciples and said, "Within this group there is a man whose canine teeth are like sword trees, whose mouth resembles a bloody plate, and who won't turn his head even when given a blow with a stick. One day he will establish my Way on the top of a solitary mountain peak."

Te-shan then took out his sutra commentaries, and, in front of the meditation hall, raised a torch and said, "Endless, deep analysis is like placing a single hair in the emptiness of space; worldly power is like throwing one drop of water into an immense gorge."

So saying, he took his commentaries and burned them.

In this kind of manifestation of Zen, I think there is something unique, something both extraordinary and artistic. When in the raising of a hand or in a single step something of Zen is present, that Zen content seems to me to possess a very specific, artistic quality. A narrow conception of art might not accept that such manifestations contain anything artistic, but to me it seems that they possess an artistic quality that ordinarily cannot be seen. In fact, in such vital workings of Zen, I believe that something not merely artistic but also beyond art is involved, something toward which art should aim as its goal.

Besides this concrete, manifestative aspect, however, Zen also has an aspect that is "prior to form." For example, when a worthy Zen monk is neither speaking nor moving but just sitting silently before us, there will be something about him that cannot be judged by our usual understanding of silence or quietude, something that is more than either talk or silence, movement or stillness, in their ordinary meanings. We can think of this quality also as being artistic.

This "prior to form" quality is far more basic than the concrete expressions of Zen Activity, for only with the presence of the former is the Activity given meaning. This quality is spoken of in Zen as "when not one thing is brought forth," "where not one particle of dust is raised," "prior to the separation of heaven and earth," "prior to the birth of one's father and mother," "utterance before voice," "not one word spoken," and so on.

Fundamentally, I feel that here something differs from ordinary art, something that art can only attain through transcending itself. From the Zen point of view, this "prior to form" phenomenon is the most basic art. It comes into being at the moment in which Zen is truly present. Compared with this, Zen dialogues, the use of various utensils, or the perception of aspects of nature, as described above, are derivative in the sense that such manifestations are infused with meaning by the "prior to form" quality.

Issuing out of this Zen Activity, the Zen use of words gradually became literary. The first Zen literature took the form of verse, the so-called *ge* or *ju*. Sometimes this verse was metrical, with conventional rhymes and tones, and sometimes it was completely free of formality. Zen Activity manifest in words favored the use of concrete and straightforward images, in a literary or poetic manner, rather than the use of analytic or theoretical prose. Zen dialogues in verse, for example, resulted in a unique literary style, which was appropriate to the full expression of Zen Activity. Poetry also has been used since the early days of Zen as a vehicle for transmitting the *dharma* from master to disciple. Thus, in Zen, the poem has played a very important role. One of the earlier, more famous examples is the poem by Hui-neng (638–713), the well-known Sixth Patriarch of Zen in China.

> *Bodhi* in origin is not a tree;
> Neither is the Mind-mirror a stand.
> Originally there is not a single thing!
> How, then, can any dust be removed?

The following quotation from the *Lin-chi lu* (*Lin-chi Record*) is another famous example in which, this time, a Zen dialogue is conducted in verse.

> P'ing, the venerable Zen Master, asked, "Where do you come from?"
> The Master [Lin-chi] said, "From Huang-p'o."
> P'ing said, "What word does Huang-p'o have [to offer]?"
> The Master said, "A golden cow last night suffered from mud and fire; no trace of it has been seen."
> P'ing said, "The golden wind blows through a jade pipe. Who hears the sound?"
> The Master said, "Penetrating through tens of thousands of barriers, not abiding even within the clear sky."
> P'ing said, "This utterance of yours is quite lofty, isn't it."

> The Master said, "The dragon, giving birth to a golden phoenix, breaks through the deep blue sky."
> P'ing said, "Be seated and have some tea."

Zen poetry of this kind became more and more refined, frequently utilized, and prolific. Thus, in Zen literary expression, poetry ranks first. In the records of the Zen patriarchs, for instance, very large sections are taken up by poetry. In China these verses were also collected into such works as the *Ch'an-tsung sung-ku lien-chu t'ung-chi* (*A Comprehensive Collection of the String of Pearls of Ancient Zen Cases in Verse*); *Chiang-hu feng-yüeh chi* (*Wind and Moon on the River and Lake Collection*); and, in Japan, the *Jūhen Jōwa-ruiju So-on Renpō Shū* (*The Second Compilation of the Jōwa Collection of Fragrances from Patriarchal Gardens*). The *Han-shan shih* (*The Poetry of Han-shan*) and *Tsu-ying chi* (*A Collection of Patriarchal Blossoms*) are also among the better known collections of Zen poetry. In later years, although no small amount of verse was written that lacked Zen content and was little more than a play on Zen terms, still, in an abundance of poetry, Zen was, and is, vividly alive. Such verse is worthy of special note in the field of religious poetry.

Further, as Zen continued to flourish, the Zen acts and words of the masters were recorded and then compiled in book form by their disciples. These are the so-called *yu-lu* (Japanese: *goroku*), the "records," or "recorded cases," of the Zen masters, such as the *Lin-chi lu*, *Yün-men lu* (*The Yün-men Record*), *Chao-chou lu* (*The Chao-chou Record*), *Pi-yen lu* (*Blue Cliff Record*), and so forth. These *goroku* contitute a literary genre peculiar to Zen. They are neither merely theoretical, didactic treatises, as found in philosophy and science, nor are they simply literary works of the order of the novel, drama, prose or poetry. Rather they form a type of work of which no other examples are to be found either in the East or West; we may consider them a unique type of literary form created by Zen. In view of their literary uniqueness, close study of the features of these numerous recorded cases of the Zen masters would prove to be extremely interesting. Unfortunately, such studies are seldom undertaken today; the results of such research would surely be of special value. Broadly speaking, this literature may be classified as religious literature; it has, as might be expected, aspects that are never met with, for example, in the literature of either Christianity or Buddhist schools other than Zen. I feel, thus, that it possesses unique interest.

As Zen literature gradually became more refined, a tendency arose for a formal literariness alone to predominate and for the living Zen content to become weak. Thus, in the Sung period, when Zen was very influential, along with a great many true Zen literary works there also appeared works in which considerations of form took precedence over content. In contrast, in the Zen works of the T'ang period something more alive and vital can be felt. T'ang period Zen literature, although not as refined in form or literary quality as that of Sung, expressed the living vividness of Zen—often in a single word or phrase. Obviously the ideal would be to combine this living content of Zen with a refined literary form, and, in fact, such works did gradually appear. It is this literature that is perhaps most expressive of Zen. Though, of course, a great deal is lost in translation, the three poems below serve to give an indication of this Zen literature at its best.

from *A Comprehensive Collection of the String of Pearls of Ancient Zen Cases in Verse*

Bodhidharma Sees Emperor Wu

The jade pipe blows, piercing the Phoenix Tower;
The old palace deep in quiet, the day does not yet dawn.
Fallen flowers filling the earth, spring already gone,
Green shade vainly occupies the same old moss.

Hsü-t'ang Chih-yü

from the *Wind and Moon on the River and Lake Collection*

Fisherman

The shore grass is green, green. In the boat on the water
Night is deep, slumber lofty; autumn of reed flowers.
The dream turns with a fisherman's impromptu melody;
The moon serene, the river vacant, a white gull seen.

Ta-ch'uan P'u-chi

from the *Blue Cliff Record*—as a commentary to the Seventh Case: Hui-ch'ao asks Fa-yen, "What is the Buddha?" Fa-yen replies, "YOU! Hui-ch'ao."

Verse

In the river land the spring wind blows; not rising aloft,
The Partridge abides, crying in deep flowers.
Over the Three Falls, waves rising high, the fish has leapt,
    transforming into the dragon;
Yet the foolish still scoop the night bank water.

Hsüeh-tou

Some of the other works that rank among the masterpieces of Zen literature are: the *Cheng-tao-ko* (*The Song of Actualizing Bodhi*), *The Poetry of Han-shan, A Collection of Patriarchal Blossoms,* and the *Ch'an-men nien-sung chi* (*A Collection of Verses Taken Up for Praise in the Gate of Zen*).

What is of greatest significance in this literature, however, is not so much that it gives objective expression to Zen, as that Zen is present as a self-expressive, creative subject. In other words, that which is expressing itself and that which is expressed are identical. If it were otherwise, this could not be called true Zen literature.

The same can be said not only of Zen literature but of the other Zen "Self-creative" arts as well, among which may be included even the appearance and gestures of a person who has attained Awakening—the postures that appear when Zen is expressed in man. These may exist only momentarily—at a particular time or on a particular occasion—and may vanish immediately after their appearance. Nevertheless, it seems to me that such postures or gestures are of incomparable interest. Rather than something carved in wood or cast in bronze, rather than the formal poses used in arts such as the theater, these naturally occurring expressions of Zen are far more basic.

Indeed, the interest aroused by such postures shares something with the interest aroused by the theatrical arts. In fact, these postures may well have been the origin of the Nō drama, which later was to develop in Japan. Actually, Nō may be regarded as the bodily expression of Zen. While the gestures of a person who has attained Awakening may be primitive and not as refined as those of a Nō performer, nevertheless, as with Zen literature, such gestures are full of meaning and life, and are of an extremely vivid and basic nature.

Descriptions of these postures from the earliest Zen days are to be found in the recorded cases of the Zen masters and in the *Ching-te ch'uan-teng lu* (*The Ching-te Record of the Transmission of the Lamp*). If we create these physical movements anew, the results surely will be new, rich and rewarding. In the Zen records and the *Ching-te ch'uan-teng lu* can also be found a great deal of material that could prove of much use to the theatrical arts, especially in helping bring about a new Oriental theater.

Art is sometimes said to be play as opposed to work. In this connection Kant uses the term *interesselos*, meaning interest-free, without practical concern, lacking any "real" objective. Ordinarily, art is of such a nature: an actor is not accused of having committed murder because he acted as a murderer in a play, nor does he receive a hero's laurels for having played a hero's role. A murder in a play, even if it seems truer to life than a real one, is not the commission of murder at all. The manifestation of Zen, however, is far from such detached play, for it is a serious, living activity. At the same time, this active Zen expression does have its own kind of detachment, which can be described as the free disport arising from the total concentration of the Formless Self (see pp. 46–48). This Zen detachment is quite different from the ordinary *interesselos* quality of art, for the former derives solely from the No Self or No Mind nature of Zen. This "unlimited disport" aspect of Zen can also be called an artistic quality of a higher level; it is a kind of diversion not to be seen in ordinary theatrical art. Rather than the detachment, so-called, of ordinary art, this Zen detachment is "interest-free" even in actual life; it is a detached daily life, a practical life of play, or, in short, a life-play. Herein may be found, as well, the romanticism of Zen.

This manner of living existed in China from the earliest days of Patriarchal Zen. Thus the Master Yung-chia (675–713), for example, in his *Song of Actualizing Bodhi* expressed this way of life as follows:

> After identifying and attaining the Path of the Sixth Patriarch,
> My realization has been that neither life nor death concerns me.
> Walking is Zen, sitting is no less Zen.
> Speaking or silent, in movement or at rest, I am quite at ease.

The venerable Master Wu-men (1183–1260) likewise, in his *Wu-men-kuan*, (*Gateless Gate*), in the nineteenth "case" entitled "The Ordinary Mind, This is the *Bodhi*," wrote:

> Spring has hundreds of flowers, autumn the moon;
> Summer has cool winds, winter the snow.
> When nothing idle weighs heavy on the mind,
> This then is man's favorite season.

This is the really free, unobstructed way of life that not only is not weighed down by right or wrong, good or evil, purity or defilement, or life or death, but does not even attach itself to a Buddha or a patriarch.

From the end of the T'ang dynasty through the Five Dynasties and the Sung periods—and especially in the latter—the cultural expressions of Zen became diverse and refined. Some striking examples are to be found in the style of painting represented in its mainstream by such works as: in the late T'ang period, the *Sixteen Arhats* (Pls. 29–32) by the great Master Ch'an-yüeh (832–912); in the Five Dynasties period, *The Second Patriarch in Repose* (Pls. 34, 35) by Shih-k'o (mid-tenth century); in the Southern Sung period, *The Sixth Patriarch Cutting Bamboo* (Pl. 39), *Śākyamuni Descending the Mountain* (Pls. 1, 37), and *Pu-tai* (Pl. 42) by Liang K'ai (early thirteenth century); *Eight Views of Hsiao-hsiang* (Pls. 73, 74) by Yü-chien (mid-thirteenth century); and *Persimmons* (Pl. 55), *Chestnuts* (Pl. 56), *Kuan-yin, Monkeys* and *Crane* (set of three paintings; Pls. 59–61), and *Eight Views of Hsiao-hsiang* (Pls. 67–70) by Mu-ch'i (mid-thirteenth century); in the Yüan period, *Grapes* (Pl. 76) by Jih-kuan (late thirteenth century); *Han-shan and Shih-te* (Pls. 81, 82) by Yin-t'o-lo (late fourteenth century); *Han-shan and Shih-te* and *T'ien-kuai* (the Toad Hermit) by Yen Hui (late thirteenth century), and so on. Paintings in Chinese ink by Hsia Kuei (late twelfth century) and Ma Yüan (early thirteenth century) are also to be included in this group.

Since Zen is a division of Buddhism, Zen painting obviously may be called Buddhist painting. But Zen Buddhist painting differs greatly from ordinary Buddhist painting. Usually the latter depicts images of Buddhas or incidents connected with the attainment of *Bodhi* or Buddhahood as described in the sutras. Zen paintings, however, do not depict otherworldly or sacred Buddha images; rather, they portray Śākyamuni, the *arhats* (Buddhist sages worthy of receiving offerings), and the patriarchs in concrete human form. Similarly, instead of the unearthly region of the Pure Land, the Buddhist Paradise, Zen paintings usually depict the actual world of mountains and rivers, flowers and birds, monkeys and oxen, fruit, and so on. Since, in Zen, "the Mind itself is Buddha," and "outside of the Mind there is no Buddha," the Buddha is nothing more than a human being who has attained Awakening. Consequently, apart from an awakened human being there is no Buddha in the sense of some other-worldly being. It is quite natural, therefore, that Zen painting does not portray unearthly Buddha images but, rather, "realistic," unsacred human beings who have achieved Self-Awakening. Liang K'ai's *Śākyamuni Descending the Mountain* is one such typical painting of an awakened man. Equally, Zen chooses to represent various incidents associated with actual Awakenings rather than with the scriptural Buddhas. The means and occasions of attaining Awakening contrast strongly with the mythical or formal descriptions of the Buddhas in the sutras. Awakening in the case of Zen may take place on any occasion, for every condition of the actual world may serve to create the possibility for such an event. Talking, silence, physical motion, a utensil or something in nature may lead to Awakening. Thus the occasions and ways of attaining Awakening are numberless.

The famous painting by the Zen monk Mu-ch'i (Pl. 55), in the collection of the Ryōkō-in temple in the Daitoku-ji Zen monastery compound in Kyoto, is a small work in which nothing but six persimmons are painted. But, from the perspective of Zen, this painting far surpasses any of the standard Buddhist paintings depicting Buddha images. Likewise, the Zen monk Yü-chien's *Eight Views of Hsiao-hsiang* are no more than landscapes, but they are far better Buddhist paintings than those depicting the unearthly Buddhist Paradise. Zen paintings indicate not a formal, idealized Buddha or Paradise, as is usual with ordinary Buddhist paintings, but directly show the true Buddha, which is prior to and free from any form—that is, the Formless Self, or the True Self, as it is called in Zen.

It is in this direct indication of the Formless Self that the uniqueness of Zen cultural expressions lies. It is for this reason that in these Zen landscape and still life paintings we feel a unique attraction or interest that we do not feel in other paintings. This attraction is not the result of casual curiosity or interest in novelty, but a result of the expression of something very profound, something that is fundamental in human beings: namely, our True—or Formless—Self.

This sort of Zen cultural expression is therefore impossible unless it arises from those persons—or in those periods—that have known the Awakening of the Formless Self, or that at least have this Awakening or this Formless Self as a prime concern. The periods in China from the T'ang through the Sung and Yüan dynasties are considered to have been periods in which such prerequisites did obtain. The conducive atmosphere of those periods, however, gradually thinned during the Ming and Ch'ing dynasties. But, meanwhile, it had passed over to Japan during the Kamakura period, and continued on there through the Muromachi and Momoyama periods.

The formation of a unique cultural complex unparalleled in the history of the world that took place in China from late T'ang through the Sung and the Yüan periods, and in Japan from the Kamakura through the Muromachi and Momoyama periods, may thus be understood to have been due to the vigorous and expressive functioning of this awakened Formless Self.

In the case of Zen painting, then, it is not, as is so often the case with other types of painting, that a consciousness not free of form (the ordinary self) paints a concrete object; nor is it that the ordinary self-with-form tries objectively to depict what is without form; nor is it that the self-without-form depicts an object-with-form; nor is it even that the self-without-form objectively paints what is formless. Rather, it is always the Formless Self that is, on each and every occasion, the creative subject expressing itself. Accordingly, the question is not how skillfully something may be realistically or impression-istically painted. It is rather a matter of how freely, as the self-expressing creative subject, the Formless Self expresses itself. It follows, consequently, that when Zen expression occurs—no matter what it is—it is the Formless Self that is, in the truest sense, being expressed. This means, finally, that that which paints is that which is painted: that which is painted is in no way external to the one who paints. Through what is painted, that which paints expresses itself as the self-expressing subject. In this sense, Zen art is neither realistic nor impressionistic, but is rather "expressionistic." But unlike the expression of that which has form, this is the self-expression of the Formless Self. The unique characteristics of Zen painting derive from this.

Zen is a form of Buddhism characterized as being "outside the scriptural teaching," and as such does not take its religious resources exclusively from the sutras, but takes them freely, according to circumstances, from any event or thing of the actual world. Even when material is taken from the sutras, the manner in which it is dealt with in Zen is qualitatively different from the forms of Buddhism said to be "inside the scriptural teaching." Such cases are, however, very few. This becomes especially evident when we note the occasions and ways by which Zen patriarchs attained Awakening. Zen, accordingly, may also be called a Buddhism of "independent Self-transmission."

Since, from its earliest days, the religious resources that Zen utilizes have been limitless, let me give here just a few examples to illustrate this freedom. To the question, "What is the Buddha?" the following answers were given: "An arse scraper," by Master Yün-men Wen-yen (864–949); "YOU! Hui-ch'ao," by Master Fa-yen Wen-i (885–958) (Hui-ch'ao was the questioner); "Three weights of hemp," by Master Tung-shan Shou-ch'u (910–90). To the same question, Master Ma-tsu Tao-i (709–88) gave as his reply at one time, "No Mind, No Buddha!"; at another time, "The Mind, the Buddha!"; and at still another time, "The Mind, this is Buddha!"; while Master Chao-chou Ts'ung-shen (d. 897) answered, "The one inside the hall." In this manner, in answering this same "religious" question as to what the Buddha is, various responses are made according to the circumstances.

But neither are the questions asked set or fixed; they also vary according to the occasion or situation, and have included such questions as:

"What is the meaning of Bodhidharma's coming from the West?"

"Apart from the four logical propositional forms, and dispensing with the hundred negations, please, Master, speak!" (asked of Nan-ch'üan by Chao-chou).

"Does a dog also have the Buddha-nature?"

"What is it like when not one thing has been brought forth?" (put to Chao-chou by the venerable Yen-yang).

"All things return to the One. Where does the One return to?"

"How does the tea taste?"

Or, when a monk has come to pay a visit:

"Where do you come from?"

Including those that appear to be very commonplace, such questions are, indeed, unlimited. However, these are no ordinary questions, for they contain the most penetrating and profound meaning of Zen.

Thus, in its "religious" resources, Zen is free from the restraints of dogma and scripture as well as anything sacrosanct and mythical. For Zen, the actual, free, verbal expressions of the Formless Self become the living scriptures of the immediate present; the man awakened to the Formless Self becomes a living Buddha, and the world, as the expression of the Formless Self, comes to be the living Buddha Land.

Accordingly, Zen paintings portray not sanctified Buddhas, but awakened men and their activities; not some fabulous world beyond, but the actual world of landscapes, flowers and fruit, birds and beasts, and the like. Zen painting has thus broken through the usual limits of other Buddhist painting, and has developed a field of Buddhist expression that is always new and free.

In technique and style also, something unique occurs in Zen painting that is suited to the expression of Zen. For unlike other Buddhist schools, which are based on the authority of scripture, Zen does not analytically pursue minute detail; it rather grasps truth at once, and then expresses it directly and immediately. Thus, the direction of both perception and expression is not from the many to the many, or from difference to difference; the direction is rather from the many to the One, from difference to unity, from the complex to the simple, from form to formlessness. Its expression is of the sort where One or Nothing directly, with the speed of lightning, freely and without restraint, expresses itself. It is not that the many expresses itself in the many, or form in form; rather, the One expresses itself in the many, and the Formless in form. Accordingly, even the many that is expressed is not meant to express the many, nor is the form expressed intended to express form. On the contrary, the many is intended to express the One, and form, Formlessness.

The Zen style made its striking appearance both in painting and in calligraphy from the later T'ang through the Sung and Yüan periods in China. Liang K'ai, Mu-ch'i and Yü-chien of Sung, and Yin-t'o-lo of Yüan represent the highest peaks among those typical of this style; Chih-weng, Lo-ch'uang (thirteenth century) of Sung, Jih-kuan, and Hsüeh-ch'uang (fourteenth century) of Yüan represent the secondary peaks; and Shih-k'o of the Five Dynasties, Ch'an-yüeh of the Later Liang, Li T'ang (early twelfth century), Ma Yüan, Hsia Kuei, Ma Lin, Ch'en So-weng (mid-thirteenth century) of the Sung, and Yen Hui and Kao Jan-hui (*ca.* fourteenth century) of Yüan, represent the lesser high points. It was these painters who invented a revolutionary style, heretical both to academic painting and to traditional Buddhist painting. Unlike the orthodox style in which, throughout, the minutest details are scrupulously painted according to the "bone" method, or are elaborately outlined so as to build up the whole, the most striking feature of the new Zen style of painting is that the whole is first painted in one stroke—in one breath, as it were—without regard for the details; it is out of the whole that the parts then emerge. In other words, instead of the many building up to form the One, the One first forms, and the many appears in it. Instead of the many or the form aspiring toward the One or the Formless, it is the One or the Formless that expresses itself as the creative subject in the many or the form. This is in complete agreement with Zen's way of Immediate Awakening. The Immediate Awakening of Zen is thus not of the direction toward the One or the Formless; it is rather the One or the Formless Awakening out of itself as the self-expressing creative subject.

Monochrome painting in Chinese ink (Japanese: *sumi*) particularly accords with Zen in that the ink monochrome actually includes many "colors." It has been said that this ink color "possesses five tints." Among *sumi* paintings, those of the "broken ink" method and the "splashed ink" method, with their inclusion of infinite detail in the whole that is executed in a single stroke, have something more suited to Zen than those of the elaborate "bone" method. In the matter of line, more fitting to Zen than thin lines are those that are as wild and thick as possible, including, as it were, ten thousand lines in each. In form, also, irregularity is more in accord with Zen than shapely, regular proportion. In technique, the broken ink method, which Wang Wei (eighth century) of T'ang is said to have originated, and the splashed ink method, first attempted, it is said, by Wang Mo (ninth century), are in perfect consonance with the Zen way of expression. Accordingly, they came to be the only types of brush technique used in Zen painting. As a result, there arose a unique, so-called standard-free style, which, because it was different from the orthodox Chinese *sumi* painting in which the "bone" method was largely used, was regarded as heretical.

Paintings typical of this unique Zen style are: in figure painting, Shih K'o's *The Second Patriarch in Repose*, Liang K'ai's *Pu-tai* and *Han-shan and Shih-te*, Mu-ch'i's *Bodhidharma* and *Lao-tsu*, and Yin-t'o-lo's *Han-shan and Shih-te*; in landscape painting, the *Eight Views of Hsiao-hsiang* by both Mu-ch'i and Yü-chien, *Landscape in Snow* by Liang K'ai, and *Landscape in Rain* by Hsia Kuei; in bird and animal painting, Mu-ch'i's *Pa-Pa Bird on an Old Pine*, *Wild Geese Among Reeds* and *Monkeys* and *Crane*; in botanical painting, Mu-ch'i's *Peony*, Hsüeh-ch'uang's *Orchid* and Jih-kuan's *Grapes*.

This same style was introduced into Japan, and, in succession, there appeared such representative Japanese artists of this style as Mokuan, Kaō, Ryōzen, Gyokuan Bonpō (all fourteenth century), Sesshū Tōyō (fifteenth century), Sōami, Tan'an, Sesson, Hasegawa Tōhaku (all sixteenth century), Miyamoto Niten (seventeenth century) and Hakuin Ekaku (eighteenth century).

In calligraphy, just as in painting, from around the end of the T'ang on through the Sung a group of works appeared with a style that differed from the orthodox school. Some of these calligraphic works were brought to Japan—along with Zen itself—during the Kamakura and Muromachi periods, and many of them are still preserved as treasures of great value. A great many of them are indeed works by Zen monks, and usually bear some Zen expression, such as a verse comment on an earlier Zen "case," a sermon for laymen, words spoken to monks, a Zen legend in verse, and so on. Their style and their manner of brushwork are wild and free, unfettered by formal rules and regulations. With distorted shapes and twisted lines, they are naïve and simple, and, at a glance, appear crude and childish, so much so that their value was not appreciated by the orthodox professionals. The same was true of the paintings by Mu-ch'i, Yü-chien and others. This calligraphic style can also be called "standard-free." Contrary to the views of the professionals, these calligraphic works are not at all childish or unskilled; rather, they possess a deeper meaning than is contained in any orthodox calligraphy, a meaning that cannot be expressed in any other style. In Japan, these works have long been treasured, not merely for having been written by the hands of long dead masters, but because they point to something that is very deep in man. In such calligraphy we feel the same beauty of subtle profundity that is evoked by the paintings of Liang K'ai, Mu-ch'i and others.

Within this genre of calligraphy, the piece known as *Flowing Yüan-wu* by Yüan-wu K'o-ch'in (1063–1135) of Sung, who is famous for his work on the *Pi-yen lu*, is generally considered to be the oldest extant. But the Kishū Tokugawa family (the former lords of modern Wakayama Prefecture, related to the Tokugawa shoguns) possesses a work ascribed to Nan-chüan P'u-yüan (748–835), which is, ostensibly, far older. The principal works of calligraphy after Yüan-wu are those by Ta-hui Tsung-kao (1089–1163), Mi-an Hsien-chieh (1118–86), Wu-chun Shih-fan (1177–1249), Hsü-t'ang Chih-yü (1185–1269), Chung-feng Ming-pen (1263–1323), Ku-lin Ching-mao (1262–1329), Liao-an Ch'ing-yü (1288–1363), Ch'u-shih Fan-ch'i (1296–1371), Yüeh-chiang Cheng-yin (1267–1350?), and others.

Then there are the works in the cursive style of Huai-su (eighth century), a T'ang dynasty Buddhist monk, and of Yang Ning-shih (873–954), of the Five Dynasties period, which could be called examples of the splashed ink technique in calligraphy. These have much in common with the paintings of Shih-k'o, Liang K'ai and Mu-ch'i. Calligraphic works by Su Tung-p'o (1036–1101), Huang T'ing-chien (1045–1105) and Chang Chi-chih (1186–1266), all of the Sung period, are also free and unrestricted. They all exhibit the full, vital manifestation of Zen Activity, and had a great influence on the calligraphy of later Zen masters in Japan.

II. JAPAN: LAYMEN'S ZEN—THE INTEGRAL LIFE

The full-scale introduction of Zen into Japan took place in the Kamakura period (1192–1333). Many monks from Japan, including Myōan Eisai (1141–1215) and Kigen Dōgen (1200–53), went to China to study Zen and then returned to Japan. So, too, did many monks from China, such as Lan-hsi Tao-lung (1213–78), Wu-an P'u-ning (1197–1276), Ta-hsiu Cheng-nien (1214–89), and Wu-hsüeh Tsu-yüan (1226–86), come to Japan to teach Zen. Zen gradually came to thrive, not only among monks but among laymen as well, and from the thirteenth through the seventeenth centuries there occurred what might be called the golden age of Japanese Zen. With the frequent comings and goings of Zen monks between China and Japan, there was a great flow of Zen culture into Japan. The large number of valuable Chinese Zen objects now preserved in Japan were brought over during this period.

Through the influence of these imported Zen objects from China, and through the influence of Japan's own creative individuality, there gradually came into being in Japan a new Zen culture. The formation of this Zen culture was centered in Kamakura during the thirteenth and fourteenth centuries, and in Kyoto from the fifteenth through the seventeenth centuries. First, in Kamakura, five great Zen monasteries, called the "Kamakura Five Mountains," were built; then in Kyoto, five more large Zen monasteries, the "Kyoto Five Mountains," were built, together with Daitoku-ji, Myōshin-ji and a number of other large Zen establishments. Then, in north-central Honshu (the Hokuriku district), Eihei-ji and Sōji-ji were founded. Each monastery had buildings and gardens built in a style peculiar to Zen.

In Japanese Zen literature, the extensive volumes of Zen prose and poetry called the "Five Mountains Literature" were written in the Muromachi period by Zen monks of the Five Mountains temples of both the east (Kamakura) and west (Kyoto). Also under the influence of Zen, Nō drama and *haikai* literature developed.

In the domain of painting, Japanese successors to the Chinese Zen painters appeared, among the more famous being Mokuan (d. 1345), Kaō (d. 1366), Bonpō (d. 1420), Josetsu (d. 1430), Sesshū (1420–1506), Sōami (d. 1525), Sesson (d. 1573), Tōhaku (1539–1610), Niten (1584–1654) and Hakuin (1689–1768).

In calligraphy, there are works extant by those Chinese Zen monks who came to teach or to live in Japan, such as the above-mentioned Lan-hsi, Wu-an, Ta-hsin, Wu-hsüeh, and others such as Ching-cho Cheng-ch'eng (1274–1340), and I-shan I-ning (1247–1317). Outstanding also are the works by Japanese Zen monks, such as Eisai, Dōgen, Daitō (Shūhō Myōchō; 1282–1377), Musō Soseki (1275–1351), Jakushitsu Genkō (1290–1367), Kokan Shiren (1278–1346), Sekishitsu Zenkyū (1294–1389), Kenpō Shidon (1283–1361), Tesshū Tokusai (d. 1366), Ikkyū Sōjun (1396–1481), Takuan Sōhō (1573–1645), Kōgetsu Sōgen (1574–1643), Seigan Sōi (1588–1661), Hakuin Ekaku, Jiun Onkō (1717–1804) and Taigu Ryōkan (1758–1831), to mention some of the more notable names in this field. It is to be noted, incidentally, that Jiun, who was not a Zen monk but a Shingon priest, studied Zen and excelled in Zen calligraphy.

While there has generally been a faithful continuation of Chinese Zen from the time that Zen first came to Japan, living Zen in Japan came to take on various forms, just as it did in China. Especially in regard to the fine arts of Zen, it may be said that it was in Japan that they were brought together and "combined," as it were, to form a composite and integral whole. What in China either had not yet appeared or was present only embryonically developed greatly after coming to Japan; this phenomenon allowed the integration in Japan of the many Zen fine arts.

Qualitatively speaking, Zen in Japan at first lagged greatly behind China in the vigor of its religious activity. In this respect China excelled, but only through the Sung and Yüan periods; during Ming and after, China had little to offer. In Japan, for the most part, Zen became either a more or less formalized *kōan* Zen, employing old recorded cases of Awakening as models for practice, or *taza* Zen, i.e., "sitting" Zen. In these developments there ceased to be, as there had been in the T'ang and Sung periods in China, a free and forceful working at any time and in any place of a Zen that could utilize any event or thing at hand as an occasion for its religious functioning. In short, Zen became extremely formalized.

Accordingly, there occurred in Japan very few instances of Zen Activity to serve as model "cases"—or *kōan*—for posterity. Nevertheless, even though *kōan* and *taza* Zen were largely practiced in the monasteries during the Kamakura, Muromachi and Momoyama-Edo periods, in these periods Zen also deeply permeated the everyday life of the people. Indeed it came to have so strong an influence that it affected the entire age.

In China, although there were many great Zen laymen such as P'ang Yün (eighth century), P'ei Hsiu (797–870), Po Chü-i (772–846) and Su Tung-p'o, and although a Chinese laymen's Zen did arise, the principal tendency there was toward monastic Zen. In Japan, in contrast, Zen became more of the masses or laymen than of monks or monasteries. This is obvious from the fact that so much of the Zen material culture of Japan is composed of objects created by Zen laymen. Certainly the output of monastic Zen is not small, e.g., Zen monks' "recorded cases," poetry, calligraphy, painting, buildings, gardens, and so on. But compared with this, the cultural expressions produced by Zen laymen are never inferior either in quality or in quantity: Nō performances, Nō music, haiku poetry, the art of swordsmanship, the Way of Tea, as well as other arts, are among the principal examples. But it was above all in the Way of Tea that a unique, integrated Zen cultural expression, the like of which was not to be found in China, occurred; and this was the creation of Japanese laymen's Zen.

Although what is now known as the tea ceremony is a deterioration into a mere pastime without any cultural value, the Tea Art that prevailed from the late Muromachi period through the Momoyama and early Edo periods is extremely important not only as a new Zen cultural expression: from the standpoint of Japanese and world culture it may rightly be said to occupy a unique and original position. For the Way of Tea, on the one hand, embraced and preserved much of the previous Zen culture, and, on the other, gave rise to a new type of "integrated" Zen expression.

What I am calling the Way of Tea is the art of tea of the school originated by Murata Shukō (1422–1502) in the Muromachi period, which was then taken over by Takeno Jōō (1502–55) and others and brought to completion by Sen no Rikyū (1522–91), after whom several derivative schools developed. This mainstream school had its golden age in the sixteenth and seventeenth centuries. The Zen aesthetic standard for the Way of Tea was *wabi*, a term that connotes poverty surpassing riches. In accordance with this Zen standard of *wabi*, which is at once a creative and self-expressive standard, the Way of Tea structured and gave form to an entire way of life, which was able to determine (*konomu*) its own resources.

The Japanese verb *konomu*, as a technical term frequently used in the world of Tea, means to evaluate, to choose, and also to create according to the Zen standard of *wabi*. Accordingly, the Way of Tea is neither merely an art nor a cultural form, but is an integrated way of life with Zen as its basis. This is evident from Rikyū's words, "Tea in a humble room consists first and foremost in practicing and attaining Buddhist truth according to Zen," and from the words of Yamanoue Sōji (1544–90), a disciple of Rikyū: "Tea, since it originated from Zen Buddhism, devotes itself to Zen Activity. Shukō and Jōō were both Zen Buddhists."

Thus, the Way of Tea includes religion, philosophy, ethics, art, manners, clothing, food and architecture; and, what is more, all of these are chosen according to a Zen standard. In other words, Tea is an expression of laymen's Zen. This cultural expression in its genesis is quite natural, and in its result can be said, without overstatement, to be the creative completion of the totality of Zen culture into a systematic and integrated whole.

Based on the Zen standard of *wabi*, the Way of Tea selected, made use of, and held in high esteem suitable objects from China, Korea and Southern Asia. Among these were large collections of Chinese Zen paintings and Zen calligraphy, as well as such objects as teabowls, tea caddies, flowerpots, jars, and incense boxes, many of which have survived to the present day. Among these, there are many that were not valued or even noticed in the lands of their origin,—e.g., China and Korea. Paintings by such artists as Mu-ch'i and Yü-chien, and the calligraphy of Zen monks, especially, are among the creations that were not appreciated in China. Likewise, such teabowl types as Ido (Pls. 177, 178), Komogai (Pl. 182) and Goshomaru (Pl. 17), which were made in Korea and which became "famous objects" of Tea in Japan, had been regarded in Korea as no more than everyday articles. Indeed, no one can imagine how many objects took on new value through the awareness of the Zen *wabi*. Furthermore, the unique cultural expressions both tangible and intangible that were freshly created by this *wabi* standard are many in kind and number. These are indeed cultural creations unique to the Orient, of which it may well be proud. They include tea-room architecture and gardens; ceramic ware such as tea caddies, teabowls, waterjars, flowerpots, etc., belonging to such wares as Raku, Seto, Shino, Oribe, Iga, Shigaraki, Bizen, Hagi, Karatsu, etc., that is, the so-called domestic wares; wooden or bamboo tea utensils like tea spoons, bamboo flower containers, tea boxes, shelves, etc.; metalware, including kettles, charcoal braziers, trivets, flowerpots, etc.; and various kinds of cloth pouches and scroll mountings. All are the special objects created by the Way of Tea, a new Zen cultural expression in Japan based on the Zen standard of *wabi*.

Tea, consequently, is not something that belongs to Zen monasteries or Zen monks, but is rather of the laity, the common people. Further, it is integral and organic. In this respect, it is uniquely Japanese, yet provides fundamental, universal suggestions concerning the ideals of culture.

ZEN AESTHETICS

I. THE SEVEN CHARACTERISTICS

Thus far we have seen that in China from the time of the rise of Zen in the T'ang dynasty on through the periods of Sung and Yüan, and in Japan from the Kamakura period until the early Edo period there existed a unique, integrated cultural complex, examples of which were discussed above. Next, the characteristics that distinguish the creations comprising this complex should be considered.

The special features of this cultural complex have hitherto been variously considered by others. For example, Okakura Tenshin (1862–1913) emphasized asymmetry as the distinctive feature; not long ago Bruno Taut (1880–1938) came to Japan and cited the beauty of simplicity as the chief feature of what are apparently the cultural expressions here referred to; and the eminent scholar of Oriental aesthetics, Ernest Fenollosa (1853–1908), seems to have considered, in his *Epochs of Chinese and Japanese Art*, that it was Zen that had the predominant influence in this area. Thus, different people have had different views; but to me it does not seem that with their variegated contents these cultural expressions are likely to yield to simple characterization. Certainly, we can recognize to a considerable degree the characteristic Okakura called "the unsymmetrical"; we can also admit that what Taut called simplicity constitutes another feature; we can also agree with Fenollosa as to the strong influence of Zen. But if a term such as "unsymmetrical," or whatever, is used only in its ordinary sense, we must say it is a very poor way to characterize the cultural forms under scrutiny here. This is true also of the term "simplicity." Further, when Fenollosa speaks about the influence of Zen, what he means by the term "Zen" appears to me to be very inadequate. In speaking thus, it would seem that there ought to be a more careful consideration of

28

what is meant by Zen, and of what kind of influence Zen inevitably exerted. Accordingly, leaving aside for the moment the question whether Zen influence was or was not present, I intend first to consider, somewhat analytically, the characteristics of these cultural expressions.

The general features of this integrated set of cultural forms are here described in terms of seven interrelated characteristics. Any example that has thus far been cited may be found to possess all of these Seven Characteristics, which in their inseparability form a perfect whole.

As an example, let us examine the Raku ware teabowl named Masu (Pl. 204), a work by Nonkō (1599–1659), which fully possesses these Seven Characteristics. All the teabowls illustrated here can be said to demonstrate these features, but Masu serves as a convenient and representative example. In this single teabowl, though with some small variations in intensity, the Seven Characteristics are present in perfect harmony. Other such examples are, from Chinese painting, Mu-ch'i's *Persimmons* (Pl. 55); among gardens, the Stone Garden of the Ryōan-ji (Pls. 173–75); among buildings, the Shōkin-tei tea house of the Katsura Imperial Villa (Pl. 11). There are, of course, numerous others.

The Seven Characteristics found in every one of these examples are: Asymmetry, Simplicity, Austere Sublimity or Lofty Dryness, Naturalness, Subtle Profundity or Profound Subtlety, Freedom from Attachment, and Tranquillity. The order of these seven does not in any sense indicate the degree of their importance; each of the seven is of equal significance.

ASYMMETRY

First, being asymmetric means, after all, being irregular. Being irregular means being crooked or unbalanced. For example, a circle, being round, is symmetrical with respect to any of its diameters. However, there are figures that are also round but which are crooked, not being balanced either lengthwise or transversely; similarly, there are quadrilaterals with sides of unequal length. Such figures are, in other words, uneven, so that being unbalanced comes to mean being uneven.

In the arts of ikebana and calligraphy people speak of three styles: the formal, or "proper" style; the semi-formal, or "running" style; and the informal, or "grass" style. Asymmetry is most akin to the informal style, for what is symmetrical is roughly of the formal style. Anything unbalanced and uneven is by definition no longer formal.

Next, in the world of numbers, odd numbers (as a set) are asymmetric while even numbers (as a set) are symmetric. Two, four, six, eight, and ten are all divisible by two, and we can say they are symmetrical; but one, three, five, seven, nine, etc. are odd numbers and are asymmetrical.

If we proceed to examine asymmetry on a higher or deeper level, we may come to understand better its meaning as a feature of the arts we have been considering. Let us consider some examples of Buddhist painting. Paintings of Pure Land Buddhism, especially those most characteristic of this school, such as the *Bhaisajyaguru Tathāgata* (Japanese: *Yakushi Nyorai*) of the Yakushi-ji, Nara; *Amitābha Crossing the Mountain* (Fig. 3) of the Konkai Kōmyō-ji, Kurodani, Kyoto; and *Amitābha and Twenty-five Bodhisattvas* (Fig. 4) of the Chion-in, Kyoto, all show very graceful figures displaying remarkable symmetry. They evoke the feeling of being perfect, well rounded and holy; the feeling of the avoidance of irregularity. Accordingly, they seem flawless, distant and otherworldly. For comparison's sake, let us examine a Buddhist painting from among the works being presented here, e.g., *Śākyamuni Descending the Mountain* by Liang K'ai (Pls. 1, 37). This will reveal the great difference between the two types. One is very symmetric and graceful, the other is in every respect asymmetric; in particular, note the irregular face of the latter. As is easily seen upon comparison, the latter, both in its colors and its brushwork, gives one the feeling of being informal.

Also informal, uneven and asymmetric are the *Arhats* (Pls. 29–32) by Ch'an-yüeh, *Bodhidharma* (Pl. 62) by Mu-ch'i and the *Bodhidharmas* (Pls. 108, 111, 113) by Hakuin. From the Zen view, these Buddhist paintings negate the characteristics of ordinary Buddhist painting, namely, perfection, grace and holiness; nor do they aspire toward such ideals. Rather, having broken through these ideal "formal" forms, these paintings have a freedom that is no longer concerned with such forms. This is the realization of what Zen calls "wordly passions fallen away, empty of all holy intent." Instead of being in "the process through which perfection is sought," as Okakura Tenshin put it, they are unconcerned with perfection. Irregularity here is *déformation*, the negation of perfection and grace; "non-holiness" is the negation of sanctity. Neither imperfect nor worldly in the ordinary sense, these paintings are imperfect and worldly in the sense of going beyond perfection and holiness.

Zen is a religion of non-holiness. Ordinarily, in religion, God or Buddha is something sacrosanct; in Zen, however, Buddha is non-holy as the negation and transcendence of holiness. Here also is the basis, in Zen art, of its *déformation*, which neither pursues nor is attached to perfection; it is of the nature, as Lin-chi said, of "killing the Buddha, killing the patriarch."

SIMPLICITY

The second characteristic, briefly, means being sparse, not being cluttered. Tea-room design, both exterior and interior, is one such example. Simplicity in color means that colors are unobtrusive and that diversity is avoided. The simplest color in painting is black Chinese ink; light and shade, if present, derive from the one color of the ink. But, for all this, such ink paintings contain much that cannot be expressed by showy coloring.

Simplicity also has something in common with naïveté and abandon. For, actually, it is abandon rather than deliberateness that is in keeping with Simplicity. The ultimate Simplicity is "not a single thing," or the One. If, as the negation of holiness results the freedom of non-holiness, then simplicity as the negation of clutter may be spoken of as being "boundless"—there is nothing limiting, as in a cloudless sky.

Austere Sublimity or Lofty Dryness

Being astringent—or dried—and sublime—or lofty—means, in short, being advanced in years and life, being seasoned. Roughly speaking, it means the disappearance of the sensuous—of the skin or the flesh—and becoming bony. An example of this is Liang K'ai's *Śākyamuni Descending the Mountain*, in which the figure's face, body and entire surroundings give the impression of having discarded the sensuous, the skin and flesh, of being advanced in years and life, of being well seasoned.

Illustrative of this, the impression of being ages or eons old, are the sturdy boughs of an ancient pine tree. In the buffetings from storm and snow such boughs have lost the greenness and freshness of skin and flesh, and have become bony, with just the pith remaining; all extraneous parts have worn away.

The frequently used term "becoming dried" expresses an important characteristic of beauty in Zen, a feature of Oriental beauty. This phrase seems to be commonly understood to mean the cessation or extinction of vitality, the drying up of a well. In the Zen concept of beauty, however, "becoming dried" means the culmination of an art, a penetration to the essence by a master, which is beyond the reach of the beginner and the immature. Such is the quality of eternal life, which, far from ending, is without either birth or death; it is an inexhaustible wellspring, which is equally free from flooding, stopping and drying up.

Whether in painting or calligraphy, "becoming dried" signifies the disappearance of childishness, unskillfulness or inexperience, with only the pith or essence remaining. Here also is involved something intensely sublime or lofty, a Dried Loftiness quite different in character from that of the painting mentioned above, *Amitābha Crossing the Mountain* (Fig. 3), and of similarly elaborate works. This rough loftiness accompanies the characteristic of Simplicity in Zen art. Moreover, together with this loftiness arises a power or strength, often characterized as sturdy—the sturdiness and hardiness of an aged pine, which is masculine and heroic. Examples of this quality are: from China, the calligraphy of Huai-su (Pl. 7), Yang Ning-shih (Pl. 114) and Hsü-t'ang (Pl. 123), the paintings by Shih-k'o (Pls. 33, 34) and Liang K'ai (Pls. 1, 37–46); from Japan, the calligraphy of Daitō (Pl. 131), Jiun (Pls. 137–141) and Hakuin (Pls. 6, 136), the paintings by Niten (Pls. 102–107), etc. These works clearly display the characteristic of Lofty Dryness. They differ in character from the Japanese calligraphy used in the "ancient *kana* syllabary." Among painted human figures, this feature of Lofty Dryness clearly appears in the *Arhats* (Pls. 29–32) by Ch'an-yüeh, the *Second Patriarch* (Pls. 33, 34) by Shih-k'o, *Bodhidharma* (Pl. 108) by Hakuin, etc.; among people it is to be found in genuine Zen masters.

Other typical examples of this Lofty Dryness are Mu-ch'i's *Pa-Pa Bird* (Pl. 2), Ma Yüan's *Fisherman on a River in Winter* (Pl. 49), and the like. The Stone Garden of the Ryōan-ji (Pls. 173–75), the Warikōdai teabowl (Pl. 16), the tea spoon (Pl. 238) used by Sen no Rikyū, and so on, also exemplify this Lofty Dryness. In vocal music, a comparison of the popular *nagauta* and *tokiwazu* ballads, for instance, will make remarkably clear the Dried Loftiness of Nō songs.

NATURALNESS

The fourth characteristic—being natural—obviously means not being artificial. While this permits of many interpretations, what is meant here is not simply naïveté or instinct. The Naturalness referred to here is equivalent to such terms as "unstrained," having "no mind" or "no intent." In this connection I can quote an expression used in the Way of Tea: "What has the quality of *sabi* [of being ancient and graceful] is good; what has been forcibly given this quality is bad."

True *sabi* in Zen beauty comes naturally; it is never forced or strained. But this does not mean that *sabi* is a natural phenomenon and has nothing to do with intention, or that it occurs innately or in nature. On the contrary, it is the result of a full, creative intent that is devoid of anything artificial or strained— of an intention so pure and so concentrated, as in "*samādhi*," that nothing is forced. In the case of an asymmetrical teabowl, unless the asymmetry is unstrained and natural, the bowl would not fit the Way of Tea. Only when its irregularity and asymmetry is natural can a teabowl be more interesting than a symmetrical one; nothing is more offensive than an unnatural, strained asymmetry.

"Intentional" Naturalness results when the artist enters so thoroughly into what he is creating that no conscious effort, no distance between the two, remains. Even such an everyday experience as laughter is forced and ceases to be natural if one does not thoroughly enter into it. This sort of true Naturalness is not found either in natural objects or in children. True Naturalness is the "no mind" or "no intent" that emerges from the negation both of naïve or accidental naturalness and ordinary intention. *important.*

SUBTLE PROFUNDITY OR DEEP RESERVE

The fifth characteristic of being both profound and subtle could be expressed as Deep Reserve, i.e., implication rather than the naked exposure of the whole. This sense of Deep Reserve is present when a man does not baldly confront us with his abilities, but keeps them within, as if they were not there.

There are examples of this in painting: the landscapes in the broken ink and splashed ink methods by Mu-ch'i and Yü-chien (Pls. 67–74) are monochrome paintings whose content is present more by implication than elaborate delineation. Unlike the paintings by Tung Yüan (tenth century) and Li Ch'eng (late tenth century), which are also in Chinese ink, but in which everything is deliberately detailed, in the former landscape paintings, crags, valleys, trees, hills, rivers, cottages, etc. are all present, but by the power of implication. This quality of Deep Reserve cannot be expressed by naïveté alone.

Looking at Mu-ch'i's *Eight Views of Hsiao-hsiang* (Pls. 67–70), we see that they are far from being anything artless and simple. The forms are simple enough; but here all is not disclosed, something infinite is contained. Such works enable us to imagine the depth of content within them and to feel infinite reverberations, something that is not possible with detail painted minutely and distinctly. Here infinity, something far beyond the actual, painted forms, is expressed. In this unstated, unpainted content lies the quality of Deep Reserve, which in turn is accompanied by an inexhaustible profundity.

At the same time this Deep Reserve, or Subtle Profundity, also contains a darkness. Darkness per se, however, is of several kinds. Consider, for example, the darkness of such Buddhist paintings as the *Red Acala* (Fig. 5) in the Myōō-in temple on Mount Kōya, and the *Vajrayaksa* (Fig. 6) (one of the *Five Great Protectors*) in the Daigo-ji, Kyoto, which are typical works of Esoteric Buddhism. The darkness in these examples savors of an abyss; it conveys gloom, threat and fear. This is the darkness of hell, of sorcery—a demonic darkness. It is true that in the *Acala* figure there is something beyond the demonic. Though in Buddhism he is considered to represent the Compassionate Buddha's aspect of eliminating evil, the darkness attending this figure nevertheless has a dreadfulness associated with destruction.

But darkness associated with the characteristic of Subtle Profundity—or Profound Subtlety—may be called a calm darkness. This is the kind of darkness that appears in Liang K'ai's *Śākyamuni Descending the Mountain*, and also in paintings by Mu-ch'i and Yü-chien. When compared with that of the *Acala*, the former darkness leads to deep composure and calm. Rather than evoking horror and irritation, it pacifies and stills the mind. For this reason, in contrast to an ominous gloom, we may call the darkness of Zen art a bright darkness.

This is also true of architecture. The inner sanctum of the Konpon-chūdō of Enryaku-ji on Mount Hiei, displays the same kind of gloom as that of the *Acala*. The darkness of a tea room, on the contrary, impresses one quite differently. Here, one is never threatened; fear or horror are never evoked.

People often complain that a tea room is too dark and murky. Certainly it is dark. However, darkness is preferred. Light is admitted only through paper screens placed for that purpose over a few small windows. If it becomes too bright, reed screens are hung outside to appropriately reduce the light. This is all for the purpose of preventing distraction, of providing a calm atmosphere, and of leading to composure of the mind. This is a natural way of expression in the Way of Tea, which has nothing other than Zen as its spiritual basis. Should a tea room be designed so as to arouse a sense of threat, fear, or gloom, it would be contrary to the true aim of such a structure. The design of a tea room—including not only its lighting, but also the arrangement of the interior, its entrance, its building materials, its colors, and everything else—is made to transform darkness into the kind that is restful, peaceful and calm. In this respect darkness in Zen art is qualitatively different from that found in Esoteric Buddhism.

But further, Zen art has a massive stability; it is never buoyant or flimsy. By massive I do not mean the heaviness of a thing that is the object of attachment, but the true stability deriving from nonattachment, from freedom. Herein, also, occurs an endless reverberation, which comes from a never completely revealed, bottomless depth. If content exhausts itself—if the process of disclosure finishes at any point—any reverberation will be similarly limited. But what appears out of a bottomless depth and never discloses its entirety—whether it appears even in the form of a spot or a line—has a reverberation beyond expression. It may be said that this quality of endless reverberation is present at its best in Zen painting. Mu-ch'i's *Pa-pa Bird* (Pl. 2), *Swallow on a Lotus* (Pl. 64), *Kingfisher on a Dry Reed* (Pl. 57), Ma Yüan's *Fisherman on a River in Winter* (Pl. 49), Tan'an's *Heron* (Pl. 88), and Niten's *Shrike* (Pl. 102) all have what may be said to be an infinite echo reverberating from a single thing, in these cases the solitary birds and the single boat. Though, ordinarily, a single thing is no more than a single thing, in these paintings a single thing, even one speck of dust, contains everything, and the "not a single thing" is inexhaustible.

FREEDOM FROM ATTACHMENT

This sixth characteristic means, briefly, freedom from habit, convention, custom, formula, rule, etc.—that is, not being bound to things. This includes freedom or "being unconstrained" in thinking and action. So long as one remains attached to something, one cannot possibly be free in it and with it.

Nonattachment is a very important characteristic of the cultural expressions of Zen, and also can be observed in man's activities. For example, the activities of a true Zen man are described as being as lively and vigorous as a jumping fish, or, in the *Lin-chi lu*, as "utterly detached" and "non-dependent."

Most religions demand adherence of some kind. Ultimately, of course, this would be commitment to God for Christians and to Buddha for Buddhists. Such is the very ultimate to which they cannot but adhere. But in the true Zen life, not only is there no adherence to such a God or Buddha, there is even a denial of them. If a man needs this reliance on a final authority, he cannot be said to be a true Zen man. What Master Lin-chi calls an "utterly detached" and "non-dependent" man is completely free of attachment either to things actual or transcendent. For this reason such phrases as "killing the Buddha, killing the patriarch" are regarded as expressions of the ultimate standpoint of Zen Buddhism. To follow a Buddha or a patriarch, as such, no longer would be the Zen way of life, which represents the most complete form of freedom.

Further, nonattachment means not adhering to regulations; not only not adhering to established rules, but also not to future ones. In Japan we speak—in a good sense—of a person who is beyond conventional regulations as one whom no single coil of rope can bind. Such a person has something transcending rules. This quality is related to Asymmetry, for leaving rules—as well as perfection—to crumble and collapse is part of nonattachment.

Sen no Rikyū, the great master of the Way of Tea, as a man and in his manner of living was part of the cultural complex displaying these seven characteristics. He is considered to have done things both wonderful and unthinkable from an ordinary view; as described by a contemporary, he could "make a mountain a valley and the west the east."

Unorthodoxy of this sort is much in evidence, for example, in the recorded cases of Zen, which are not fettered by the ordinary rules of language. By saying that language in Zen does not necessarily follow ordinary usage, I do not mean that it is an unlettered or ignorant violation of linguistic rules, but rather that it transcends ordinary word usage because of its nonadherence to the latter. Since the records of Zen cases abound in such examples, it is no wonder that those records cannot be read, if one was ever to try, according to the ordinary rules of language or logic. This means that there is present in the Zen records a rule-transcending meaning, which emerges where the regulations have been broken through. This is often called the "Rule of No Rule," and also constitutes a very important element in the cultural expression of Zen. It is in this Rule of No Rule that what is called "unrestricted freedom" establishes itself.

Although freedom or being unconstrained *within* the rules may ordinarily be important, this is still living according to and having one's will dictated by the rules. For instance, being rationally free means living freely according to the rules of reason, without violating them; this is freedom within the rules of reason. The Zen freedom being described does not mean being free rationally and volitionally according to the rules, but is freedom in the sense of not being under any rules. It is this latter kind of freedom that has made its appearance in the cultural expression of Zen and appears as the characteristic of Freedom from Attachment. Such paintings as Hakuin's *Monkey* (Pl. 4) and Sesshū's *Winter* (from *Landscapes of Autumn and Winter*; Pl. 3), and such calligraphy as Ryōkan's "Mind, Moon, Circle" (Pl. 9), I-shan I-ning's *Poem on a Snowy Night* (Pl. 8) and Hakuin's *Mu* (Pl. 6) are works in which this characteristic of Freedom from Attachment is present to a remarkable degree.

TRANQUILLITY

The seventh characteristic is that of quiet and calm, and of being inwardly oriented. Tranquillity means, negatively, both not being disquieted and not being disquieting; certainly, the movements of a Zen man are not disturbing but are full of Tranquillity and composure. In a Nō play, for example, *yōkyoku* is the term used for the vocal music, which is accompanied by flute, drum and other instruments. Certainly all this is—if we are to use the term—noisy; but when one listens to *yōkyoku*, even the accompaniment does not disturb. Nō music, either vocal or instrumental, instead of being disquieting, results in composure and Tranquillity. In this respect, it differs greatly in character from *nagauta* and *tokiwazu* music. Hence, to sing and to make sounds and yet, at the same time, to bring calm and composure, constitutes one of the features of the cultural expressions of Zen.

Thus, in a painting like Liang K'ai's *Śākyamuni Descending the Mountain* the impression one receives from the whole scene, as well as from the figure, leads one's mind to infinite Tranquillity. Never, as is often the case with an ordinary landscape painting, will such a painting give only a superficial experience. Similarly, with Mu-ch'i's *Persimmons* (Pl. 55), the painting permeates the mind with quiet. Although belonging to the general classification of still life, it possesses this special quality. In calligraphy, such works as those by Ryōkan (Pls. 142 ff.) and Jiun (Pls. 137 ff.) are also of a quality that leads to infinite Tranquillity. Though manifestation in form is analogous to making noise, the very form itself of these works negates noise and induces calm. This sort of calm or composure seems also to be excellently expressed in the phrase "rest amid motion." Further examples that clearly possess this feature are, in painting, Mu-ch'i's *Pa-Pa Bird* and Sesshū's *Winter*, and, in calligraphy, Hakuin's *Mu*.

Thus far the explanation of the Seven Characteristics, I am afraid, has not been sufficient. As already pointed out—and this is a very important point—these characteristics are not separate from, or independent of, each other; rather, they indivisibly form a perfect whole. Consider Asymmetry, for example. As discussed here, it is not mere asymmetry, but an Asymmetry that contains within it Simplicity, Austere Sublimity, Naturalness, Profound Subtlety, Freedom from Attachment, and Tranquillity. For this reason, the same term "asymmetry" as used in connection with Zen culture, has, unlike its usage anywhere else, a manifold content. I would not necessarily oppose the idea of having the term "Asymmetry" represent the entire uniqueness of Zen culture. But I do feel that the kind of asymmetry that does not include the other six characteristics cannot properly be said to characterize the cultural expressions of Zen.

Concerning Simplicity, the same is true: if it is the Simplicity of Zen, it must include Asymmetry, Austere Sublimity, Naturalness, Subtle Profundity, Freedom from Attachment, and Tranquillity. But the simplicity meant, for example, by Bruno Taut does not include in itself the other six characteristics in the manner stated above. If, therefore, we should use a phrase like the "beauty of simplicity" to characterize Zen culture, the Ise Shrine, which is simple—as Taut thought it to be—would seem to belong to this culture, since both are characterized by the same term. But to my way of thinking, the Simplicity spoken of in the case of Zen would never include the Ise Shrine, and the Ise Shrine cannot be included in the same category as a tea room, which is simple in the all-inclusive sense used here. The Ise Shrine, although certainly simple, lacks such qualities as Asymmetry, Freedom from Attachment, and Lofty Dryness.

Recently in the West, in the fields of architecture and the decorative arts, people have come to talk much about simplicity; but that simplicity does not seem to include—or, rather, I would say, definitely does not include—the other six characteristics. Zen art necessarily includes all Seven Characteristics as an inseparable whole, and the cultural forms we have been talking about do in fact possess all of the seven features.

Today, in Japan, a great many of these objects and cultural forms are preserved as cultural properties, both tangible and intangible. In this respect Japan remains a treasure-house of this cultural complex, and, I can say, almost nowhere else—including the West—does there exist another culture with such characteristics. I cannot say absolutely that there is no other such culture, but, generally speaking, among the Western cultures there is none that so perfectly possesses such characteristics.

In the East, this cultural complex did not appear at random, scattered here and there, but in a great, unitary system. Further, it permeated every aspect of human life—painting, calligraphy, ceramics, and the people's daily life. That Japan constitutes a treasure-house of these cultural expressions should be a matter of great pride for her. To continue the study of such expressions still extant is of great importance. Although today the living contents of these traditions have almost disappeared, some still remain—not only as museum relics of the past or as cultural properties of yesterday, but as living traditions in the present.

II. FOUR BASIC PROBLEMS

THE FUNDAMENTAL SUBJECT OF EXPRESSION

Proceeding one step further now, the question inevitably arises as to what formed or created the cultural complex possessing the Seven Characteristics. We have just considered a certain complex of cultural expressions that existed in the past, and still exists today, and have endeavored to make as clear as possible the nature of each of its characteristics. But as to what constructed or created this complex, to answer merely by saying that it was Zen would be much too simple. That would only be to refer to the Zen that appeared in a certain age without going into the matter in depth. Further clarification is needed concerning what it is within Zen itself that led necessarily to the creation of such expressions, or, to put it another way, the reasons why Zen should necessarily have taken on such characteristics when it expressed itself culturally. For this purpose, we must consider what Zen is, at the same time making it clear why the Seven Characteristics have Zen as their source, and why, whenever Zen expresses itself, it necessarily emerges with these characteristics. If this is not made clear, it cannot be established, in a strict sense, that the manifestations having these Seven Characteristics are either expressions of—or influenced by—Zen.

Probing deeper into the seven indivisible and integrally expressed characteristics discussed above, I would like now to consider the nature of the Fundamental Subject that expresses these features in one perfect whole. In other words, since the creative subject of this expression is also the source of the expression, it ought to contain the basis for bringing forth these Seven Characteristics in "what is expressed."

That this group of fine arts has these seven features would allow one, a posteriori, to suppose the existence of some foundation for them. Logically, whatever it is that expresses itself with these features ought to be their source, and must contain the basis for their integral nature. But logic alone does not lead to an understanding of such a basis, for it is a living subject that expresses itself thus. Unless it is clearly understood to be living and existent, it remains a mere idea and has no reality. This is why the question of a Fundamental Subject of expression is very important.

Here a basic problem is encountered in this group of fine arts. People vaguely say that the root source is probably Zen. But the mere conjecture—or logical deduction—that it is probably Zen is not the same as knowing definitely that it really is Zen. From this it follows that if we want to assert that it is Zen, we must thoroughly *ascertain what Zen is*; why, since Zen is of such and such a nature, it can be the root source of the Seven Characteristics and contain their basis; and how it comes to express itself. This, then, is one of the basic problems involved.

A second problem is that the fine arts with Seven Characteristics are not limited to art in the narrow sense of the term. Rather they cover the whole of human life or human nature. In Buddhism, man's activities are classified into six *vijñāna* or perceptions; i.e., perception through the five sense organs—eyes, ears, nose, tongue, and body—and perception through *manas*, which is commonly called consciousness. This six-fold process may roughly be said to represent the functioning of human nature in all its spheres. Now, this group of fine arts extends throughout all these spheres, including, for example, even moral principles and philosophy, both of which take on very unique forms. This being the case, the root source of these fine arts is expected to be something that expresses itself in all spheres of human existence. It cannot be anything that appears only in art in the narrow sense, or only in what is theoretical or ethical. Rather, whenever and however it expresses itself, what is expressed must have broad significance. In this sense, the Fundamental Subject of this group of fine arts is not so much artistic as something that is beyond art. What such a Fundamental Subject is, or, *what can express itself in all spheres of human life*, becomes an important problem.

A third problem is that of the geographic areas in which this group of fine arts has appeared. The areas are limited to the East, and further, to China, Korea, and Japan. This cultural complex did not appear in India, Tibet or Central Asia. In Europe and America, it goes without saying, it never appeared, nor did anything immediately similar. Thus it follows that the Fundamental Subject expressing itself in these manifestations ought to account for the fact that it has existed only in these limited areas. Here, again, arises the question of *the nature of the Fundamental Subject that satisfies these geographical conditions*.

Fourth, it is to be noted that these cultures appeared in specific periods in history. They appeared for about ten centuries, roughly from the sixth through the sixteenth century. Accordingly, the Fundamental Subject of expression must be something that was at work expressing itself during these ten centuries. Once more, the problem is, *what is this Subject that meets these temporal conditions?*

These are the four questions to be answered concerning the problem of the Fundamental Subject of this culture. To begin with, I shall state definitely and conclusively that it is nothing other than Zen. Accordingly, I shall take up the above-mentioned four questions, relating them to Zen, beginning with the last question first.

Periods and Areas: The Historical Basis

First, it can be said that Zen satisfies the fourth condition indicated above perfectly. Zen arose in China around the sixth century, since Bodhidharma, who is regarded as the patriarch who brought Zen to China, came to China at that time, in the reign of the Emperor Wu of Liang. From the sixth century on through the seventh, eighth and ninth centuries, Zen developed steadily; in the period of the Sung it reached its zenith. This unitary group of fine arts, concurrently, also went through the same developmental process in China.

During this time, Zen also entered Korea. There, likewise, it led to the creation of a Korean culture with the same special characteristics. Then, in the Kamakura period, Zen entered Japan. There the same cultural complex flourished together with Zen through the Muromachi and Momoyama periods. It was toward the end of the Momoyama and during the early Edo periods in Japan that these fine arts reached one of their peaks. Thus, in terms of historical periods, there is a parallel development between the rise and fall of this cultural complex and of Zen.

In addition, viewed from the aspect of the atmosphere or the spirit of the times, it was Zen that reached a high point of influence in China in this period, so that we can say that this era was the era of Zen. Accordingly, considering the conditions of the times as well, we can say that there existed a historical necessity for this culture to arise.

Next, concerning the third question about areas, the existence of these unique fine arts in China, Korea, and Japan accords perfectly with the germination, the rise, and the decline of Zen. It was in the areas where Zen flourished that the manifestations discussed here appeared. We can say that this indicates the necessary regional relationship between Zen and these arts. Further, the lack of expressions of this sort in other areas is also considered to derive from the lack of the appearance of Zen anywhere else than in China, Korea, and Japan. Zen did not exist either in Tibet, India or Central Asia, even though they are areas of the East, just as it did not appear in Europe or America. So it can be said that in those areas where Zen did not exist neither did the fine arts under discussion, and that, consequently, this singular group of fine arts—together with Zen—is unique to the Oriental countries of China, Korea and Japan.

Fig. 1. Mu-ch'i • *Pa-Pa Birds in the Rain*

Fig. 2. Kao Jan-hui • *Flying Swallows and Landscape*

Fig. 3. artist unknown • *Amitābha Crossing the Mountain*

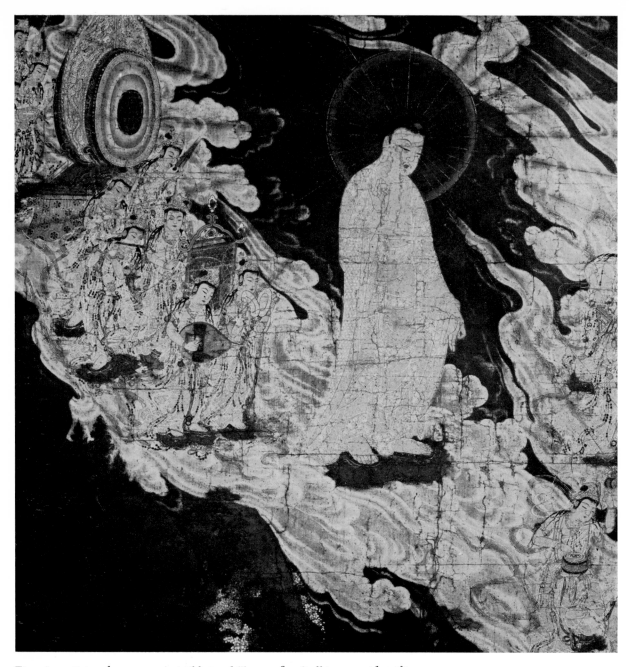

Fig. 4. artist unknown • *Amitābha and Twenty-five Bodhisattvas* (detail)

Fig. 5. artist unknown • *Acala* (known as the *Red Acala*)   Fig. 6. artist unknown • *Vajrayaksa*

Fig. 7. Inner sanctuary, Ise Shrine

Fig. 8. Tōhaku • *Maple*

Fig. 9. Warikōdai-type teabowl • Yi dynasty

Fig. 10. Kōetsu • Raku ware teabowl, named Fujisan

THE ZEN BASIS

I. THE MEANING OF ZEN

THE FORMLESSNESS OF TRUE SELF-AWARENESS

The first and second problems mentioned toward the end of the last section, concerning the nature of the Fundamental Subject of expression, can only be considered in the context of Zen. So let us examine Zen itself to the extent necessary, and see whether it is able to provide a clear answer to the two problems posed in connection with the cultural expressions that are the subject of this book.

While the question of what Zen is requires careful steps in the manner of elucidation and comprehension, in brief, I think it can be said that Zen is the Self-Awareness of the Formless Self.

Although commonly the term "formless" means lack of form, in Zen it comes to have a different meaning, though the common meaning also is included. Though the voice is said to possess no fixed, readily observable form, Zen Formlessness is not limited to this meaning. Again, the human mind is commonly considered to have no form, and, partially, this is true. But we can speak of formlessness in a different sense from the way in which both mind and voice are said to lack form. Accordingly, the Zen term means, briefly, that there is no form of any kind, either physical or mental. For while it may be true that neither voice nor mind possess spatial form, they cannot be said to lack all form; any mind, any mental phenomenon, has form.

The ideas of truth, beauty, and goodness, for example, which cannot be said to have form in the spatial sense, nevertheless do have form as ideas. Ideas can be differentiated and defined. The ideas of good, evil, of beauty, ugliness, of truth and falsity are all ideas that are differentiatable. If they were not so, they would remain cognitively unknown. Accordingly, insofar as they have to be—and are—defined, they must be regarded as having form. In this case the form is ideational or mental. Concerning the mind, therefore, the question is if there is any mental activity that is beyond differentiation—that is, is there any mind that is without distinction or beyond definition.

Ordinarily, such a possibility is not considered. Nevertheless, there is a mind that can be considered to have no form: what is ordinarily called self-consciousness. Being conscious of itself, it is what is called "self." Self-consciousness—or self—ordinarily can never be defined or limited to anything specific. Of course, there are instances in which self-consciousness is treated as an object of study; for example, in psychology, scientific research into consciousness, or in philosophy, where it is treated as the psychology, the science, or the philosophy of self-consciousness respectively. Here too then, self-consciousness is defined to the extent that it is treated objectively; if it was not defined, it could not be an object of study. So far, therefore, if it is considered differentiatable, it must have form.

It does not follow from this, however, that self-consciousness is something objective or that it can be defined. Self-consciousness in itself, despite all attempts, can never be differentiated or made objective because it is always the subject. When self-consciousness is treated objectively, for example, as mentioned above in the science of consciousness or psychology, that which becomes the object of study can no longer be self-consciousness; rather, that which entertains the object of study as *object* is self-consciousness. Self-consciousness is that which never becomes an object, but which at all times and on all occasions remains the subject. Otherwise it would not be *self*-consciousness. And, all human beings possess such self-consciousness; although it generally may not be clearly understood, our self-consciousness, upon close examination, is of the nature described. When one tries to objectify one's self, the "objectified self" is no longer one's true self, but a shadow, a something left behind. Self-consciousness, thus, can never be pushed "over there," however hard one may try to force it. As soon as one does try, it returns "here," or, better, is always "here."

Therefore, while the ordinary mind that is limited and defined has form, the mind as self-consciousness has no such form. It is in every respect beyond form, beyond definition. The true mind, consequently, is not the various differentiatable mental phenomena, but is the self, which defies and eludes definition and objectification. It is this mind that may be called pure mind. When it is said that man is mental, it means that he is this self. To recapitulate, the mind that we ordinarily say has no form, not even mental or ideational form, is self-consciousness.

However, even this self-consciousness that is pure mind still cannot really be said to be totally formless; a limitation still exists. Though self-consciousness per se apparently is unlimited, confrontation occurs between one self-consciousness and another: one formless self-consciousness stands opposite another formless self-consciousness. Such self-consciousness contains a distinction and opposition between itself and others. I am not now referring to any "objectified" self-consciousness, but of self-consciousness itself. Thus, although form is seemingly lacking in ordinary self-consciousness itself, there is still the distinction between this formless self-consciousness and another; there is always the difference of me and you, or of me and him. It can be said, therefore, that self-consciousness is extremely pluralistic—in fact, nothing is more pluralistic than self-consciousness. The basic reason is that no self-consciousness is ever the same as any other self-consciousness, so that at no other time in history, at no other place, is there any other "I" except me: there is no other person the same as "I." To say that in all respects "I am I" fully describes the individual character—or independent nature—of self-consciousness. Everyone is to himself a first person.

When it is said that however many people there may be in the world, no one among them is the same as "I," it is on the basis of self-consciousness. But here self-consciousness is always a particular self-consciousness as distinguished from all others. In this sense I feel that this distinction constitutes the root source of all distinctions—a point I find extremely interesting. Self-consciousness, which in itself is without form, without definition, is, despite its formlessness, distinguished from all the other self-consciousnesses by being a self. Thus, even as regards self-consciousness, differentiation occurs. And where there is differentiation, there is form and objectification. Such objectification in the case of self-consciousness, however, is quite different from that of ideas, which are always objective, as discussed above.

But Zen Formlessness does not even refer to the formlessness of self-consciousness. For while this self-consciousness must also be said to have form, the Self-Awareness of Zen is totally formless. Here, there is no form in matter, body, mind or self-consciousness. Since the earliest days of Zen, this is what has been described as Formlessness.

Sometimes the Formlessness of Zen is expressed as "body and mind fallen away." "Fallen away" means being free from both body and mind or not being of body or mind, since there is neither body nor mind. In Zen there is the expression, "Zen practice [*zazen*] is body and mind fallen away." "Zen practice" here does not mean the form of sitting in meditation (the usual meaning attributed to *zazen*), but true, Formless Zen. "Body and mind fallen away" thus means the Self That is Not Anything.

Zazen

We human beings are ordinarily considered to be of a mental as well as physical nature, of having both a body and mind. The ordinary self or self-consciousness is the fundamental subject of such forms as the body and the mind, and in that sense only is it formless. It is the discarding of this self that, again, is meant by "body and mind fallen away." Considered in this way, Formlessness means the discarding of this ordinary self, of the self that still has form and still can be differentiated.

THE FUNDAMENTAL SUBJECT OF SELF-AWARENESS

Speaking, as I have been, of discarding the ordinary self and of awakening to the formless Fundamental Self—or Subject—might appear to be no more than an intellectual negation of the self, and the bandying about of concepts such as a Formless Self. Being without form of any kind, however, is certainly conceivable as an idea. But something being conceivable is one thing; its reality, its existence, is quite another. This matter of existence, however, also constitutes a big problem; it may be said that where there is no form there is no existence. Thus we are obliged to think of a manner of existence in which nonexistence (Formlessness) exists. "Being without form of any kind" spoken of in Zen is not just the thought, concept or idea of no form, but refers to the actual Self being without form.

"Body and mind fallen away" never means anything other than the Formless Self, which has cast off body and mind—that is, other than my Self with my "body and mind fallen away." This *I* differs from the ordinary "I" that stands in opposition to other selves; this is the *I* that has eliminated the ordinary "I." This *I* no longer simply distinguishes itself from other selves. Therefore, Formlessness in Zen is not the *concept* of being formless, but rather the *reality* of the Self that is formless. It is this True or Formless Self that we call Zen.

Zen, therefore, is nothing "particular." It is, in the ultimate sense, non-particular, totally undifferentiated; what, again, in the true sense, never becomes an object never can be objectified. Zen is the Self that is ultimately and wholly beyond objectification; in brief, Zen is the Self-Awareness of Formlessness. It is this Self-Awareness—or Self—that Zen calls Buddha.

In Zen, Buddha is not anything we can see, believe in, or intuit, externally or objectively, and has no spatial, temporal, physical or mental form. While the ordinary Buddha of Buddhism is often regarded as something external, the Buddha of Zen is far from that. In Zen, Buddha is Formless Self-Awareness. Accordingly, Zen teaches that the Buddha should not be sought externally: "Never seek elsewhere!" or "Outside the Mind, no Buddha!" The Mind here referred to is the Mind that is Self, in which "body and mind [are] fallen away"; this is not what is ordinarily called mind, which must be broken through. I think that nothing is more spiritual, nor anything purer than this Self. Further, in the ultimate or deepest meaning, when compared with this Self of Zen, everything else falls into the category of things—that which is objective. What is, will be, or has been objective are all things.

Accordingly, the purest mind is nothing other than the Self of No Form, as explained above. And since this is Self, it cannot be taught to others. But even the ordinary self, if it is self-consciousness, cannot be conveyed to others. It is, as the term "self-consciousness" indicates, what only one oneself can be conscious of. This unteachability, applying even in the case of the ordinary self, holds true all the more with the ultimately intimate, fundamental True Self. There can be no objectifying or defining of this Self, and what cannot be defined cannot be directly taught. There is no other way than to become awakened to it for—and by—oneself. The truth is that this Self is what we really are. So it is that Zen says the Self should not be sought outside the Self. However far and wide one may go in search of it, there is not any possibility of coming across this Self externally, either in the world of mind or matter. It can be realized only through itself, never through another.

What can be differentiated can be taught, but whether differentiated "inside" or "outside," it is "outside." The Self-Awareness of Formlessness, in sharp contrast, can never become anything "outside"; to be even more precise, it can never become either "inside" or "outside." When it is said that it does not exist externally, this might be taken to mean that it exists internally. But if it were said to exist inside, that would be to distinguish inside from outside, which would therefore be subjecting it to limitation. This inside, in contrast to outside, is inside yet not truly inside. The true inside is the inside not having inside or outside, and the true Formless Self-Awareness, accordingly, also possesses neither position. Further, in Self-Awareness there is neither self nor others. It is this Self-Awareness that Zen calls Awakening or *satori*.

Satori is nothing other than this Formless Self, or Self-Awareness: it is only with Awakening that such a Self comes into being. *Satori* means Awakening to —and thereby being—the Formless Self—i.e., our own original being. Hence Zen speaks of what is "Original," or the "Original Self." Compared with this Formless—or Original—Self, the ordinary self is derivative, a mere manifestation; it is not ultimate, and must be overcome.

The attainment of *satori*, then, distinguishes Zen from ordinary religions. To attain *satori* is an activity quite different from intuiting, believing, knowing by intellect, or emotionally feeling, which usually obtain with ordinary religions. In the attainment of *satori*, the attainer and the attained are not two but one, this "one" being what is Original. The expressions often used in Buddhism to the effect that all men "have the Buddha-nature," or that "every sentient being is originally Buddha," should be understood in this sense. If it be taken to mean that although one is in essence Buddha but at present has not achieved Awakening, then Buddha cannot be the truly Original Buddha, for there would be distinction between the Original and the manifest. Clearly, this is no longer the true Buddha. Therefore, the ultimate or true meaning of the expression "every sentient being is originally Buddha" is that the Formless

Self that I am—the Self of No Form—is aware of itself. Since Self is synonymous with Self-Awareness, to say that the Self of No Form is aware of itself is redundant. Accordingly, it is simply the Self of No Form that is meant by the expression "every sentient being is originally Buddha."

Buddha always and everywhere expresses itself; it is never concealed. But if it is not transcendent, so, neither, in the ordinary sense of the term, is it imminent. Buddhahood is not a matter of transcendence or imminence, but of "Presence." Since this Presence is that of the Formless Self, it is not of the kind that belongs to any temporal sequence; that is, it does not exist only between what is called the past and the future. Rather, this Presence means there is no temporal distinction of past, present, and future. Thus the Buddha does not exist in any particular division of time, nor, in terms of space, does the Buddha dwell in any particular place—such as in heaven or in some other world. If this were not the case, the Buddha would be particular and limited. The True Self exists "here and now." Existing "here and now" transcends space and time—this existence is Presence, the true time.

In my own terminology, I have expressed this Self as the Fundamental Subject that is Absolutely Nothing. Here the word "Nothing" should be understood in the sense of Formless. Nothingness, as it is ordinarily spoken of in the West, seems to be derived from the concept of negation. Also in Japan, in philosophy and other fields, the word is commonly used in the sense of negation. As to the Nothingness of Dr. Kitarō Nishida (1870–1945), my most respected teacher, it is, according to my understanding, no mere negation, but the "No" of the Self of No Form. Very often, however, it does not seem that the term is clearly understood in this latter sense.

As for myself, I have sometimes used the single word Nothingness to express the Fundamental Subject that is Absolutely Nothing. For example, I have long spoken of "Oriental Nothingness" with precisely the aforementioned meaning in mind. I qualify it as Oriental because in the West such Nothingness has never been fully awakened, nor has there been penetration to such a level. However, this does not mean that it belongs exclusively to the East. On the contrary, it is the most profound basis or root source of man; in that sense it belongs neither to the East or West. Only as regards the actual Awakening to such a Self, there have been no instances in the West; hence the regional qualification "Oriental." Certainly the Formless Self itself has nothing to do with anything regional. Thus, it is appropriate to express it as the Fundamental Subject that is Absolutely Nothing.

THE ACTIVITY OF SELF-AWARENESS

Thus, the Fundamental Subject that is Nothing is the Formless Self. With this term, however, people tend to conceptualize this Formless Self as possessing the form, as it were, of formlessness. That is, there is a general tendency to think that because the Formless Self is the deepest and most fundamental manner of man's being, man remains in this state. Similarly, what is expressed in Buddhism by the term *śūnya* or Void, which is nothing other than the Formless Self, is taken as mere emptiness and so as something quite distinct from *rūpa*, or Material Form, or from *sat*, or Being. But the Formless Self is not only without form; it is *Self* Without Form. Since it is Self, its Formlessness is active; being without form, the Self is also active. Therefore Zen uses such terms as "rigidly void" and "merely void" for the kind of formless self that remains only formless. Again, when the self is never active and remains within formlessness, this is called "falling into the devil's cave."

The Fundamental Subject that is Absolutely Nothing can never be static, but is constantly active. By "Fundamental" is meant being the "matrix" or the "root." The Fundamental Subject that is Nothing is thus the "active root-matrix," in other words, the True Self. The term "Fundamental Subject" can be replaced by the term "Self," with all the implications discussed above. In respect to its activity, the Fundamental Subject that is *Absolutely Nothing* is also the Fundamental Subject that is *Actively Nothing*.

Further, in regard to activity, there is the Self that has activity and the Self that appears through activity. By "appearing through activity" I mean that which has no form comes—through activity—to have form, and that only this can be said to be true form. What simply "has form" has no freedom from, but is attached to, form. Lacking this freedom, form is manifest solely from the form of form. The form that constitutes the activity of the Formless Self, however, is the form of No Form. For this kind of formless form, Zen has the term "wondrous being." This term signifies that, unlike ordinary being, this is at once being and nonbeing. Here, being never remains static, but is constantly one with Formlessness. So it is that the Formless Self is characterized as the True Void, and its appearance in form as "wondrous being"; and thus the Zen phrase, "True Void—Wondrous Being." This means that whatever is manifested by the Formless Self is a "wonder-full" being; and the Fundamental Subject that is Nothing and free from ordinary being takes on being. For example, the Zen expression "The willows are green and the flowers glow" means that after one attains Awakening the willows are green and the flowers glow as "wonder-full" beings, in the sense of constantly arising from the matrix of Formlessness; but before Awakening, willows and flowers are only forms.

In Awakening, thus, two aspects may be discerned: the process or direction of attaining freedom from what has form and of Awakening to the Self Without Form; and the process in which, through its activity, the Self Without Form comes to assume form. In the matter of devoting oneself to Zen training, it means that the aim is to attain—to be awakened to—the true Formless Self, and thus become thoroughly freed from form. When this is attained, a new kind of form arises: not ordinary form, but that which is "wonder-full." For Zen, therefore, it is this world of "wonder-full" being that constitutes the world of differentiation.

Such a world, however, is impossible unless based on the Formless Self—that is, the Formless Self expressing itself in everything means that this expression occurs both in the totality of the spheres of our five senses and in the mind or consciousness. Thus, both the physical and mental activities of man after Awakening come to be the activities of the Formless Self. That is to say, the Formless Self functions in the perceptual spheres. When, consequently, a tree is seen, the seeing is the activity of the Formless Self, and the tree that is seen is the tree that has being there. Since in the *perceived* tree the Formless Self expresses itself, it is no ordinary tree; it is rather a "wonder-full" tree seen as the self-expression of the Formless Self, and is not separate from the perceiver. As the self-expression of the Formless Self, the tree now comes to have a meaning that it did not have previously, just as the perception of the tree through the eye is now realized to be an activity of the Formless Self.

It is in this sense that the world in which the Self Without Form expresses itself becomes the world of the Buddha; for by the Buddha is meant nothing other than such a Self. In this connection, we may note the ancient lines:

> The mountain colors are the Pure Body;
> The voice of the mountain stream is the broad, long tongue.

This means that the colors of the mountain are those of the Buddha, and that the murmuring of the mountain stream is his voice. All this has its basis in what has been explained above. It does not mean, animistically, that an object such as a mountain or a tree is inhabited by a soul, nor does it mean that the Buddha is such a soul. Such an interpretation would reduce Buddhism to a primitive religion, such as animism or fetishism. Such expressions mean that the self-expression of the Buddha is no other than the expression of the Formless Self; Buddha is not an image or the like, but, rather, whatever is seen or heard or arises in the mind is the Buddha.

II. ZEN AND THE SEVEN CHARACTERISTICS

From the Formless Self it follows that the world is essentially One, and all men are equal. This has its metaphysical basis in the Fundamental Subject that is Absolutely Nothing—the Fundamental Subject that is Actively Nothing—which constitutes the bottomless depth of the human being, and which is absolutely One. Every human event, whether individual, social or historical, arises from and ultimately returns to this Fundamental Subject that is Actively Nothing. Ordinarily, however, since we abide in the world of differentiated phenomena, we have distinguished and separated ourselves from each other. Any identity is no more than an identity on the basis of difference; it is not the Absolute identity that is the root source of difference.

In the phenomenal world, the world is plural, and men inevitably suffer from inequality. But just as it is said in the West that in God's presence everything is one and all men are equal, so in the East, because the bottomless depth of man is the Fundamental Subject that is Actively Nothing, everything is one, and all men are equal. By penetrating into the bottomless depth of the phenomenal world, man can be free from plurality and difference, and can actually attain the immanent "noumenon" that is absolutely One and equal. Here man is free from the plurality of phenomena, and yet is, in his Self, the root source of plurality; he is plural without ceasing to be One. In being One, man is the Formless Fundamental Subject that is beyond every limitation and characterization. In being plural, he is the Active Fundamental Subject that is not confined even to the One. Plurality is the One; the One is plurality.

While Oriental culture may be spoken of as the culture of Nothingness, this Nothingness does not mean mere nonexistence or negation; it rather stands for the Fundamental Subject that is Absolutely and Actively Nothing. The religions unique to the East have no such God as that of Christianity, who is other and objective, in whom one has faith, and upon whom one relies. The "religion" of Zen is rather the *life* in which man, by returning to his root source —that is, the Fundamental Subject that is Actively Nothing—breaks through everything differentiated or with form, and becomes himself the Formless— Absolutely One—Fundamental Subject that is totally free. Now, as the True Subject, he, in reverse, manifests his Self in every form of distinction. It is in explicating the ultimate nature of man in such a life that we have a philosophy unique to the Orient; it is in the artistic expression of this Fundamental Subject that is Absolutely and Actively Nothing that we have the creation of a uniquely Oriental art.

From this nature of Zen, of necessity, the Seven Characteristics already mentioned arise. In other words, the expression in form of the Self Without Form necessarily produced the aforementioned singular group of arts that necessarily possess these Seven Characteristics. It was because the Formless Self came to awaken in a certain period and area that such a group of arts were formed there. Accordingly, we can safely conclude that these expressions are the result of the activities of the Self Without Form and, further, that since the Self Without Form is the root source of the Seven Characteristics, it expressed them in these arts.

I should like now to consider in what aspect of the Formless Self each of the Seven Characteristics of Zen art is rooted.

No Rule

While the first characteristic, Asymmetry, means the lack of regularity, it also means the negation of fixed form. For example, in Buddhism generally the Buddha is considered to be the perfect form of being. Consequently, the Buddha image, when represented, regardless of the kind of material used, is ordinarily depicted as being as close to perfection as possible. In Zen, however, any such perfect shape, insofar as it is that which has form, must finally be rejected. This, then, is a rejection of perfection. Indeed, Zen even rejects what religions ordinarily characterize as holy, if it still has form.

While ordinarily any form is revered if it is perfect, in Zen, perfection of form, no matter how complete, is not true perfection. On the contrary, it is No Form, as has here been explained, that is perfection, if we are to use that term. Accordingly, when perfection is spoken of in Zen, "perfection of negated form" is true perfection. This, of course, differs from the ordinary meaning of the word. Thus, it is in the negation of every form that we have the ground for Asymmetry.

Consequently, in Zen, when a human figure, such as a Buddha, is painted, it is not painted with the attempt at perfection as is the case in Pure Land Buddhism. Such an august or noble Buddha image as is observed in the *Amitābha Crossing the Mountain* (Fig. 3) will seldom be seen in Zen painting; instead, such perfect forms are negated. This can be seen in Ch'an-yüeh's *Arhats* (Pls. 29–32), which we noted as an example of the characteristic of Sublime Austerity. In Zen art, paintings like these *Arhats* are preferred, and the so-called *arhat* face, rather than the magnificent face of an ordinary Buddha image, is thought to be more appropriate to a Zen monk. The *arhat* face is decidedly crooked, as can be seen in Ch'an-yüeh's paintings. Some of the *arhats* have too large a head, others an excessively large jaw, and still others extremely long eyebrows; all have countenances that, from the ordinary viewpoint, are very far from being well proportioned. But although not what one would call shapely, they express freedom from form.

Furthermore, the term "becoming rounded" refers, for example, to even numbers, which are rounded, proportioned, and well balanced. But Zen negates even such a completed "roundness." Thus Zen prefers odd to even numbers. In tea room architecture, too, it is always the odd numbers, never the even ones, that come into play. This is no mere imperfection. Rather, it is a negation of whatever has form, no matter how perfect, expressed as Asymmetry. This expression of that in which form has been negated, or the expression of that which has no form—of Formlessness—is the natural manifestation of "wondrous being." And, again, this takes on the characteristic of Asymmetry.

Concerning Zen calligraphy, its lines or characters are never straight or symmetrical. The characters have no common axis, and the strokes are crooked and misshapen. But this is not mere distortion. This crookedness, in negating the perfection of form—what is commonly called orderliness or shapeliness—is expressing what is without form. In short, it is the negation of shapeliness and, in its place, the manifestation of No Form. Accordingly, we can say that Asymmetry means not adhering to the kind of perfect form, which, by being symmetrical, tends to make symmetry something ultimate. In brief, then, Asymmetry is the manifestation of No Form as the negation of adherence to any perfection of form.

No Complexity

Next, concerning Simplicity, actually nothing is simpler than the Formless Self. In my opinion, this is the ideal kind of Simplicity, which form per se excludes. A familiar expression of Zen says, "Not a single particle of dust is raised." The presence of any "dust"—even a single particle—prevents simplicity in the deepest sense of the term. It is only having no form that is true and ultimate Simplicity, which cannot be anything other than the Formless Self.

Accordingly, when such a simple Self—that is, Nothingness—manifests itself within something, the being or the form of that something is also simple. To put it another way, true Simplicity appears both within what people ordinarily call simple and within what they ordinarily call complex. That is, true Simplicity is never exhaustively explained as being simple in the ordinary sense. True Simplicity comes into being by, and through, the expression in complexity of the Self that negates complexity, i.e., of the Self that is Absolutely Nothing. It is this sort of Simplicity that is to be found in the singular group of arts we have been considering. Since this Simplicity, like Asymmetry, has Formlessness as its basis, we would be greatly mistaken to take it in the ordinary sense of plainness. The latter is not the kind of simplicity that characterizes this unique cultural complex.

While No Form is thus the simplest form, no color is, likewise, the simplest color; and what is simple in the sense of having no color cannot be anything else but the Formless Self. When this Formless Self expresses itself, it expresses, in that self-expression, such Simplicity. This Simplicity, then, is not only at work in what is expressing itself, but is also to be found in what is expressed.

As regards color, consequently, true Simplicity obtains when in color there is no color. That is, when no matter how many or varied the colors, all colors are negated as the expression of the Formless Self so that there is No Color in spite of there being colors, then we can say that we have true Simplicity.

Accordingly, Simplicity does not mean ordinary simpleness. In fact, everything in nature, including all the complicated things that make up this entire world of ours, when viewed as the expression of the Self Without Form, is simple. Such Simplicity is certainly on a level higher than—or at least different from—ordinary simplicity.

While I have already indicated that not a few of the paintings that belong to this cultural complex are in Chinese ink, they, too, express in themselves the negation of color. Further, the broken ink method of some of these ink paintings also expresses the negation of form. True Simplicity, then, in my opinion, is not something that disappears when there are colors or when the shapes are complex, but is that which can express itself whether there are colors or not, and whether shape is or is not complex.

Thus, the Simplicity of tea room architecture is one thing, while that of the Ise Shrine with its *torii* gate is quite another. Actually, tea room architecture, with its ceiling of different planes (absent in ordinary houses, which, instead, usually have a single, board-covered plane) and with the varieties of materials used, looks very complex in the ordinary sense of the term. Yet its complexity has a kind of severe Simplicity that is not to be found even in such a simple structure as the Ise Shrine.

This is also true in the case of painting. For example, although Hasegawa Tōhaku's *Maple* (Pl. 5), a painting on sliding doors, is ordinarily to be described as elaborate and opulent, and although Simplicity would seem to be the last term for describing it, yet, in spite of the complicated colors, my feeling is that the painting is expressive of a Simplicity of a much higher level.

However, by this Simplicity I never mean only unity. Of course, without unity there cannot be true Simplicity. But, ordinarily, unity means a unity of form, and a unity of form on the basis of form per se cannot be true Simplicity. True Simplicity must be the unity of that which has no form; that is, the "unity of No Form," which must therefore be a unity of a higher level than the unity of mere form.

Such Simplicity has found expression not only in architecture and painting, but also in the activities of those whom we call true Zen masters. The Simplicity common to the matured detachment of a Zen master is the form that the Self that is Absolutely Nothing invariably takes in its activity. In the Nō play, also, I see true Simplicity. Although the costumes of Nō are very gorgeous and far from simple in the ordinary sense, the dancing figure in such a costume, unlike the dances to *nagauta* and *tokiwazu* music, expresses Simplicity, as it is meant here; this is true of Nō not only as regards its dance, but also as regards its music.

No Rank

As to the third characteristic, Sublime Austerity, briefly, as has already been explained, this means being without sensuousness. Although reason is also devoid of the sensuous, it is not wholly free from it. That is, since reason contrasts with sensuousness, the former is not entirely independent of the latter. It still has something to do with the senses. Complete emancipation from the senses, therefore, is realized only in the Self Without Form. Thus, when weakness, immaturity and the like are thoroughly eliminated, there appears a Sublime Austerity, which is most thoroughly realized in the manner of being of the Self Without Form.

This singular group of arts expresses such a Sublime Austerity. While this quality means being advanced in years and life, being seasoned, being "ancient and graceful" (*sabi*), or having a "poverty surpassing riches" (*wabi*), all these features derive from the nature of the Formless Self. Becoming advanced in life or years means undergoing seasoning and removing weakness. Although being weak means being subject to injury, where does the true elimination of weakness occur? It is, I would say, in the Formless Self that weakness ceases. It is only there that true freedom from all insecurity is acquired. Hence this Self also contains the meaning of advancing in years, or becoming eons old.

Becoming eons old is also accompanied by something best called sturdiness. In becoming sturdy or seasoned, there appears something that is not expressed by the ordinary term beauty. When we see works of art that are self-expressions of the Self Without Form, we find that they all contain that quality beyond beauty. Whether in a portrait or in a landscape, in this art this Sublime Austerity is always expressed.

No Mind

The fourth characteristic, Naturalness, means not being artificial. In this connection, we also speak of No Mind or No Intent. But what is really meant by not being artificial? I presume this means "being as we originally are." Then the question arises, "What is most original just as it is?" I would answer that it is the Self Without Form that is the true, Original manner of being. People often say "it is just as it is." While this phrase means being as we are originally, it is not to be taken in the simple sense. Being natural in the ordinary sense is rather artificial, since it is not being truly Original. Accordingly, Naturalness, in my opinion, must mean the truly Original manner of being. It is Naturalness of this kind that appears in this art.

No Bottom

Profound Subtlety, the fifth characteristic, includes profundity, darkness, reverberation, Deep Reserve and the like. Profundity is also a characteristic shown by the Formless Self; indeed, nothing is so profound as this profundity of the Self Without Form. So with Deep Reserve; there is nothing that surpasses the Self Without Form in its being infinite beyond exhaustive expression, as has already been noted.

Darkness also belongs to this Self; a darkness full of calm, a darkness that leads to composure. It is the darkness found inside the tea room; a darkness that calms and leads to ultimate tranquillity—a darkness very different from ordinary darkness. This darkness highlights profundity and composure and thus negates mere brightness; as such it also exhibits Deep Reserve.

What, also, is the nature of endless reverberation (see p. 33)? Since by endless reverberation is meant the incapability of being totally expressed or exposed, it could also be characterized by the word inexhaustibility, implying not lack of resource but the quality of being bottomless. In my understanding, it is in the Self Without Form, which cannot be exhaustively expressed in form, that we have the basis of true, endless reverberation.

NO HINDRANCE

The sixth characteristic, Freedom from Attachment, is also an important feature of the Formless Self. The term "nonattachment" does not refer to any attitude or concept, which is limited and bound to the mind. The Formless Self is not bound to any form. As the living Fundamental Subject free from all form, it is free of adherence or attachment. While being concerned with what has form, it remains formless. Only this formlessness in form is true Freedom from Attachment.

While there are many interpretations of these terms, I do not, for example, think that rational freedom is true freedom. In so far as one has form, one does not have true freedom; freedom is actualized only by one who is free from form. The Fundamental Subject, even when out in the world, never adheres to form. In the sense that he is free from attachment, a true Zen monk has freedom in both thought and action.

The activities of a Zen man—or Zen Activity—are said to be those carried out at lightning speed, too quick to be caught by the eye or even by the mind. If there is any attachment, such speed cannot occur. Only the Self that, while in the midst of the world, is yet unattached to and free from it is capable of being unrestricted and free in dealing with it. So long as we remain "something," we can never be free. Thus, by being nonattached is meant the freedom to take on any form because of not having any form. This freedom, when it is actualized in both what is expressed and what is expressing itself, is also what is meant by nonattachment.

No Stirring

The seventh characteristic, serenity or Tranquillity, means, negatively, not being disturbed. Disquiet is completely absent from the Formless Self. Since being something, or having some form, involves disquiet, even the slightest bit of "being" is disquieting so long as it has form. Accordingly, one can truly be free from disquiet only when there is no form.

Ordinarily, even hearing sounds or seeing things may disturb. Thus, in the ordinary sense, one is truly free from disquiet when there is no sound to hear, no thing to see, or nothing to stimulate the five senses. But even in this state of sense deprivation, the mind is in action, which, of course, also can be disquieting. Only if nothing appeared to the five senses and nothing stirred in the mind would there be true freedom from disquiet. In the actualities of life, however, no such condition exists. Even when we are alone and our mind, in the ordinary sense, is calm, the existence of body and mind with form is itself disquieting. Consequently, as long as "I am," as long as there is the ordinary self, there is disturbance. Except in the Formless Self, there is absolutely no condition of freedom from disquiet. It is this Self that is Zen; and it is this Self that is true Tranquillity.

This true serenity is nothing objective; it is not merely being tranquil or not being disturbed. It is rather being what may be called the Fundamental Subject or Absolute. Only by being the Fundamental Subject can one be free from disquiet in all conditions. For this Fundamental Subject—or Self Without Form—even in a place that is "noisy," in the broadest sense, negates the noise and quiets it. Thus, being tranquil in every action, or being "at rest amidst motion," as the expression goes, is true serenity. It is this kind of Tranquillity that is expressed in every work of true Zen art.

As has already been noted, since these Seven Characteristics are no more than attributes of the manner of being of the Self Without Form, they are one and inseparable. The oneness of the Self Without Form is their basis. Hence, the seven, each being an expression of this One, are each included, inseparably, in all the others.

When this Self Without Form awakens (to itself), it not only directly influences the arts—as, for instance, in the formation of the group of arts that is being considered here—but it influences everything else as well. That in the times and places this Awakening occurs the entire society comes under the influence of its expression in culture or art is because this Self Without Form is man's true and ultimate manner of being. In this sense, we can speak of the essential culture of Zen and the derivative culture arising from its influence.

CONCLUSION

The nature of the cultural development called Zen art, and the conditions of its occurrence only in the East, may now generally be understood, I hope, from the foregoing explanation. What I wish to emphasize, however, is not so much a peculiarity to the East, as that this Formless Self is the ultimate manner of being of man and therefore should be awakened in every man. Since the manner of being of the Formless Self ought to be that of every man, the Awakening to and of this Self in the West (assuming that in the West such a Self has not been awakened) would at least make up for the lack of such an Awakening heretofore. With this Awakening, the West, which has hitherto had its basis only in being, and which has known only the world of the self that has form, will, I am sure, achieve a still greater profundity. And, if this new Awakening is attained, there will then be great change in Western art, culture, and its very nature of being, all of which have traditionally been based on the self with form.

Such a change would be quite natural; for it would necessarily be toward a future true manner of being of Western art or culture. When, in the West, the "culture of form" changes to one in which the Self Without Form expresses itself, then something will emerge that has not been seen before outside the Orient. There will then be a new awakening to what man *ought* to be as man—even if he seems to have forgotten it. This will mean a culture advanced and deepened. Such a development would be a very great and basic contribution to—or influence upon—the West, coming from Zen.

Ordinarily, however, when Westerners distinguish East from West and talk about contributions the East will or can make to the West, generally they do not think along these lines. It seems to me that Arnold Toynbee, for example, because of his insufficient understanding of what Zen—that is, the True Self—is, presents only a very shallow view when he speaks of possible contributions by the East—or by Buddhism—to the West. To hold that tolerance and the like are what the East can contribute is really too superficial. In my view, one should go somewhat deeper into the source of human nature and become awakened to what hitherto in the West has not yet been awakened, even though it ought to have been. Here is to be found the most significant possible contribution that the East, Zen culture, or Zen art, can make to the West, for only with this influence can the West awaken to its lack of Awakening. When this occurs, Western culture can then proceed to a new and very stable Fundamental Subjectivity, which alone will transform its very substance.

APPRECIATIONS OF SELECTED PLATES

ZEN PAINTING

Examples of the various subjects of Zen painting are presented in the following order: human figure, bird, landscape, animal, and color painting of tree and flowers.

1. Liang K'ai: *Śākyamuni Descending the Mountain* (Pls. 1, 37)
This depicts Śākyamuni, who has pursued Awakening (*satori*) on the mountain, descending after its attainment. At least that is how Zen people view it. In his discontent with the way of the world, man finds it impossible to remain there and "enters the mountain" to find his way free from suffering. As the result of his six years' search, Śākyamuni discovers the way to live the actualities of life by being free from them, and leaves the mountain. This painting of *Śākyamuni Descending the Mountain*, thus, can be said to symbolize most excellently man's true way of being.

While there are many works on the same theme by other painters, for me none expresses this symbolization more clearly than this work by Liang K'ai. It has the deepness of the mountain from which the figure descends; indeed, even the background scene expresses well the profundity of the spiritual environment. The entire figure of Śākyamuni unmistakably tells us that he has attained the serenity of *nirvāna*. We cannot help but feel that the presence of a person awakened to the True Self and living in the actualities of life really ought to be like this. Although the Nō drama may be called the dramatic art of Zen, the origin of the movements and poses in the Nō performance are rightfully similar to this *Śākyamuni Descending the Mountain*. A Nō performance begins with an actor entering by way of the long passageway from the wings on the andience's left (*hashigakari*) onto the stage. We can say that the *Śākyamuni* of

Liang K'ai exemplifies a figure thus emerging. In the same sense, the pose of Liang K'ai's *Śākyamuni* is the basis of all the poses in the Nō drama.

The painting is in Chinese ink, with the clothing of the figure lightly colored in red. The color is very thin, far from being obtrusive, and has an extremely subdued feeling. The manner of execution is also appropriate to a Zen painting. Although in some areas the depiction is detailed, one is not conscious of elaborateness; the overall effect comes rather from the broken ink style unique to Zen painting. Ink paintings before the appearance of the Zen paintings of Liang Ka'i and some others were carefully and painstakingly detailed but little more —elaborate detail dominated. Rather than careful elaboration, Zen grasps the whole in one breath, and the whole is suggested and reverberates at once. This means minute detail is present in the roughness and harsh irregularity.

This painting contains all of the Seven Characteristics of Zen art. The entire painting expresses very interestingly the characteristic of Asymmetry, with the diagonal formed by the mountain backdrop as one element in this. The whole composition in this manner of painting manifests Asymmetry.

Sublime Austerity: It is as if blood, skin, and flesh have been cast out, and the pith has emerged from within. The eyes, unlike those looking *at* something, are very introspective. They are the eyes, we may say, of depth itself, or of Nothingness. Nor could the ragged and unkempt face be described as refined, although such words as ragged and unkempt are not sufficient in themselves to describe it. Although the dishevelled hair is painted with a sure touch, it is in a broken ink style that denies it any grace. The folds of the clothing also reveal the sureness of Liang K'ai's brush. Such brushwork negates detailed preciseness by means of what the man possesses in himself, by means of Oneness. And yet something detailed and precise still emerges.

Freedom from Attachment: *Śākyamuni Descending the Mountain* is invested with the most basic freedom, freedom even prior to nonattachment; it is the "final deliverance" of the Formless Self, which is absolute freedom from all things. Here is the expression of complete nonattachment.

Of the Seven Characteristics, Tranquillity is best expressed in this painting; that is, it expresses what is prior to appearance, by means of what has appearance. Moreover, here this is manifested in the man, a fact highly appropriate to a painting of *Śākyamuni Descending the Mountain*.

2. Mu-ch'i: *Pa-Pa Bird on an Old Pine* (Pl. 2)

There are many Zen paintings of birds; usually such depictions are of a single bird rather than many. Mu-ch'i's *Pa-pa Bird* is representative of such a painting. His *Swallow on a Lotus* (Pl. 64) is another. Tan'an's *Heron* (Pl. 88) and Niten's *Shrike* (Pl. 102) also depict solitary birds. In these paintings the bird depicted gives the impression of containing within itself the whole world, of being the Oneness that harbors the whole world within itself. Thus in this painting the solitary bird tightens the whole composition and makes clear the central theme. It is a monochrome in the broken ink style, and dispenses entirely with elaborate representation. Instead, the legs of the bird, the vines, and the pine branch reveal a well-seasoned and well-tempered strength and, employing the effect of the broken ink style, form a composite unity.

Austere Sublimity is remarkably present here, as, also, is Tranquillity—for instance, in the bird's shape. The pine branch with its enveloping vines gives the feeling of "unrestricted freedom in activity," Freedom from Attachment. The bird seems to express an undeniable and inviolable dignity, a Sublime Austerity. We may call this a classic example of Zen bird painting.

In this depiction of a solitary bird, no mere singleness but the Zen Self finds its natural expression. For example, let me liken this bird to a dot. Such a dot, though but a single point, contains the universe in itself. A dot drawn by the True Self contains the whole. Mu-ch'i's *Pa-Pa Bird* has this quality. Viewing this painting from its compositional and stylistic aspects, that is, when we take a good look at it as a whole with the bird as nucleus, the world contained within can be seen. The same is true of *Śākyamuni Descending the Mountain*. In one, it is expressed in a bird, in the other, in a human figure. Ordinarily speaking, a depiction of Śākyamuni is a Buddhist painting, whereas flowers and birds are representations of natural life. But here this distinction does not hold true. Both are essentially the same.

The eyes of the *pa-pa* are sharp and penetrating. They are the eyes of Liang K'ai's *Śākyamuni*. Here nature as well reveals the Seven Characteristics common to Zen culture. Most discernible are Tranquillity and Sublime Austerity, with Simplicity, Asymmetry, and Freedom from Attachment, much in evidence as well. To me the distinguishing feature of this painting—a feature of extreme power—is the way in which the whole is intensified by the small area of dark black ink.

3. Sesshū: *Winter* from *Autumn and Winter Landscapes* (Pl. 3)
This work, by the Japanese painter Sesshū, is an expression of Zen. Although there have been many such Zen landscapes by Chinese artists, no doubt the two examples of *Eight Views* of *Hsiao-Hsiang*, one by Mu-ch'i (Pls. 67–70), the other by Yü-chien (Pls. 73, 74), are typical. They are characteristic of broken ink or splashed ink type landscapes as well. While Japanese landscapes in this style do exist, they are generally not executed entirely in the same fashion as the *Views of Hsiao-Hsiang* of these two Sung artists.

Sesshū's composition in this painting exemplifies well the qualities of Asymmetry and Subtle Profundity, the feeling of mountain depths. The shapes of the rocks and trees clearly reveal Austere Sublimity. More than simply being depicted as wizened forms, the powerful appeal of an austerity here equivalent to sublimity is present. Another characteristic is Profound Subtlety, a kind of dimness or darkness, never secret or gloomy, but a darkness that imparts a calmness. It could never evoke fear. The figure in the painting, wending his way deep into the mountains, also evokes serenity. The towering mansion in the distance, so calm and restful in the bosom of the mountains, seems to be a place where one might pass a tranquil existence. Here, surely, the figure will be afforded a good rest. The situation and composition of the deep mountains closely resembles that of *Śākyamuni Descending the Mountain*. In the latter, the roots of the trees express Sublime Austerity; in the former it is found in the rock formations. Here Tranquillity and Asymmetry reign. What we have is not the minute detail of the early Chinese schools of landscape, but rough, jagged brushwork. Simplicity is another element that comes to mind. All is perfectly natural, without any forced, studied quality, and singularly reveals Sesshū's outlook as a painter. There is a freedom from contrivance, where nothing is forced or overdone. The brushwork and composition also both manifest Naturalness: no design or purpose is to be seen, either in the technique or in the composition; it is rather a kind of "purposeless purpose." No worldly considerations intrude into such an environment or situation. It is apart from the dust of the world, and nonattachment emerges in the landscape scenery.

4. Hakuin: *Monkey* (Pl. 4)

There are numerous paintings similar to this composition of a monkey reaching out for the moon in the water. Water with the moon reflected on it is usually drawn below. This example is probably of such a design. The ink tone here is neither very dark nor very light. Hakuin often used a sized paper, which accounts for the appearance of light and dark splotches in the inked areas of some of his works.

Here a monkey is used to give expression essentially to the same thing as that expressed by the *pa-pa* bird of Mu-ch'i. The broken or splashed ink brushwork is extremely simple, as if the work were painted at a single stroke. Austere Sublimity is well expressed. Subtle Profundity is there also, in something very deep and infinite evoked by the tip of the reaching hand. The stretching arm, with a remarkable strength, seems to constitute the important *moment* of the painting. The arm, which is reduced to just a thin stroke, manifests Sublime Austerity. A painting such as this could easily become merely coarse and naïve; in this case it has achieved Profound Subtlety.

In the untrammelled composition and style, there is a carefree quality that echoes the characteristics of Naturalness and Simplicity. There is something in it that is reminiscent of Hakuin's calligraphy. The inscription of Chinese characters and the picture itself—for example, the twigs of the willow tree— form a perfect, harmonious whole, without the slightest discrepancy. The monkey's face has the feeling of nonattachment; its eyes are innocent and natural. This same style pervades all of Hakuin's calligraphy and painting.

The composition is crossed by three diagonals, which express well the quality of Asymmetry; the one running from above is cut vertically by another, which in turn is then cut aslant. This evokes a feeling of appropriateness, with nothing forced. Thanks to this, the painting brings forth in one vital breath that which is in us, namely, that which fundamentally possesses the Seven Characteristics, and inspires a sense of close familiarity with the work. This is not just a monkey; it is as if I myself had assumed the form of a monkey and taken this pose. Hakuin's talent was really outstanding. In the energy of the Asymmetry as well, the vitality and activity of Zen are distinctly apparent. Since Asymmetry involves the breaking or negating of what is ordinarily termed straight and correct, and the going beyond and detachment from regulation, Zen art invariably involves the working or activity of Zen. So superlative was Hakuin in every respect that we may look in vain throughout Japanese Zen for someone to excel him. This is the reason his works possess an extraordinary sublimity as well.

5. Tōhaku: *Maple,* left two of four sliding doors (Pl. 5)
There is a definite reason for the inclusion here of this sumptuous painting. Zen paintings are generally ink monochromes, since, as has been stated, this medium is highly suitable for the pictorial expression of Zen. Indeed, nearly all of the paintings selected for this book are monochrome. However, this does not mean that Zen cannot be expressed except by paintings in black ink; it is not at all such a simple matter. Certainly it is monochrome and not color—above all the monochrome executed in the broken or splashed ink styles—that has an essential relation to Zen, yet there is no specific reason Zen cannot be expressed in polychrome as well. The problem is, rather, if Zen should express itself in a colored painting, what would be the nature of such a painting.

The paintings in which Zen is truly expressed, even those of the Sung period, ought to have the Seven Characteristics, even if they are in color. So essential are these characteristics, they may as well be called the characteristics of Zen. Thus, if they have these characteristics, even polychrome paintings express Zen. The fact remains, however, that there are few such paintings in color. In Japan, the works of the Tosa school, so minutely and beautifully colored, do not possess the above characteristics. On the other hand, Tōhaku's *Maple,* painted on two sliding doors in the Chishaku-in temple, is fully endowed with them, in spite of its unusually strong coloring. In terms of the composition, of the arrangement of the trunk and of the branches, the Seven Characteristics are clearly revealed. This can be understood even better by looking at a black-and-white photograph of the work (Fig. 8).

The Lofty Dryness of the branches and trunk discloses to a high degree the special quality of Zen painting, a quality that is given expression as well in the asymmetry of the lines of the composition. This emphatically is not beauty in its ordinary sense, such as in Tosa opulence. Here is a strength derived from Lofty Dryness, a mature, dry quality that the color does not negate. The attributes of Sublime Austerity, of Simplicity, and of Subtle Profundity are explicit in spite of the thickly applied color. The tree, for instance, is now an aged trunk displaying Profound Subtlety. At the same time, the pond beneath the trunk plays a highly significant role in the expression of this Profound Subtlety. Tranquillity and depth are present here as well. In spite of its sumptuousness the work gives a feeling of extreme Tranquillity, which, far from disquieting us, calms and sets our mind at rest as we gaze at it. This can be best understood by experiencing the actual painting, which so clearly manifests the Seven Characteristics.

I find it interesting that while Tōhaku painted this gorgeous work, apparently so different from Chinese ink paintings, he also has works in the latter style that can even be said to rival Mu-ch'i; his *Monkeys on an Old Tree* (Pl. 98), belonging to the Ryōsen-an temple in the Myōshin-ji Zen monastery precincts, for example. Here Tōhaku was possibly influenced by Mu-ch'i's *Monkeys* (Pl. 61), one of the set, *Kuan-yin*, *Monkeys*, and *Crane*. But far from being a mere imitation, Tōhaku's work is a free expression of the artist's own personality, and is fully worthy of comparison with Mu-ch'i's painting.

In a way, Tōhaku's painting seems to be even freer and bolder than its Chinese counterpart. The branches and trunk are executed so well that we may call this an ideal Chinese-ink painting. Another work by Tōhaku, *Pine Trees* (Pl. 98), is also an extraordinary example, and shows what Tōhaku was capable of as a painter in this genre. Or rather, it might be said to show that Chinese-ink painting was his basic medium. In other words, what he did in his *Maple* was to execute an ink monochrome painting in color. The truth of this statement can I think be verified in the present work. In this respect, it is different from ordinary Zen paintings, and of course it is vastly different from ordinary polychrome paintings. But above all I would like to regard it as a Zen painting in color, a colored painting of Zen.

More explicitly, although ordinary Chinese-ink painting negates color, a Zen Chinese-ink painting negates even the ink color, since it is still considered as an ordinary color. For this reason, Zen paintings are not just ink paintings in the ordinary sense; they are Zen ink paintings. Thus, what I mean by a polychrome Zen painting is a product of Zen Activity, which, as a renunciation of Zen ink painting, has taken color but has never lost the character of such Zen painting. There is a relationship with Nō costumes and with the materials used in the pouches for the tea caddies and in scroll mountings, all of which may be termed works of Zen art in color.

Comparing the painting of the maple with actual gardens, it has the same feeling as, for example, the Takasago Beach area of the garden of the Katsura Imperial Villa. This area (Pl. 167) has a stone lantern at the end of a promontory, which projects into the pond from a setting of stones. Not only are the compositions of the two similar, but they share a common source. This similarity thus inevitably appears in the compositions arising from this common origin, in elements such as the arrangement of some rocks, or the aspect of a certain pond. The rocks in the upper part of the Takasago Beach photograph produce an effect similar to that of the maple in Tōhaku's painting. This similarity also extends to the relationship between the pond and the blank spaces of the painting. This explains why the Takasago area of the Katsura garden has about it that same sense of Profound Subtlety experienced so strongly in the *Maple*. All is wonderfully simple and natural; there is nothing forced in the composition. Since artificiality is not a factor here, Simplicity is strongly in evidence. The Seven Characteristics are all included in the painting.

ZEN CALLIGRAPHY

Next we turn to some typical works of Zen calligraphy. Calligraphy is classified according to the following three general styles: the regular or block style (*kaisho*), the semi-cursive or "running" style (*gyōsho*), and the cursive or grass style (*sōsho*). Zen calligraphy is found more in running style than regular style, and more in grass style than running style. Even then, old pieces of calligraphy by Zen monks that appear to be written in *kaisho* style are really quite different from ordinary *kaisho*: sometimes the characters slant, at other times their lines are distorted; the overall feeling is never one of regularity, but rather of distortion. For these reasons, Zen calligraphy may generally be said to be of the grass style. Most of the specimens included in the plates are in this style.

6. Hakuin: *Mu* (Pl. 6)
This piece by Hakuin in grass style is of the single Chinese character *wu* (Japanese: *mu*). I think it may be said that this is Chao-chou's *mu*. It appears in a well-known *kōan*, and has been used since the *kōan* was first adopted as an aid to attaining Awakening. A monk once asked Chao-chou if a dog has the Buddha-nature. Chao-chou simply retorted, "No"—*mu*. But this reply transcends "no" in the word's ordinary sense. When the meaning of *mu* is realized truly, the True Self, the Formless Self, is awakened. In other words, far from simply meaning "no," *mu* is Zen itself. The true and living Self, the Self in the Zen sense, is *mu*. Thus when Hakuin wrote this character he attempted to depict this Self. He was writing *mu* not in its usual sense but Chao-chou's *mu*. As Chao-chou's *mu* assumes written form, it is Chao-chou's *mu* that is writing. *Mu* writes *mu*. The *mu* that is written and the *mu* that writes ought to be, and in fact are, wholly One. So this *mu* by Hakuin is itself Hakuin, Hakuin himself. Or it could be said that Hakuin himself took the form of this character *mu* and

therein manifested himself. This is "form without form." The style of this character is unique. It seems to belong to Hakuin alone. The entire form is alive, and somehow seems to be something more than a mere character. We feel that here *mu* is actually manifest, alive and vital.

As can be seen in the reproduction, the ink area is strangely mottled. This was possibly caused by unsuccessful sizing, with dark splotches appearing where the sizing did not take. Yet to me it seems these spots break up the monotony of the light ink wash and, in the manner of the splashed ink style, become a natural part of the whole. It appears as if ink had been daubed on in splotches or flung about in drops. It is, in a manner of speaking, splashed ink calligraphy.

Although this character imparts an impression of grotesqueness, it is not that alone; rather, it attains to the quality of Sublime Austerity, replete with strength, constancy and a masculine vigor. Both the form of the character and the tone of the ink express Subtle Profundity. There is only a single character drawn on the paper's surface, a character of extreme Simplicity lacking any association with worldliness. Here this element of Freedom from Attachment is particularly strong. Within its vitality we feel a calm and reposed subtlety of limitless profundity. It expresses the same serenity that is expressed by Chao-chou's *mu*. It can be regarded as energetic Zen Activity, manifested in a manner that is peculiar to Hakuin.

7. Hakuin: *Sanskrit Character*, symbolizing Acala (Pl. 136)
The style of this character is the same as that of the preceding *Mu*, and the impressions received from both works are also the same. This writing symbolizes (as a substitute for the actual name) Acala Vidyārāja, "the Immovable One." But it seems to express a Zen interpretation of Acala, different from that of Esoteric Buddhism. It is a Zen Acala. Acala in Esoteric Buddhism is a form assumed by Vairocana Tathāgata (Japanese: Dainichi Nyorai), the principal or patron Buddha of that sect. Vairocana is represented as a Buddha whose exceedingly refined and gentle expression makes his compassion and love known to men. Nevertheless, Acala is the destroyer, a form that Vairocana assumes in order to annihilate evil and subjugate every evil demon or obstruction to Awakening. At the very sight of his terrible form, all demons are stricken and, overcome with terror, driven wholly away. He is called the "Commanded Wheel Body" (Japanese *Kyōryō-rin-shin*) of Vairocana Tathāgata; that is to say, at the command of Vairocana he becomes wrath incarnate as the subjugator of evil. Acala thus represents the evil- or demon-quelling activity of Love or Compassion; accordingly, the sense of fearfulness he evokes is natural.

What is interesting here is that although the actual character (Sanskrit: *hmmāṁ*) symbolizing Acala belongs, strictly speaking, to Esoteric Buddhism, when it is written by Hakuin it loses its Esoteric Buddhist quality and becomes Zen. To take this work as a specimen of Esoteric Buddhist art, simply because the character derives from it, is to limit it only to its traditional significance. It is an interpretation contrary to the intention of the calligrapher Hakuin and in opposition to the calligraphy as an expression of Hakuin. Despite the fact the character for Acala is Esoteric, Hakuin's rendering of it nevertheless possesses the Seven Characteristics. Hakuin has not only written the character, he also has painted the picture of Acala. To my mind this picture is not in the least Esoteric; it is a painted exposition of Zen. Hakuin's *Mu* and this character are identical in nature.

Concerning Freedom from Attachment, the work has such intensity as to be free from all things, and to have all things return to this freedom. People think of Sōtō and Rinzai Zen in terms of the former stressing tranquillity and the latter emphasizing activity. Hakuin (Rinzai) tends strongly to break through mere tranquillity; Zen Activity is vigorously in evidence in this work. Yet it is not merely severe, for in it infinite Tranquillity and Subtle Profundity are vividly and dynamically expressed. In my opinion, the Tranquillity contained in Liang K'ai's painting is the basic Tranquillity from which such activity arises. This is the Tranquillity in the first step of the descent from the mountain. Hakuin greatly disliked Esoteric magic. Zen is an activity that, in thoroughly negating such magic, possesses a "bright darkness," that is, Subtle Profundity, and, moreover, never loses this quality.

As I previously stated, that which is written is also that which writes. What is directly manifest here is that that which writes is what is written; that, instead of form producing form, form is produced by what is without form.

8. Huai-su: Excerpts from *Autobiographical Notes* (Pl. 7)

These portions of the autobiographical notes of Huai-su, a Buddhist monk of T'ang China, are a typical expression of Zen. There is a feeling of Austere Sublimity, of becoming seasoned and dried, in the wonderful "thirsty brush" of the grass style characters. And the irregular, broken symmetry is certainly clearly manifested. Plate 7, for example, is not simply a straight row of characters; the characters are of all different sizes, veering off to the right, distorted and misshapen. Yet this distortion has nothing nervous or annoying about it at all—the letters are remarkably natural. The distortion is not intentional, it is a natural result. Nowhere does the *déformation* appear forced.

Notice how free and wild the brushwork is. This is detachment, adherence to "no thing." The wildness derives, after all, from Freedom from Attachment. The remarkably large appearance of the characters stems from the presence of Subtle Profundity and Tranquillity; the freedom and abandon belong to detachment. For example, though the character 戴 (Chinese: *tai*) has many strokes, the feeling it gives here is of Simplicity. The movement of the characters is free and lively, but also the composition is somehow dominated by an infinite serenity, which is grounded in Subtle Profundity.

We feel in the attitude of the writing the deep realm of the calligrapher's concentration, which leaves not a glimmer of discrepancy between the writer and what is written. This is both the naturalness in the concentrated activity of writing the characters and nonattachment to things; it is also the expression of the monk Huai-su himself, who was an unattached, wildly free spirit.

The brushstrokes have the same feeling and tone as the painting of the tree trunk in Tōhaku's *Monkeys* (Pl. 98). What is sensuous, what is blood or flesh, all has fallen away, leaving the bone exposed. We feel this is something with no opening, no fissure at all, something that has gone through a hard and uplifting discipline, and been thoroughly tempered.

The question of the relationship between the blank space and the areas of applied ink is one that recurs in all Zen art. For all its apparent dissimilarities with the garden, when it is compared with, for example, the garden of the Ryōan-ji temple, Huai-su's calligraphy seems to express a feeling similar to the latter—that is, in the relationship between space and what fills space. That the blank space is a complete whole, with no openings whatever, is a natural result of something possessed of Zen. Here, in my opinion, the space is Nothingness, that is, the Self. The way in which the Self Without Form comes to express itself in Chinese characters is consequently inevitable. So, a sculptor, for example, if he is a true sculptor, must virtually become the very space or mass he would carve. If the space is objective, it is not true. In true sculpture the space forms itself; it is form without form: form is created from what has no form. For a sculptor, the space is his Self. Insofar as he keeps the space apart from himself he cannot be a true sculptor. For the sculptor to whom space is objective, the space never becomes his Self and the sculpture never becomes an expression of his Self, no matter how much he may carve. For the true sculptor, such space is his Self; in forming that space he is forming his Self. In fact, a sculptor is a "living space."

It is the same with calligraphy. A man of Zen in the act of writing is the Formless Self in action. Without the working of this Formless Self, space becomes something with form; form expresses form. Thus the space is limited space, and cannot be absolutely formless. In Zen, however, space is not like this, for the Self is the Self Without Form, and it is the Formless Self that is space. And since the Formless Self always expresses itself in what appears in this space, it can be said that the Formless Self expresses itself fully and completely in the whole. The feeling thus produced is not to be encountered in anything else. This is the fundamental basis, and Zen painting, Zen Activity and everything else have their source here. The Seven Characteristics I have formulated are merely an analysis of that fundamental source.

9. I-shan I-ning: *Poem on a Snowy Night* (Pl. 8)

The calligrapher I-shan I-ning was a Chinese Zen monk who came to Japan, where he became naturalized. His calligraphy's distinguishing feature, which is of course inseparably included in the characteristics, is nonobstruction, an unstemmed flow that is unrestrained and unconventional. It is Freedom from Attachment. The brush moves with an unhindered fluidity, without stagnation, unrestricted. Compared with the style of Huai-su's work, we find that it does not have the former's sturdiness born of seasoned austerity. One may feel initially something of the smoothness and continuity seen in examples of the ancient Japanese *kana* syllabary. But upon reflection, it turns out to be qualitatively different from the gentleness of the *kana* script. The difference lies here: although written with a flow and freedom, these qualities contain the Seven Characteristics. Of course, the Japanese syllabary is also asymmetrically balanced, but its asymmetry is not of the kind to include the other characteristics within it. Sublime Austerity, strongly expressed in Huai-su's work, is not lacking in this work by I-shan; it is simply included within the whole in a different form. Profound Subtlety seems to be fully expressed here as well.

Looking at this work, we never feel it to be complex or tedious; it retains its Simplicity in spite of the numerous characters. Its unreluctant Naturalness is evident at a glance. It possesses something liberating, something detached, that imparts to us total freedom. Though written with apparent rapidity, it gives the feeling of Tranquillity: it is not in the least disquieting. In my opinion it differs basically from the writing style of ancient Japanese calligraphers (such as Ono no Tōfū [894–966] and Fujiwara no Yukinari [972–1027]). And while work of this kind did exist in China, in Japan features similar to it are seen in the brushwork of Musō Soseki (Pl. 134) of the Tenryū-ji temple and, in later times, in the calligraphy of Ryōkan (Pls. 9, 142–44).

On the other hand, the works of Hakuin give an entirely different feeling. They have a sense of weight and maturity, a rough, bold thickness. I-shan's work rather reflects neatness, but the basic substance would seem to be identical.

10. Ryōkan: "Mind, Moon, Circle" (Pl. 9)
Although Ryōkan lived centuries after I-shan, the tone of his calligraphy is highly reminiscent of the latter. It is light and easy, neat and simple, frank and openhearted. Looking at it, we have the feeling of Freedom from Attachment. It is the expression of calmness, "no mind," and the spiritual realm of Ryōkan, bouncing a ball, playing innocently with children. Here, of course, nothing is forced or excessive.

Simplicity: into the circle of this engraved wooden potlid the characters fit tidily and simply. It is not regular, expressing instead that which negates regularity—Asymmetry. An austerity is fully present, but Austere Sublimity, a remarkable feature of Huai-su's calligraphy, is not conspicuous here. Still the real characteristic of Ryōkan's writing is this seasoned sublimity, and not

Freedom from Attachment. To be sure, there is clear expression of non-attachment, but unless one has arrived at this state of maturity or ripeness, characters such as these simply cannot be written. They are products of seasoned, sublime austerity. Although Ryōkan often played with children, his childlike quality is completely different from theirs; his innocence was gained as the result of a total process of maturation.

The other works by Ryōkan included in the plates (Pls. 142–44) also express something that is more than mere softness or plasticity; there are also the wiriness, pithiness, and thinness of extreme strength. Ink rubbings of his works also reveal the Seven Characteristics, but preeminent among them is Sublime Austerity.

CALLIGRAPHY AND PAINTING

In painting, Zen generally has taken for its "Self-expression" some objective, external form, e.g., the things of nature, such as trees and birds, but this is not photographic realism. In Zen painting, to "copy" external things is to express in them the True or Formless Self, this Self-expression appearing as a human figure, a bird, a landscape, and so forth. Zen painting is never either realism, or symbolism. Symbolism involves representing something here by means of something there, and considering the latter as the symbol of the former. Thus I would like to call Zen not symbolism, but "expressionism." Moreover, this "expressionism" expresses not the external world, but man's infinite depths, the infinite variety of his Formless Self. Because the Self does the expressing, it expresses itself in all things; because this is an expression of the Formless Self, what expresses is what is being expressed, and what is expressed is "formless form." This is why I prefer to call Zen painting "expressionism." This expression is the Self-expression of humanity's ultimate manner of being. Besides, since the Self that expresses itself is Formless, it is free, and manifests itself anywhere at will. There is no copying of externals, but rather the expression of the Self in what is external.

With regard to painting, "external things" refer to forms in the external world. Calligraphic forms, however, do not exist in nature, in the natural world, but are man-made. In this respect, they come from within rather than are supplied from without. Although it is possible that pictographic writing was originally developed from external forms, it belongs to an early stage of writing. The characters that later emerged from these pictures were made by man. In this respect, calligraphy does not express external forms: its forms are internal—they come from within man. But even as forms expressing something internal, as words—as having existed since ancient times with a definite form—they retain a kind of form, though not one derived from the external world. Yet precisely because this form is not of the external world, calligraphy may well be said to be something man-made projected upon the external world. As such, it is altogether independent of realism. So, despite the old limitations of written language, it is here that I find the interest in calligraphy to be different from that of painting. It is this that allows the calligrapher to abandon himself in his calligraphy, which, in turn, results in the splashed ink style. Accordingly, I personally find calligraphy more interesting than painting.

In calligraphy there is usually a form or formality to be followed; in this it is no different from realism. But this is not true of Zen calligraphy, which is never bound by the preestablished forms of letters. The unconstrained facility of Zen springs from this freedom. It matters not in the least whether the characters are distorted or not. And yet, by having the Formless Self as its base, what is thus written somehow keeps an orderly arrangement. Since the arrangement comes from this base, it springs forth unintentionally. When one goes on writing without thinking of doing this or that, the spacing of the characters will be orderly. When one holds the brush poised over the paper, there, already, space is established as one's Self, that is, as the space of Nothingness. Then, when the characters appear, because of the presence of the space of Nothingness, they spring forth clearly, with characteristics different from those of ordinary characters.

ZEN ARCHITECTURE

Among the various kinds of architecture, none expresses Zen as well as the architecture of the tea room. Of course, there has been much Zen monastery architecture in China. The architecture of the Five Zen Monasteries (built by Emperor Ning Tsung [1194–1224] of the Southern Sung), for example, seems particularly fine, and today these buildings still remain. Therefore, one cannot limit Zen architecture to the tea room alone. Japan, as well, retains numerous examples of Zen architecture in her monasteries. The monastery architecture of the so-called Gozan ("Five Mountains"), both of Kamakura and Kyōto, and that of other temples as well, can also be called Zen architecture.

In China, the Zen monasteries are architecturally different from those of the other Buddhist schools. Yet, the architecture of the tea room, even more than the Chinese Zen monasteries, is inseparably associated with the seven characteristics. In other words, architecture that accords with the characteristics of Zen did not appear until the creation of tea room architecture in Japan. In this sense, the tea room is a more essentially Zen-type structure than the Chinese Zen monasteries.

Tea room architecture has features in common with the works of painting and calligraphy already considered. They are all in perfect accord; but this is not necessarily the case with a Zen monastery. For instance, compared with Mu-ch'i's *Pa-Pa Bird*, a Zen monastery evokes feelings of a different order: there is no sense of dry maturity, freedom in activity, Simplicity, or Asymmetry. The Five Zen Monasteries of Kyoto, for example, strike one as being well proportioned. They are more symmetrical than asymmetric, do not possess Austere Sublimity, and somehow appear only massive. They have no unrestrained quality, no lightness or Simplicity. In this they differ from the aspects of Zen culture that have these qualities. Yet the tea room is in perfect harmony with each of the paintings and calligraphic specimens dealt with before. The painting of the *Pa-Pa Bird* will never be out of place hanging in the *tokonoma* of a tea room; hung in a Zen monastery, that harmony somehow collapses. Thus, I find it highly significant that the tea houses came to be built not as monastery adjuncts but as lay architecture.

Tea room architecture appeared when Zen entered the lives of the common people; it was a structure based upon that life, and not the creation of Buddhist monks or monasteries. What kind of men were these lay Buddhists who developed a taste for such tea rooms? They were people of Zen. The earliest tea structures were built in the Muromachi period, following the shogunate of Ashikaga Yoshimasa (1436–90), by men such as Murata Shukō, Takeno Jōō, Sen no Rikyū, and Kobori Enshū (1578–1647). Although they were laymen, Zen was the main element in their lives. That is the reason Zen appeared in architecture, and the reason for it doing so through a form of lay life, specifically that of the Way of Tea. This is tea room architecture. The Tōgu-dō of the Ginkaku-ji temple, a tea room-type structure built earlier, during the beginning years of Yoshimasa's rule, still bears the stylistic influences of Buddhist temple architecture. Its qualities do not yet manifest the Seven Characteristics.

11. *Tea room (shoin style), Zangetsu-tei, Omote Senke (Pl. 10)*
There are two structural styles in tea rooms or tea houses that can be said to manifest Zen: the *shoin* "study" or "writing house," and the *sōan* ("grass hut"). It is the *sōan* style that truly reflects in architecture the formation of the true Self of Zen. The *shoin* style is more proper and formal than the *sōan*, and thus has a sense of being well proportioned and ceremonial. Typical of this *shoin* style is the tea room of Zangetsu-tei ("Lingering Moon Arbor"), belonging to the Omote Senke school of Tea. Other examples are those located in the Katsura Imperial Villa; they are called the Old, Middle, and New Shoin, and all have a very formal and proper appearance. Nevertheless, their formality is endowed with the Seven Characteristics. In respect to Asymmetry, for instance, a *shoin* structure is comparatively more symmetrical than a tea house of the *sōan* type. Though relatively more symmetrical, when closely examined it

is seen to be not quite symmetrical, for example, in its ceilings or in the construction of its windows and walls. Moreover, other characteristics—Sublime Austerity, Subtle Profundity, and Simplicity—are present as well, if only in their broadest meanings.

Although in the *shoin* style, the tea houses of the Katsura Imperial Villa have a sense of complete Simplicity, a feeling of Freedom from Attachment that is extremely light and facile, a serenity, and a touch of Profound Subtlety, all appear in a harmonious whole. In this they are unique, and defy comparison with any other structures.

Therefore, the Katsura Imperial Villa's *shoin* tea houses constitute a distinct and separate form of architecture. The formality of this *shoin* style when made "cursive," into a "grass" style, as it were, is the *sōan* style of tea room architecture. The *shoin* style probably dates from before the introduction of Zen to Japan in the Kamakura period. An architectural style similar to *shoin* was introduced into Zen monasteries prior to the appearance of tea rooms in that style. As Zen monastery architecture, it was very ceremonious and imposing. By making this style "cursive," I mean taking it beyond the *shoin* style and bringing it closer to the Seven Characteristics.

The *shoin* style tea house came into being in the following way: a man of the Way of Tea had these Seven Characteristics within himself; wishing to build a tea house in the *shoin* style, he critically chose according to his own sense from the elements in this style as it already existed.

A tea house in the resulting style might be called an intermediate architectural stage between the *shoin* style of the Zen monastery and the *sōan*-style tea house. Its style is not so formal or proper as the former and it is thus closer to the "grass-hut" style. But it includes all the structural elements of the Zen monastery, whereas in the *sōan* style, it is fair to say, such elements are completely absent.

12. *Shōkin-tei tea house (sōan style), Katsura Imperial Villa* (Pl. 11)
The *sōan* style is completely free of the architectural elements of the Zen monastery. It comprises what has been selected according to the Zen characteristics and is in genuine and full accord with them. Tea houses in this style are still being built today. When the Way of Tea became a pastime of the manorial lords and little more than an indulgent luxury, instead of keeping the quality of *wabi*, a "poverty beyond riches," the tea house evolved into the *shoin* style and tended toward the *shoin* architecture of the Zen monastery. Rikyū said "The true essence of Tea lies in the Tea of the *sōan*," and in that respect the Shōkin-tei ("Pine Harp Arbor"), a *sōan* tea house for *wabi-cha*, the "Tea of *wabi*," seems to be the truest expression of the essence of Zen. In other words, the *sōan* tea house may be considered the finest architectural form in which Zen has ever expressed itself.

The roof, instead of being formal, seems wanting in symmetry. Some roofs are triangular, others rectangular, and some look as if they had been chopped off irregularly. Totally lacking in symmetry, they are truly asymmetric. The Asymmetry of the roof, blending with the tea house garden, produces an effect appropriate to Zen. The placement of the rocks in the garden is not exact; they are "random" and irregular. A stone wall is never made of well-fitting stones: some are small, others large; some are protruding, others recessed—all asymmetric, and simple as well. The entire structure has a sublime, austere quality, for all wooden materials are well aged.

Then there is the Profound Subtlety of the tea house, which I consider of particular importance. The tea house is indeed deeply reserved. This feeling permeates the interior greatly. Dark as it is, the darkness is not the darkness of a temple of Esoteric Buddhism, or the darkness of an image of Acala (see p. 33). It is not fear or uneasiness that we feel, but a calm and a Tranquillity that turns us inward and invites us to return to the root of our being. It might be called a quiet, composed darkness, wherein we find an expression of the infinitely deep Formless Self of Zen. The entire tea house, interior and exterior, is designed to that end.

The architectural simplicity is apparent at a glance. There are some who say the tea house is unnatural, but they are referring to poor construction. When, as sometimes happens, foreigners try to copy tea house architecture, the result is invariably tasteless, and exceedingly unnatural. A true tea house is in no way unnatural: it is Naturalness itself. It has a Freedom from Attachment evoking a separation from the world as well as a liberation of man's mind. The Tranquillity of the tea house needs no further exposition here.

Besides the tea house, it is unlikely one will find any structure possessing all these characteristics. Of course this does not necessarily mean the tea house must always be as it is now. If a structure with these basic characteristics were constructed today, it would probably become, as Zen architecture, a new architecture in a new style. Such changes have already appeared in painting and in calligraphy. They are, to say the least, conscious attempts to create something lacking in the West. But since they show a fascination in what comes from the depths of humanity, it seems inadequate merely to aim consciously at such a goal. In architecture, too, I think that if someone, even without possessing in himself the Seven Characteristics, tried to construct a building with these characteristics, he would be likely, at least, to end up with a structure approximating his original intention.

ZEN IKEBANA

Ikebana is divisible into *chabana* (floral art for the Way of Tea) and *ryūgibana*, (that associated with the ordinary ikebana schools). The art has been practiced in Japan from ancient times, originating as floral offerings on Buddhist altars. This early "ikebana," however, was a formal style, which demanded that the flower setting be formally correct, well balanced, and never unshapely in order to be fit for offering before the Buddha. Flowers set in such a manner are called "standing flowers" (*rikka*), whereas the type I will be dealing with here is called *nageire* (literally, "thrown in").

Not formally set, *nageire* flowers are of the "grass" style, the *déformation* of the *rikka* style. They are in full accord with the nature of the Way of Tea. Placed in a tea house possessed of the quality of *wabi*, they never look out of place; they match exactly the tea house architecture. Flowers in the *rikka* style, on the other hand, seem altogether disconnected and in disharmony with such a structure. The *nageire* style of flowers can be said, I believe, to be a special genre of ikebana created by the Way of Tea. Since Tea became popular, flowers for it have been called *chabana*, to distinguish them from standing flowers and other types of flower arrangement.

Although ordinary ikebana includes some styles that may be described as irregular, the irregularity is very different from that of *chabana*. Among the schools of ikebana, such as of the Ikenobō school or the Mishō school, there are irregular or uneven styles; for example, the running style, and the even more cursive grass style. But they all differ from flowers for Tea in their manner of *déformation*, though they do, it is true, possess a kind of deformity. The *déformation* of the Tea ikebana shown in the plates possesses those same qualities I have been using to describe painting and calligraphy; that is, they possess the Seven Characteristics. Basically, therein lies their wide difference from other ikebana. Today various styles are used in ikebana, but few of them seem to have the Seven Characteristics.

13. *Chabana* (Pl. 13)

The flower shown here is what is called *tessen*, a Japanese variety of clematis. The clematis is placed in a rough, unglazed pot of Nanban ware with a surface pitted by tiny stones. The flowerpot is to be hung on the wall. In it there is a snow-white flower, surrounded by five leaves, which—growing of course on the twisted stalk of this plant—are not set symmetrically. Rather, the manner in which the flower and the five leaves are set negates symmetry.

Austere Sublimity: The three most prominent leaves seem to express something tightened and dried. The lowest leaf, facing upward and producing a strong, firm effect in response to the overhead flower, though but a single leaf, expresses qualities of strength and sturdiness. The leaf extending to the right along with the tendrillike stem also seems to impart a sense of tightness, of being dry. The stems above the flower are sturdy-looking as well, imparting no sense of fragility. The leaves stretching out in three directions centered around the flower produce the effect of dryness, of being somehow quiet, with an air of antiquity. In the midst of these seemingly dry stalks is the simple snow-white flower in full bloom. Instead of being sensual, bright and colorful, its form is neat and simple, expressing a noble and sublime attitude. The feeling of Sublime Austerity is amply expressed.

When we compare this with Mu-ch'i's *Pa-Pa Bird*, we feel that there is a fundamental consistency. The single flower is analogous to the solitary *pa-pa* bird, and the leaves that extend in three directions are similar to the pine twigs or vines of the painting.

There is an abundance of Profound Subtlety; and gentle restraint, modesty and understatement are manifest in this ikebana. There is something here akin to darkness, with the white flower imbued with a kind of luminous darkness that never appears shallow or superficial.

Simplicity is also expressed. The leaves are few; of the five, only three are conspicuous, and they are asymmetrically placed without severing their mutual relationship. With the preservation of a concise unity there is no feeling of repetition or complication.

No artificiality: Nothing is forced; no leaf that should be facing upward is facing down, and vice versa. The stems, though curving and bending, show no unnatural aspect; they are placed in complete Naturalness.

Freedom from Attachment: The flower, its pure whiteness undefiled by the dust of the world, avoids ostentation, and emerges trim and well shaped; we naturally feel its Simplicity. Never would it give rise to worldly thoughts. This is not only true of the flower but of the ceramic pot as well, in its color and shape.

Serenity: No one is likely to receive a feeling of disquiet from this ikebana. Seeing it makes one calm, brings quiet to one's mind. None of the Seven Characteristics is lacking, nor is there present here anything to detract from them in any way. Thus this ikebana is in keeping with the other articles reproduced in this book, and forms with them a harmonious whole. Placed side by side with the *Pa-Pa Bird* painting, the presence of this harmony will be apparent to all.

Further, no qualitative difference would be felt if this ikebana were placed beside a work by Ryōkan, I-shan I-ning, or Huai-su. The irregular arrangement of Huai-su's characters, for example, is entirely congruent with the three-pointed array of the clematis leaves; the sinuous strength of the clematis tendrils can be identified with the dry sturdiness of the calligraphic lines. Thus, there is no incongruity when the flower is hung in a tea room—especially when that tea room is of the *sōan* type—either on the main pillar of the *tokonoma* alcove or on the *tokonoma* wall in place of some hanging scroll, such as a piece of calligraphy from the brush of a Zen monk. A flower in a ceramic pot, a piece of calligraphy—the two are dissimilar only in being different objects; fundamentally they are identical: in both Zen expresses itself.

To reiterate, ikebana of this kind is altogether different from that of the standing style, or from any ikebana not possessed of the Seven Characteristics. The *chabana*, among all the forms of ikebana, stand out as having this unique quality. Since flowers are ephemeral, examples from past ages of course have not come down to us—although hereafter photography will enable them to be preserved for posterity. We know about "standing flowers" of the past through numerous examples depicted in old books, but since such works do not exist for *chabana*, we have no means of knowing what they were like.

Chabana are not formal arrangements made according to set rules. The flowers are placed in a vessel without rules, or, according to the "Rule of No Rule." With standing flowers and the like—those which are formally "arranged"—there are certain rules by which the flowers are placed, and according to which instructions may be given. But with *chabana* no such instructions are possible. In this very impossibility the interest lies, and in it as well we see the nature of the *chabana* "rules" that are freed from rules. Accordingly, what is required is to truly realize this nature for oneself and to place flowers freely, independent of all precepts; in other words, what is required is Zen Activity. When the Seven Characteristics are inseparably fused within the person who places the flowers, so as to constitute his Fundamental Subject, then even a single flower set in a pot will be an expression of these seven qualities. That is the ultimate rule, the essence of *chabana*. Thus this may be termed an ikebana beyond instruction.

Since this is beyond instruction, it is exceedingly difficult. Devotees of ikebana schools, who follow rules for flower arrangement, are often heard to remark at the difficulty of *chabana*. Such words have great meaning in that they are uttered by those who are trying to arrange flowers according to established principles. They know better than most the limitation of the rules they follow. They are, let me say, well aware of the restrictions of the rule-conforming way of being. In that awareness we notice an inner need to break through the rules. Thus their comment on the difficulty of *chabana* is the genuine utterance of one aware of his confined circumstances. Herein we can see the great importance of a "leap" in bringing this type of ikebana to life.

Of course this is not simply a matter of picking flowers in a field and throwing them into a vase. Although ordinary ikebana can be properly done only after years of practice, there seem to be some who think that *chabana*, or *nage-ire*, are very easy, that all they have to do is to put some flowers into a vase. Such "arrangements" are far from being true *chabana*. Rather, they proceed in the direction of regularity; they are but very naïve ikebana tending toward the adoption of rules. Yet, it appears that many consider such creations to be *chabana*. It is a fact that we seldom come across arrangements that impress us in their transcendence of rules, as forms unrestricted by regularity. This is because the high level, the profundity of such ikebana, that is, that which is prior to or transcends rules, is lacking in the person who sets the flowers. "Prior to rules" does not suggest naïveté, but rather that from which rules are derived and which is never a feature of the rules per se. It involves, therefore, what is constantly in the process both of negating and forming rules. In other words, rules are here applicable only once. Rules that emerge are good as far as they are appropriate, but should what pertains now be such that it goes on to dominate what follows in succeeding moments as well, such a "rule" is only restrictive, and once formed, will endure and continue to bind us. Thus, the rules for *chabana* are appropriate only once. Because of this very transience of their validity, they possess eternal meaning. Of all rules, those that are true are the ones that are eternal in themselves but never restrict what follows.

Further, the subject from which such rules ensue conforms with them, what Zen refers to as "being master of every situation." Each time a rule is formed it is true. The rules that never dominate the subject that forms them, the rules that are formed by the subject that creates or forms but is never dominated by it, rules newly formed and yet that alter moment by moment, flexible rules (for no true rules are fixed)—such are the ultimate, crowning rules. Such rules will be impossible to achieve so long as their nature remains external to us. They are possible only when the rule-forming subject *is* the Rule of No Rule. This is not necessarily applicable to *chabana* alone: all Zen art has this quality at its source. Only then can rules be rules in which Zen expresses itself. Because Zen possesses a basic freedom, this results quite naturally.

14. *Chabana* (Pl. 12)

Once again, the flower is the clematis; here there are two blossoms and seven leaves. The odd number of leaves coincides with the quality of Asymmetry. The five leaves of the previous work helped to produce the asymmetric but unified effect of the three prominent leaves; without the two leaves just above the blossom the whole effect would have been lost, and the remaining three would have lost their coherence with each other. The two apparently meaningless and not exactly leaflike leaves there play an indispensable role.

The seven leaves of the present work face in various directions, thus breaking any symmetry. However, this effect is in no way deliberately intended. Five of the seven are visible, also an odd number, and, though facing in different directions, they look unified. Had the tendril stretching to the left ended at the juncture of the two leaves above the flower, the whole plant would in a sense be dead. But the curved end of the thin vine gives life to the leaves, providing them with a kind of resonance. Although these leaves do not play as asymmetrically powerful a role as those of the previous work, they tighten and pull together the two flowers.

The upper flower, surrounded by leaves, seems to be blossoming out of them. It is one with the leaves, never isolated from them; they are in complete harmony. Alone, the upper flower would have cut the overall effect in half; without the lower flower the leaves on the tendril would lose their vitality. It is due to the lower flower that the leaves above come to life. On the other hand, without those leaves the flower underneath would be without support, as if somehow hanging in transit. As it is, there is a complete unity with the flower hanging downward, the tendril extending sideways, and the leaves. The upper flower faces the lower, the lower flower looks up as if the two were conversing.

The shape and color of the black Seto ware flower vase make the flowers come to life in the manner they do. They come to life precisely because of the jar's blackness, because of its small, swollen body and its narrow neck. Reciprocally, the vase is greatly enhanced and brought to life by the flowers. We may say that through this reciprocity the present work has been brought into being.

I will not in this case dwell upon each of the Seven Characteristics. If the work is observed as carefully as the previous one, its Zen characteristics will be seen to be harmoniously included. For the previous *chabana*, a hanging wall container was employed, the flower being placed in the manner appropriate to the container. Here the vase is placed below, on the floor of the *tokonoma* alcove, and the flowers are set in a manner entirely suited to this position.

In the West the term "flower arrangement" is used because the flowers are simply arranged in the sense that they are gathered in an orderly manner. Setting *chabana* is nothing like flower arrangement in this sense of the term. The former means giving flowers life, true life. This does not imply bringing home wild flowers and fixing them as they grew in the fields, true to nature. No mere arrangement or skillful reproduction of nature, a *chabana* setting must, necessarily, be the Self-expression of Zen. This Self-expression involves the Self Without Form temporarily borrowing the form of flowers—infusing them, so to speak—thereby enabling the flowers to arrange themselves. The result of such Self-formation is true *chabana*. Living the life of Zen should also be of such a Self-formative nature; what does not have this quality is not Zen art. So it may be said that *chabana* is extremely exacting in nature. In this sense I do not consider *chabana* as flower arrangement in the term's usual sense. Rather, I believe it to be a penetration into the life of the flowers by allowing the essence, or Nothingness, of the flowers act to make them express themselves.

I have already mentioned that the grass style is the *déformation* of the formal or proper style, yet there seem to be two kinds of *déformation*. One may be said to be naïve, and has no regularity from the very beginning. The other is what negates fixed rules and the restrictions resulting when rules become set and crystalized. What is free is what has passed through rules, what has gone beyond rules. Something beyond rule is inevitably subjective, not objective. Further, there are diverse kinds of subjectivity. I am speaking of what is fundamentally subjective and formless continuing to give birth to rules without becoming attached to them. What is thus engendered states the relation of the grass style to the formal style.

ZEN GARDENS

Gardens also are of various kinds, having existed in the West and in the East as well since very early times. As the term "landscape gardening" or "landscape architecture" would indicate, gardens are not so much natural as artificial creations, so that in a manner of speaking they are works of art. Among such gardens are included those in accord with Zen. In discussing some typical Zen gardens, I would like to consider their characteristic elements.

In Japan Zen gardens have been built roughly since the Kamakura and Muromachi periods, and may be divided into two kinds. One, consisting of gardens that are ordinarily attached to Zen temple-monasteries, is designed for the most part to be viewed and appreciated from inside the buildings. Of course it is possible to walk in such gardens, but most are constructed more to be viewed from a temple room or the *shoin* style tea house of a temple than for walking. Of this type examples abound—for instance, the gardens before the head priest's quarters (*hōjō*) of the Daitoku-ji, the Nanzen-ji, or of other temple-monasteries too numerous to enumerate here. These gardens were built by Zen priests. One monk well known as a landscape gardener is Musō Soseki. He is responsible for the construction of the gardens of the Saihō-ji and Tenryū-ji temples in Kyoto, the Eihō-ji temple on Mount Kokei in Gifu Prefecture, and many others. Some of these are merely attributed to him, but most of them are unquestionably his work. His gardens were made for viewing, and in them is seen what conforms with Zen, the expression of Zen.

The second type is that commonly called the *roji*, also referred to as a "tea garden." There are no definitive Chinese characters for the word *roji*, so that while we usually have 露地 ("exposed ground"), sometimes it is 路次 ("passage-way"), or 廬路 ("cottage path"), or others. Since the time of Sen no Rikyū, the characters that represent "exposed ground" have often been used with a particular meaning, derived from a phrase in the Lotus Sutra: "a white ox on the exposed ground." This makes it clear the significance of the garden has undergone a change—a change in concept—since Rikyū's day. It was with a very deep meaning the characters 露地 ("exposed ground") came to be used, for from the Zen standpoint, they refer to the garden as an expression of Zen.

The garden of the Katsura Imperial Villa is at once for viewing and for walking. It is designed not only for admiring the view while walking through it, but also just for walking to or from a tea house; in that sense it is a pathway. A garden like this is more important from the aspect of walking than from that of viewing. So for the walkers' convenience, stepping-stones, paving stones, and veen shoe-removing stones are employed. Yet all the stones are alike in being expressions of Zen. Although the builder surely constructed the garden in order that people might walk in it, it may also be said that it was built so that walkers may feel something of Zen.

When stepping-stones are arranged in accordance with Zen sense, they will naturally be such that from them one feels what Zen is. Of course the composition of stepping-stones, etc. is accomplished in accord with the Seven Characteristics. This is clearly noticed when we see a truly well-realized garden.

15. *Stepping-stones below the Tsukimidai ("Moon-Viewing Platform"), Katsura Imperial Villa* (Pl. 14)

Even with stones, those of similar appearance are not used; every stone is different in shape, and there is rich variety. Few symmetrical—square or rectangular—stones are used. Even among those that look like checkered paving, there are no truly square stones used. Some are large, some are small, some long and some short. All are fit together so that no stones of the same size are used; thus the symmetry is broken. When cut stones are used they are somehow arranged without the impression of symmetry or regularity of shape. The arrangement nowhere forms a straight line or single direction; rather, zigzag lines prevail. Of course this stems from the practical consideration of making it convenient for people to step upon them; but that is not the only reason, for in this way the stones also assume an asymmetric pattern in a natural way. It is this point that is clearly felt in the composition of the stepping-stones in the *roji* of any tea house. I chose the present garden because it seems to express eloquently the attraction and interest of the Asymmetry of stepping-stones.

Their interest lies not only in the breaking of symmetry, but also in the remarkable unity they reveal in spite of their apparent isolation from each other. The unity of symmetry is of a simple order, whereas symmetry that is broken and yet retains its unity is of a higher level. In this light, since the present composition of stepping-stones genuinely reveals the unity of Asymmetry, they may be termed unassailable, invulnerable. It would not be possible to move any of the stones. Move one and the whole would become monotonous and symmetrical. Due to the presence of each stone, the overall symmetry is broken, bringing the whole composition to life. Each stone in that manner is necessary and indispensable. This is Naturalness, the lack of artificiality.

It is not deliberately intended, but is a natural outcome of the expression, the natural expression without conscious striving, of Zen, which is living and functioning vitally within. Herein we see the true greatness of such landscape architecture. In that respect a symmetrical tea garden is a failure. In a tea garden, square-cut stones might be appropriate for stepping upon but would be too alien to merge into the whole. Only gardens such as those shown here are able to match the structure of the tea house. Thus the feeling one gets from the *roji* garden while walking through it never alters even upon entering the tea house; instead the tea house is the culmination of this feeling. Neither inside, in the tea room, nor outside, among the stones, is the feeling ever broken. Building such a garden is extremely difficult, but such gardens actually do exist.

What is true of the stepping-stones is true as well of the disposition of the trees. Not any tree will do; they must be well chosen: this tree is not interesting here, that tree is just right, and so on. Some varieties of trees are chosen especially for particular uses. And among similar varieties of trees, specific ones are chosen for their particular shape or height and planted in an asymmetrical manner. Stone lanterns, water basins, and other objects to be used in the *roji* will not be chosen if they are of regular shape. The stone lanterns used in the Katsura Imperial Villa are truly appropriate in taste for a tea house. Stepping-stones, trees, stone lanterns—with these the *roji* garden is in every respect expressive of the characteristic of Asymmetry. The feeling produced is not one of formality, but of the *déformation* of the grass style.

Austere Sublimity: The rock steps are not rounded or full, as if, for example, they were flesh and blood, but are angular, dry, and hard. All the rocks give a feeling of dryness and make us feel something sturdy or strong at the same time. Most are manly and rugged, not frail and feminine. The rock steps are indeed strong exponents of lofty dryness.

Trees of great age rather than those green and fresh are suitable for the *roji*. As for pruning, some prefer to leave the trees natural and do not like to have a gardener shape them. They are afraid naturalness will be lost. But here again, shaping the trees never means making them artificial or unnatural; even though this involves the hand of man, the trees are transformed into what is "natural." Properly done, they are far from anything approaching artificiality. Instead of merely growing in abandon, they are transmuted into what agrees with the spirit of the Way of Tea. It is sometimes said that trees should be shaped to be "just as they are in nature." But this does not mean mere nature, nor mere imitation of it. It means, as in the previous case of the *chabana*, trimming the trees so they might express the Seven Characteristics of Zen art. And actually this is what happens; the trees are found to possess the Seven Characteristics, free from unnaturalness or artificiality.

A tea garden has about it a gentle restraint—Profound Subtlety. There is never a sense of superficiality. The moss of the garden clothes and leaves the ground unexposed, producing the effect of Deep Reserve. The beauty and deepness of the moss express Subtle Profundity. Placing rocks and stones as if they were resting on the ground is avoided, for the natural grace and restraint is increased when the stones are placed so they appear to be emerging from deep beneath the surface. The greatest portion of each stone seems to be buried, with only a relatively small area visible above ground. The way in which the stones are tastefully set in place is very important.

The base of the stone must be kept from sight, concealed, for example, by mosses, or as is many times the case, covered with short fernlike plants or low underbrush. The tasteful effect of the stepping-stones greatly varies according to whether moss is present or not. In the Katsura gardens, the stepping-stones would appear quite different without the distinctive ferns. The high degree of gentle restraint we feel in this garden may well be dependent on them. Thus such plants were not included in the garden simply because, as things of the natural world, they look natural, but were planted in order to establish a tone of tasteful reserve or Profound Subtlety. Beside every stone wash basin without exception some ferns or other small plants are planted in order to keep the foot of the basin from being exposed. This makes it possible to give expression to the profundity of the stone.

Stones are said to have *sabi*, the quality of being seasoned enough to appear tranquil, serene, antique and graceful. To leave the stones fully exposed would deprive them of Deep Reserve. When stones communicate newness instead of age or *sabi*, they give the sense of full exposure and lack of Profound Subtlety. Subtle Profundity demands using stones with as much *sabi* as possible, and if new stones are employed, making them look serene, antique and graceful as soon as possible. Thus the tea garden is constructed to be gracefully reserved. A tea garden that is too bright and clear is unpleasing. A darkness of a sort, a "calming darkness," is needed. Trees are planted to lessen the effect of light. The garden should not be dark to the point of gloominess; a "light darkness," a "calming darkness" is the suitable atmosphere for a tea garden. No other garden resembles a *roji*.

The tea garden is not in the least complicated. Its Simplicity, as in, say, the asymmetrical scattering of the stepping-stones, evokes no sense of tedious complication. The present garden gives the feeling of somehow being simple; but it is not delicate. It is rough and uneven; but more than that, it has a simple quality that includes the other six characteristics.

Naturalness: The Simplicity, Asymmetry, roughness, etc., of this garden have none of the annoying artificiality found in those tea houses or tea gardens whose presumption renders them unfit to quality in this category. Instead, here we feel the presence of No Mind, of an unintentional quality that is artless and natural, the kind of Naturalness beyond mere naturalness, made by man but nevertheless truly natural and far from any element of exertion.

Freedom from Attachment is also a highly important quality in a tea garden. There is a verse on the *roji*:

> The *roji* is the path
> Outside the world of restlessness;
> How could the dust
> Of the mind be scattered there?

According to this, the *roji*'s nature is such as to enable one who enters to rid himself of the dust of the world and to forget completely about worldliness. Were it not built to accomplish this, it would not be a *roji* in the true sense of that word.

In the Lotus Sutra the *roji* is no other than the world of Awakening. The word *ro* (露) indicates "exposure" of the "Mind Ground," or, in my expression, the exposure of the Formless Self or the Fundamental Subject that is Absolutely Nothing. This is the true *roji*, and it naturally must be a place where one is freed from worldliness. It is important upon entering the *roji* for one to remember that since it is a place free from attachment, one is there to remove the dust of the world. Yet in spite of this, it is one of the marvels of the Zen garden, one of its most significant aspects, that even should one enter it without any preconsideration, one will, naturally, become freed from worldliness. In other words, here the Mind Ground will be disclosed, in the same sense that the word *roji* is used in the Lotus Sutra. And this disclosure will come about in a completely natural manner, for the *roji* has just such a detached characteristic.

Tranquillity: Of course, it goes without saying that a *roji* ought to be calm; a disquieting *roji* is simply not a *roji*. A tea garden is free from all disquiet. Therefore, even the placement of stones must not cause any agitation. Nor should the distortion or *déformation*, the garden's Asymmetry, result in anything but total peace. Quietude is implicit in Simplicity, so that even if there are a great many stones, they should be simple, and their shapes and placement should also give rise to calm and serenity. A fine tea garden is possessed of a calm able to quiet the mind.

The garden of the tea house may be built anywhere adjacent to the structure, in however abbreviated or narrow an area, even in the middle of a city—though the gardens in the Katsura Imperial Villa are quite spacious. Even located amid a bustling downtown area it will make one who enters forget all the noises. If it is unable to lead us to such calmness it is not a true *roji*.

In the *roji* there is a structure called a *machiai*, or waiting arbor, in which a bench is provided. The stone steps of the *machiai* in the Katsura gardens (Pl. 168) are arranged with really admirable skill. The grouping of stones in front of the Shōkin-tei, and the surrounding area, is so constructed that anyone seeing it will feel his mind growing quiet.

16. *Path between the Tsukimidai and the Gepparō, Katsura Imperial Villa* (Pl. 15) Generally speaking, in all the *shoin* structures in the Katsura Imperial Villa—not the Shōkin-tei (*sōan* structure)—the tea rooms are rather formal in style. The *roji* leading to them are also of the same style. The stepping-stones of this *roji*, which lead to the Gepparō tea house, for example, are suited to *shoin* architecture; they possess the *shoin*-like touch we find in the *roji* itself, which

serves as a pathway to and from the *shoin* tea house. The Gepparō, viewed from the far end of this *roji*, looks truly deep and secluded. Although the tree in the background is neatly pruned into a cylindrical form, its symmetry is broken by the diagonal slant of the roof of the Gepparō, and the overall appearance is not one of regularity. The somewhat retired, graceful and tasteful appearance of the Gepparō, which does not reveal itself in its entirety, gives the feeling of true Subtle Profundity and Tranquillity. There is somehow a sense of Sublime Austerity, which is very much enhanced by the sturdy constancy of the garden trees. The arrangement of the stepping-stones negates the straight line of the stone path. The presence of these rocks gives the garden the informality of the *sōan* style. From this discussion, the essential qualities of the tea house *roji* should have become clear. An indication of the typical *sōan* style *roji* appears in the plate of the Shōkin-tei (Pl. 11).

With the tea house there is a gate or *kuguri*. Plate 170 shows the inner gate or *naka-kuguri* of the Zangetsu-tei at the Omote Senke school of Tea. The gate helps to give the *roji* depth, and a restrained, reserved gracefulness. It imparts the impression of partitioning different realms, as if it were dividing the worldly from the detached; the impression is given that, in passing through it, one enters a region of tasteful reserve, an utterly new world. In this sense I am very fond of *naka-kuguri*, especially one as admirably constructed as that in the Zangetsu-tei. At the tea house of the Shinju-an temple in the Daitoku-ji Zen monastery compound (Pl. 171) a guest washes his hands at a stone water basin after, not before, passing through the gate. Such an arrangement is unusual, for here a stone water basin, which is ordinarily found outdoors, is set indoors. This finding the outdoors indoors gives a feeling of Deep Reserve or Subtle Profundity. The *roji* garden is of this same nature.

Whereas *shoin* gardens, even those only for viewing, are of various kinds, some having trees or water and others without water, gardens of Zen temple-monasteries have characteristics different from those of gardens that existed prior to the introduction of Zen, i.e., Zen characteristics. But in my own opinion, the *roji*, the tea garden, of all gardens most clearly expresses such characteristics; therein, we may say, the Zen characteristics are consummated.

17. *Stone Garden, Ryōan-ji, Kyoto* (Pls. 173–75)

This well-known, *shoin* style, Zen temple garden has not a single tree; it is bordered on two sides by an old earthen wall from which emanates a sense of Subtle Profundity and of dryness. Rectangular, enclosed by the earthen wall topped by tile, the Zen interest of this *shoin* garden is to be found in the Seven Characteristics that constitute its essence.

The garden stones themselves and their arrangement into five groups both exhibit Asymmetry. Note the odd number of the grouping. Further, each group itself is a far cry from anything that could be called symmetric. Nor does the rectangular shape, even though with its straight lines it is quite regular, ever appear conspicuous. This is due to the disposition of the stones. Symmetry, even when present, never dominates, but is broken by the placement of the stones. The whole area is completely transformed into asymmetric space.

Austere Sublimity is definitely present in the mode of being and shape of the stones. Every stone is truly dry, with a kind of inviolable dignity: each has a feeling of constancy, of being seasoned and aged, of calmness. Regarding Profound Subtlety, the entire garden suggests a depth of unknown profundity. In this sense, although the term *seki-tei* or "stone garden," is perfectly appropriate for this garden, I prefer the term *kū-tei*, "empty garden." The term "empty" refers to the depth of the garden, the depth of the Fundamental Subject that is Nothing, of the Formless Self. The Ryōan-ji garden, in that sense, is incomparably expressive of the Formless Self of Zen. The profundity of the garden is felt all the more because of the sparseness of the rocks. Too many stones, or too much variation, would absorb all our attention and render it difficult for us to sense Nothingness or Emptiness: in this garden the number of stones is kept to the absolute minimum. That is why I prefer the term empty garden to describe what makes its appearance here.

Two ancient lines well illustrate a special point.

A bird cries. The mountain quiet deepens.
An ax rings out. Mountain stillness grows.

A verse reading "Not a bird cries. The mountain is very quiet" would be bereft of life, indicating nothing more than a naïve and shallow quiet. The quiet that appears from the bird's cry is qualitatively different from that where no cry is heard. It possesses at its base a limitlessness of expression, while the latter is nothing but a monotonous and simple absence. Only with the quietude and depth that forms the basis of this source, what I call the Fundamental Subject that is Actively Nothing, is true profundity or Profound Subtlety possible. To me the rock groupings in the Ryōan-ji garden indicate the feeling of the mountain, becoming even more deeply quiet when a bird cries, or the effect of Subtle Profundity as the sound of the ax rings out amid the deep forest trees. As we gaze upon the overall disposition of the five groups of stones, putting aside individual stones as such, we come to feel the unknowable profundity of this garden of sand. Their placement bespeaks the incomprehensibility of the depths from which these stones emerge. One never feels that the rocks are floating on the surface of the sand; the garden is so composed that even though the base of the stones might actually be rather shallow, we feel them to be unfathomable. The stones that are so set as to make them appear buried deep in the ground are covered around their bases by hair moss in order to hide their shallowness;

this moss plays an important role in the manifestation of Subtle Profundity.

Simplicity is of course one of the characteristics of the garden. Most people will probably feel that Simplicity is the garden's outstanding feature, but I find that the presence of Subtle Profundity is also strong and even more remarkable than that of Simplicity, Nothingness is truly well expressed here. Also present is a genuine Naturalness, for we feel nothing unnatural or artificial in this garden. I can think of nothing else so charged with the ability of removing of all affectation and of freeing us from all artificiality.

The stillness of the garden is truly felt. Certainly, the grove of cryptomerias surrounding it, and its location at the foot of a high hill help produce this effect, but they all are outside the walls. The garden within is very calm and still, and in that it needs no help from anything else. The garden of the Ryōan-ji temple can be said to have the Seven Characteristics; although it is different from the *roji* garden and although it is generally to be classified as being in the formal style, its excellence is in everything extraneous having dried up, thus exposing the very pith and essence. The feeling of the stones' placement is similar to that of the stepping-stones of the *roji*. Looking at this garden—since walking about in it is not permitted—just by looking at it, one clearly feels the Seven Characteristics of Zen.

In a way this is hard to appreciate simply because it is so basic, so essential, because there is no deception or camouflage, as there might be, for example, if some trees or bushes were in the garden. It includes only what is genuine, which makes it all the more difficult to understand. It is really an exceptional garden; Simplicity alone could not draw to it the attention of so many persons who do not fully understand it. Not only is it difficult to understand, but it also contains something that eludes yet somehow appeals directly to the depth of our being; this indicates the excellence of this garden as an expression of Zen. It appeals directly to the depth of our being because, I feel, it touches the Formless Self.

Since the garden of the Ryōan-ji is of the *shoin* style, it is formal, somewhat different from a *sōan* garden. In spite of this difference, the formal style of this rock garden appears to basically constitute the essentials of the grass style. Thus, if one were to take only the bones of a *sōan* style garden, the result would be something like this garden. In this sense, though formal in style, it has assumed the pith and marrow of the informal.

The interest of Zen gardens and of Zen calligraphy and painting seems to be basically the same. The only difference is in the medium of manifestation. In the one case it is natural things; in the other the things are man-made. There is a myriad variety in nature, and Zen takes these things to itself as ways or means or moments of Self-expression. As such it is absolutely free. In the most real sense, Zen can express itself in man's making, seeing, hearing, in the entire world of his activity. It is precisely because of this that we say Zen can become man's life, that the Fundamental Subject of such expression is all, is total, is nothing "special" or "particular."

Zen art is multifarious. From the Zen point of view, the usual paintings of Buddha are not the only type of painting to be venerated. My idea of true worship is to become one with or to truly understand the Fundamental Subject as it expresses itself in, for example, Mu-ch'i's *Pa-Pa Bird*. Thus, were I to choose something for purposes of worship, I would prefer Mu-ch'i's painting to some poorly done and readily available image of *Avalokiteśvara* or *Amitābha*.

ZEN CRAFTS

There are various kinds of ceramics in the West and in the East. Among the many types of Eastern ceramics, the so-called Tea ceramics, or *chatō*, refer to the diverse earthenware objects used in the Way of Tea: teabowls, jars, flowerpots, incense containers, tea caddies, etc. The craft of Tea ceramics involves somewhat special processes of shaping, firing, and glazing. The texture of Tea ceramics, as well, partly due to the nature of the glazes or clays adopted, differs from other ceramics.

This unique variety of ceramics is what the great Tea masters such as Takeno Jōō, Sen no Rikyū, and Furuta Oribe (1544–95?) "critically chose" (*konomu*) according to their "Tea sense." As mentioned on page 62, the term *konomu* has great meaning in the Way of Tea. More than mere liking, it means being active, creative, or formative. *Konomu* is ordinarily used in the general sense of appreciation, but in the Way of Tea it involves choice, creation, and formation rather than mere passive appreciation. It thus encompasses the important meaning of "creating the fine art of Tea." Thus, in the Way of Tea, one speaks of Rikyū's, Kobori Enshū's, or some other Tea master's *konomi* (the noun form of *konomu*), or critical choice, which partly signifies the individual's creativity by which he forms what is unique and original to himself. Not necessarily limited to ceramics, *konomi* is used in every aspect of Tea; a tea house of Oribe's *konomi*, Rikyū's *konomi*, Jōō's *konomi*, etc. Tea ceramics, generally speaking, also are what Tea masters made or had made according to their own *konomi*. Such products are truly tremendous in number.

Today there are a large number of tea utensils that are designated as masterworks, and they are surprisingly expensive. A single teabowl, after the war, and especially in recent years, has come to cost millions of yen; the same is true of a single jar; a small incense box may cost hundreds of thousands of yen. Few things are as expensive as tea utensils. But they are also very highly esteemed. So numerous and highly regarded have these objects been, one wonders what would be left if they were excluded from Japanese ceramics. Not a few people—especially ceramic specialists and art critics—depreciate

Tea ceramics, esteeming instead what they consider to be superior pieces of Chinese ceramic art. To me, Tea ceramics have such profound characteristics as to go beyond the understanding of those who undervalue them—unique characteristics common to all Tea ceramics but never noticed in the above-mentioned Chinese pieces. These characteristics are, after all, what we have spoken of as the Seven Characteristics. Perhaps every piece of true Tea ware possesses them. Zen, which is the source of these characteristics, in manifesting them has made its appearance in and through such Tea ware. This is positively not so with other ceramics; no Western ceramics, for instance, seem to bear comparison with such pieces. Single pieces may resemble them, but there is no group of ceramics consistently displaying such features. Except for incidental resemblances, I find none but Tea ceramics possessed of these Zen characteristics.

For examples of Tea ceramics fashioned by the aesthetic standards of the Japanese Way of Tea, I shall first cite the Raku ware pieces critically selected by Sen no Rikyū. Some feel that Raku ware is without value as ceramic art. Of course, the Raku ware that in later ages became mere imitation is not worthy of mention, and there is no need for us even to discuss it. But the earliest Raku ware, fired by Chōjirō (1516–92) under Sen no Rikyū's guidance and according to his critical choice, have characteristics that in many ways were unknown prior to its appearance. One of these characteristics is practicality; it was made for use in the Way of Tea.

For example, in order to make it easy for the powdered tea to be whipped with the bamboo whisk, the bottom of a Raku teabowl is wide and capacious— it is called a "tea-pool" or *chadamari*. It is difficult to use a bamboo whisk at the bottom of a cone-shaped bowl. Thus, with his spatula as well as on the wheel, the potter makes the lower inside area of the teabowl large enough to facilitate easy whisking. Though this may occur in the teabowls of other wares as well, it was in Raku ware that it was first incorporated. A Raku teabowl has an irregular lip, meant to prevent the bamboo whisk from falling inside. A Raku teabowl does not convey the heat of the hot water as directly as porcelain does, because it is made of porous, low-fired clay, minimizing the absorption and transmission of heat. Since it is held in both hands, it should not allow the irritation excessive heat would involve; there should be a warming sensation that comes faintly and slowly. Such considerations—practical considerations —were factors involved in the choosing of the clay as well as of the glaze.

But Raku ware was not the product of utilitarian motives alone; nor were such motives the chief incentive. The choice of the clay used and the shape the bowl assumes are regarded and praised as being highly suited to practical use. But with Tea ceramics these are not matters of primary importance. What is of first importance is that standard or sensibility by which the ceramic piece is made in order that it may suit such practical considerations. It is not practical use, but rather in what manner it is realized, that matters most. Actually, practicality is realized so as to agree with, instead of to go against, the Seven Characteristics. The latter, after all, manifest themselves by making practicality the "motive" of their appearance.

Since Zen becomes daily life, practical use also constitutes the motive of its activity. We could think of various ways of building a tea house as a dwelling place if we considered only the practical aspects involved. But of highest importance is *what* it is that lives therein; and naturally the subject that makes a choice in building it is important. Depending on what chooses, or what kind of criteria it is that chooses, the resulting tea houses will greatly differ. That is why Tea ceramics are made according to the Zen standard and at the same time are so made as to suit practical use.

As to "motive" or "opportunity," various things come to be the motive for Zen to express itself, usefulness being one of them. With a tea room, Zen takes the matter of dwelling as the motive of its architectual expression. With the ceramics of Tea, in the case of an incense container, for example, Zen assumes the motive simply of making a box for incense. Thus expressing itself, Zen creates what would be otherwise impossible without its unique sensibility. Japan possesses numerous examples of pottery for Tea that were produced according to this sensibility. Of course there are some pieces of porcelain of this nature, but teabowls are mostly earthenware.

While *konomu* implies both creating and choosing, I feel it is necessary to stop and consider the distinction between creating and choosing. Among teabowls that have been greatly prized up to the present time, those made in Korea have been particularly numerous; some have been singled out as masterpieces—the Ido type bowls named Kizaemon and Tsutsu-izutsu; the Goshomaru, Irabo, and Komogai types, and so forth. These were not made or commissioned by Tea masters according to the latter's *konomi*. They were not created according to the standards of Tea by men of Tea, but were made and existed in Korea before they had any connection at all with Japanese Tea masters.

What was significant in this case was the activity of choosing on the part of the Tea masters, choosing what suited a certain standard—the standard of the Seven Characteristics—from what was already in existence. We can say that what in Korea had been almost without value was discovered and esteemed by the Tea masters as works of "new" beauty. The uncovering of this beauty in a bowl involves a change in the value of the bowl. Therefore their beauty, overlooked in their native land, was found, or, one might say, was given to them, by Japanese Tea masters, according to the previously noted standards.

18. *Warikōdai-type teabowl* (Pl. 16)
Although this is a Korean teabowl, due to its interest as an article for the Way

of Tea, it was singled out and used with esteem by a Japanese Tea master, thus coming to be treated as a masterpiece of ceramic art. Truly it is an uncommonly excellent teabowl. Both in its whole and in its parts its shape is asymmetric and original. Its lip is uneven. Its foot, or *kōdai*, which is higher and larger than ordinary, broadening toward its base, gives a sense of stability, of massive composure, to the whole vessel. As the illustration of the underside shows (Fig. 9), the four bold notches cut in the foot moderate its otherwise exaggerated effect. At the same time they impart an original aspect to the whole teabowl.

With an ordinary bowl much attention is paid to the shape or silhouette of the body, and little to the lip or foot. With a teabowl for the Way of Tea, however, importance is attached to the lip, inside surface, and foot. When one appreciates a teabowl, one turns it upside down in order to closely inspect its base. A tastelessly formed foot deprives a teabowl of its suitability for use in Tea. Thus, when a tea vessel is made for the Way of Tea, great pains are taken in the shaping of its foot, and, as a result, diverse forms have evolved. The notched-foot teabowls made in Japan in later ages were appreciated for their relation to these Korean precedents. Its foot not only well expresses the interest found in Asymmetry, but is very simple and primitive, without a trace of complication.

A well-mellowed, Austere Sublimity that truly defies description is felt in the uniqueness of the shape and in its quietly exquisite grace. Its uncommon shape and texture, moreover, do not in the least appear artificial—they are natural, without traces of being made to look antique. Its lack of superficiality, its shape and color give a sense of reserve and grace and depth. There is something beyond mere surface appearance, the resonance of something inexhaustible; the more one looks at it, the richer it seems to become. Each time it is seen, one discovers another of its aspects. There is no way one could ever grow tired of it.

The quality of being unconstrained is also well revealed. Looking at the shape and texture of the bowl and at the notches in its high foot, one feels in it a sense of liberation, of unconventionality and amusement, an uncommon detachment, which could never be duplicated in a symmetrically correct, smoothly textured teabowl. Its counterparts in painting would be Mu-ch'i's *Bodhidharma* (Pl. 62), Hakuin's *Bodhidharmas* (Pls. 108, 111, 113), Sōami's broken-ink *Landscapes* (Pls. 94–97), and so on. Additionally, the teabowl has a massive serenity, silent stability, and deep self-composure.

A teabowl is not only for admiring but also for making tea in and drinking from. The feeling one gets from making tea in it, or from holding it and drinking from it, is sure to be quite the same as that received from looking at it. And with this experience one naturally understands why this teabowl was chosen by Tea masters, and has been treasured ever since.

19. *Goshomaru-type teabowl, named Sekiyō* (Pl. 17)

This Goshomaru teabowl, like the notched-foot teabowl, is Korean, chosen by men of the Way of Tea and brought to Japan as a unique work for use in their art. The Goshomaru type includes several varieties of diverse shapes and glazes, but they are all wonderful vessels of the Way of Tea. Goshomaru teabowls, such as Sekiyō and Hibakama (Pl. 181) are representative of the type. Goshomaru teabowls are said to have been adopted, chosen, and habitually used by the Tea master Furuta Oribe, a student of Sen no Rikyū. The teabowls produced in Japan that belong to what were later called Oribe and Shino wares, especially the "shoe-shaped" ones, are considered to have had these Korean models as their prototype.

The Sekiyō and Hibakama bowls are elongated and irregular in shape, like an old shoe, and their inner bottoms are wide and large, their feet pentagonal or polygonal; their glazing, firing, and coloring harmoniously produce a primitive, broken ink style coloration. Perhaps no other teabowls are more asymmetric and have shapes of more abstract beauty than these. Another uniqueness is the feel of these oblong bowls fitting perfectly into the palms of the hands when held lengthwise to drink from.

In the Sekiyō bowl, the varied colors of the glaze and the effects of the firing process give a feeling of the spontaneous, broken ink Simplicity. Nothing is complicated. Its workmanship looks tight and powerful, devoid of all slackness. The quiet and antique-looking glaze and color mark the whole vessel with Austere Sublimity. The Naturalness could not be surpassed; there is nothing in its shape or color to make one feel anything unnatural. There is also a quality of unrestraint, such as is observable, to take one example from painting, in the *Dancing Pu-tai* of Liang K'ai (Pl. 42). Just as the *Dancing Pu-tai* has an infinite calm and stillness at the bottom of the liberated activity of his dance, so beneath the splashes of this broken ink style coloration, this teabowl discloses a calmness antecedent to the application of the glaze—it is deeply imbued with Subtle Profundity.

20. Hon'ami Kōetsu: *Raku ware teabowl, named Fujisan* (Pl. 18)
21. *Cylindrical, Oribe ware teabowl* (Pl. 19)
22. E-*Shino ware water container* (Pl. 20)

The examples in this book include a particularly large proportion of Shino and Oribe ware pieces, the reason being that they seem to me to embody the Seven Characteristics best of all the Tea ceramics produced in Japan. Other wares satisfying these conditions are Raku, Hagi, Karatsu, Shigaraki, Iga, and Bizen wares, all original ceramics closely associated with the Japanese Way of Tea.

Raku ware began when Sen no Rikyū requested Chōjiro, a potter of Korean descent, to produce Tea ware according to Rikyū's *konomi*. Later ages produced many imitations far less creative than these early works. The original works were those produced according to the critical choice of the Zen layman and great Tea master, Sen no Rikyū, so as to suit the Tea standard of *wabi*—that which possesses "poverty surpassing riches." So, unlike the Korean wares selected, which had been made independently of the Tea standard of wabi, Raku ware was entirely the creation of the Japanese Way of Tea, and has significance accordingly. As such, Raku ware far excelled any of the best Korean wares. The Raku ware pieces made by Chōjirō, founder of the Raku lineage of potters, and by Dōnyū, the third generation (1599–1659; also called Nonkō), are creative works of the spirit of *wabicha*, the Tea of *wabi*, and are exemplary of teabowls embodying the Seven Characteristics.

Furthermore, great attention was evidently given to their design from the practical side of tea making and drinking. To keep the whisk from falling into the bowl, irregularities were molded into the lip, which also has a slight inward turn to facilitate drinking. To aid in whisking, the inner bottom is made flat and wide. Instead of being cone shaped, it swells outward toward the base to give it stability and to enable it to fit naturally into one's hands, making it easy to handle. The clay and glaze were chosen carefully for durability, to produce a mildly warming sensation to the hands, and to avoid the irritation excessive heat might bring.

Raku ware was to the taste of Sen no Rikyū, and was his invention; later, this ware was favored by Sen Sōtan (1577–1658) and others of the mainstream tradition. Thus they may be called unique works created in Self-awareness by the Way of Tea. Yet this quality is not limited to teabowls alone: it is true of all utensils used in Tea. Besides the main kilns used by Chōjirō, there were many secondary kilns. Among some of the Raku teabowls made by Hon'ami Kōetsu (1558–1637) and others prominent in Tea, not a few rival those made by Chōjirō and Nonkō. In later times much Raku ware was fired, both at the main kiln and secondary kilns, among which a great many worthless pieces are to be found. But there were still very many wonderful pieces produced that are unrivaled by other wares. Judged just as ceramic art, Raku ware is wonderfully original. A look at the Raku ware included in these pages will fully confirm such a judgment.

23. *Tea caddies* (Pls. 216–20)
24. *Tea spoons* (Pls. 233–39)

Another important ceramic tea vessel is the tea caddy, or *cha-ire*. Tea caddies, which are used chiefly for the stronger teas, include many works—the so-called *kan-saku*, or *kara-mono*, that is, "Chinese wares"—brought from China, as well as many native Japanese pieces of unique worth adopted by Japanese men of Tea.

Many bamboo and wooden works are included among the choices of the men of Tea. Most important of the bamboo wares are tea spoons, or *chashaku*. Thin bamboo wafers less than a foot in length, these are used only for transferring powdered tea from the tea caddy to the teabowl, yet they are a most important implement in the preparation of tea. Men of Tea naturally go to great pains over their choices, exerting much care to have each and every article expressive of the requisite individuality.

Since the beginning of the Way of Tea, there have been excellent professional *chashaku* carvers; many implements were made by such men under the direction of the Tea masters according to their *konomi*. But also numerous are those carved by the Tea masters themselves. Preserved today are a fairly large number of spoons famous as being hand-carved by men such as Jōō, Rikyū, Furuta Oribe, Kobori Enshū, Sōtan, Hosokawa Sansai (1563–1645), etc.

Tea spoons were originally made of metal, but after they began to be carved from bamboo, they became suited to the standard of *wabi*. Bamboo was selected according to the *konomi* of the Tea men and worked into various shapes, in which appeared not only the individuality of the creator but also that of the tea spoon itself. The result has been an extremely rich variety in this single, thin piece of bamboo. Another matter of deep interest is the tasteful and suitable names given to such pieces according to their respective features.

There are also metal, ivory and wooden tea spoons, but the ones of bamboo are most numerous and most suitable to their role. The shape and line of a bamboo tea spoon is very simple, the long grain of the bamboo adding neatness and sharpness. It is somehow reminiscent of the Japanese sword. It is said that the posture taken by Rikyū when he held a *chashaku* resembled that of an expert swordsman with sword in hand, allowing no point to remain unguarded or open to attack. The historical accuracy of this description aside, I find the associations highly plausible. A bamboo tea spoon is not only simple but is possessed of all the various characteristics becoming tea utensils. A masterpiece will be seen to contain dry and inviolable loftiness, composure, unconstrained freedom, and graceful reserve. Placed upon an extraordinary teabowl such as the Warikōdai, it never appears isolated from it; it rather seems to increase the value of the vessel.

25. Kobori Enshū: *bamboo flower container, named Sairai,* (Pl. 21)
The bamboo tea utensils considered next in importance to tea spoons are bamboo flower containers. Flower vases previously had been mostly copper, earthenware or bamboo basketware. Ever since Rikyū developed a taste for the famous bamboo flower container named Onjōji, bamboo cylinders befitting the Tea of *wabi* have come to be prized by the men of Tea. Many possess a unique quality not to be seen anywhere but in bamboo vases. Together with bamboo tea spoons they constitute valuable cultural properties created by the Way of Tea. Sairai and Fujinami, both direct products of Enshū's *konomi*, possess an unmatched beauty of *wabi*, which far excels any fine celadon porcelain flower vase. Sairai, the uppermost node cut off lest it appear obtrusive, fully displays

the simplicity of bamboo and appears very neat and trim. It is shaped like Jurōjin, the God of Longevity, with a high "forehead" entirely out of proportion to the short body. But this shape is all the more interesting for the sense of detachment it conveys. It also expresses calm, composure, and a *konomi* that is in no way commonplace.

26. Kobori Enshū: *one-windowed bamboo flower container, named Fujinami* (Pl. 240)
Fujinami is typical of "one-windowed" flower vases, a common style among such tubular bamboo vases. The thickness of body, the firmness of the cane, its nodes protuberant and sturdy, its grain "graceful and ancient" looking and coarse, even with natural splitting, all this makes bamboo a natural and highly appropriate material for use as a vase for *chabana*. In this work, the manner of cutting also shows excellent skill. The length of the tube in proportion to its thickness is neither long nor short; swelling slightly at the top, the upper end looks clear and tight, with the clean knife cut at the node. The "window" for inserting flowers is boldly cut into the cane in a straight line, beneath the top node. The body is tightly secured by its two nodal "belts." The workmanship is truly irreproachable. A bamboo tube of such excellence compares quite well with ceramic flower vases possessing *wabi*, even with rare works of Nanban or Iga ware.

There are also basketry flower vases. Flower baskets for *chabana*, unlike Chinese wares, which are delicately woven from thin strips of bamboo, are finished in a form suited to *wabi*, with thin and thick bamboo strips intertwined in an "offhand" manner. There are also bamboo stands on which to place a kettle lid (*futaoki*), which are in no way inferior to those made from metal or clay. Other bamboo tea utensils include kettle hooks, ladles and tea whisks, but, essentially, tea spoons and flower containers are considered the most important.

Wooden tea utensils include the *daisu* (shelf for tea utensils not in use; of Chinese origin), *tanamono* (a shelf devised in Japan after the *daisu*), *natsume* (powdered-tea container), *robuchi* (hearth rim), trays, etc. Both in kind and in number, wooden articles are perhaps more numerous than those of bamboo, but since they lack the interest of the latter, I have included here only one example: a grained tea box, or *kiji-natsume* (Pl. 242), that was prized by Rikyū. The *daisu* and *tanamono* are the most important of the wooden wares. Some, brought from China and liked and used by men of Tea, predate the Tea of *wabi*. The rest were created by Tea masters according to their own *konomi*.

27. *Iron kettle with tortoiseshell pattern* (Pl. 22)
Next comes metal ware chosen by the Way of Tea, the most important of which are the kettles. Here, as well, many remarkable works dating prior to the Tea of *wabi* were singled out and used by Tea masters. But gradually a class

of professional kettle makers evolved, and kettles were cast after the instructions of these masters. The materials used vary; gold, silver, and copper pieces were produced, but iron products are most numerous, since iron is the material most befitting the Tea of *wabi*. Kettle shapes are extremely diverse, including, round, flat, cylindrical, and square-shouldered, etc., ones. There are wide and narrow mouths, and *ubakuchi* (sunken like the mouth of a toothless old woman). Some are of fine texture, others are coarse, some have a studded surface, and still others are embossed with various designs. Varieties are numerous, but all agree with the *konomi* of Tea. Plate 22 is a kettle embossed with a tortoiseshell pattern; the kettle in Plate 244 has "hailstone" studding and calligraphy designs. Since a kettle is one of the chief utensils in a tea room, standing out as prominently as the hanging scroll and the flowers in the *tokonoma* alcove, men of Tea take great care in selecting them. Two books with illustrations of tea kettles, *Ashiya-gama* (concerning kettles cast in the Muromachi period) and *Tenmyō-gama* (kettles of the middle Muromachi and Momoyama periods), are noteworthy. The very appearance of such books testifies to the unique position occupied by kettles in the Way of Tea.

28. attributed to Hon'ami Kōetsu: *inkstone box*, (Pl. 23)
There are many lacquer ware tea utensils; chief among them are *natsume*, incense containers, cake plates and containers, *daisu*, *tanamono*, and *robuchi* (see above). Because lacquer ware has a naturally smooth and beautifully finished surface, it would seem to have an unlikely connection with *sabi* or *wabi*. But the lacquered "papier-maché"—*ikkanbari*—has a great deal of *wabi*. Unlike ordinary lacquer ware, this consists of layers of paper pasted together and coated with lacquer; it has a coarse surface and antique look, a taste of Simplicity and freedom. It has the most *wabi* of all lacquer-ware products, perhaps deserving to be called a grass style of lacquer ware. Another variety producing the flavor of *wabi* uses a raw surface of split wood, instead of the beautiful smoothness of planed wood, as the ground to which lacquer is applied. In addition there is *Kamakura-bori* (Kamakura-style carving, so called for the era in which it was first made), which is a comparatively roughly finished work, carved in low relief and then coated with red lacquer. Incense cases and hearth rims of *Kamakura-bori* are often greatly prized.

Articles of *maki-e* (lacquer using gold or silver dust, etc.), the most gorgeous and exquisite of all lacquer ware, are used for tea utensils such as *daisu*, *natsume*, and incense containers. *Maki-e* are generally of the *shoin*, or "proper," style, and thus not wholly suitable for the Tea of *wabi*. Yet *maki-e* of a mat or lusterless finish do possess the taste of *wabi*. The box depicted in the illustration, by Hon'ami Kōetsu, has an uncommon, rounded and full shape, which gives it a solemn, serene, and composed appearance. The painted design on the cover of the box is free and large, rather than minutely executed; it can be said to possess fully the characteristics of Subtle Profundity and Sublime Austerity.

29. *Pouch for a tea caddy named Yamazakura* (Pl. 24)
30. *Pouch for a tea caddy named Akatsuki* (Pl. 25)
31. *Pouch for a cylindrical tea caddy case* (Pl. 26)

Pouches (*shifuku*) are made for holding tea caddies, teabowls and incense containers; but the most important kind is that used for the tea caddy. Since at times the tea caddy is displayed in its pouch, fine old materials possessed of *wabi*, and suitable for the tea caddy in question, must be used. Men of Tea choose and greatly value materials such as gold brocade, satin damask, fine silks, and rare, ancient imported fabrics, making them into pouches to encase exactly the article to be inserted. Existing pouches are of course innumerable, and the variations of kind and design have unending interest.

32. *Scroll mountings* (Pls. 246–49)

Another craft associated with the Way of Tea, which uses fabrics similar to those employed in the pouches, is that of the *kakemono* or hanging scroll. Since the scroll is a tea article to be hung in the *tokonoma* alcove for appreciation, the paper upon which the calligraphy or painting is to be done is, I think, the matter of prime consideration. The material to be used for the mounting of the scroll and the manner of mounting must also be given great care. However fine the chosen paper may be, it could not be termed a good scroll if either the mounting material or the way of mounting is bad. Hence, men of the Way of Tea try to employ the materials and style most appropriate to a *kakemono* for Tea, and have invented a style of mounting called *chagake*, or "Tea mounting." Although hanging scrolls have existed in China and Japan since early times, men of Tea created a new mounting style, using distinctive materials imbued with *wabi*. Although a mounting for a *kakemono* is roughly equivalent to the frame of a Western painting, to me the Oriental beauty and variety of the Japanese-style frame is incomparable.

I have taken up the principal crafts created by the Way of Tea; I could continue, but there would literally be no end. Although the present book has been limited to what is visual, in the Way of Tea there are also many diverse, intangible elements, such as *temae*, the procedures for preparing tea; *kaiseki*, the simple, light meal served before tea; and the manner of address between host and guest. Thus, Tea encompasses a highly refined, and primarily Oriental, way of life. This life culture, with Zen as its Fundamental Subject, is a culture of the ordinary people, formed entirely by the men of Tea, the laymen who based their lives on Zen. It must be said that this life culture was realized for the first time in Japan.

In China, Zen culture attained an extremely high level. Especially, the essence of Zen Activity in China was far beyond the reach of Japanese Zen. But

Chinese Zen was a culture limited to monastery-temples. Even allowing that the whole Sung period was imbued with Zen, Zen culture still remained centered in the monasteries; a Zen culture centered entirely in the lives of the common people did not come to be established in China.

The Way of Tea is Zen culture separated from Zen monasteries, newly formed and directed at the common people. It is Zen culture assimilated into the culture of the common man, and created into a life culture of the people. In this respect one may be justified in considering the Way of Tea in Japan as occupying a unique position in the history of Zen culture. Thus, I do not think it too much to say that the Way of Tea brought the entire existing Zen into its domain. Further, according to its spirit, Tea created a new life system of Zen culture, and that the finest artifacts of Zen culture still in existence were not only given value, but created and preserved as well, by the spirit of the Way of Tea.

ZEN DRAMATIC ART

33. *Scene from the Nō play* Matsukaze (Pl. 27)
34. *Scene from the Nō play* Sotoba Komachi (Pl. 28)

To conclude, I would like to discuss the Nō drama, a dramatic art unique to Japan, as an aspect of Zen culture. This is Zen expressing itself in dramatic art, dramatic art formed by Zen. But let us set aside the process of its formation for the moment. In Nō, the mental posture of the performers, their movements, the chants or *yōkyoku*, and the instrumental music of the hand drums, stick drum, and flute, are all formed by Zen becoming their Fundamental Subject. As such, other types of Japanese theatrical art—the dance, kabuki, *nagauta*, *tokiwazu*, *kiyomoto*, etc.—are clearly different from Nō as regards their respective fundamental subject of expression. Of course some of them, including kabuki, have adopted the style of the Nō, but in spite of the outward similarities they differ in their subject of expression. Nō differs qualitatively as well from the Chinese *ching-chu*, and, of course, is vastly different from the operas found in the West. The Nō is a dramatic art with unique and incomparable characteristics, the basic ground for which is the fact that the Fundamental Subject of expression in Nō is Zen.

That Nō is based on Zen can be seen by attending a performance. Historically, Nō came to completion during the Muromachi period, a time when Zen was especially flourishing. Its originators Kan'ami (1333–84) and Zenchiku (fifteenth century) were Zen influenced. Treatises on Nō by Zeami (1363–1443) and by Zenchiku reveal the Zen roots of this drama.

The photographs included show but the stopped motion of the performers, yet they still enable one to grasp the feeling of Zen expressed in the Nō performance. The pose depicted in Plate 27 reminds one of Liang K'ai's *Śākya-muni* (Pl. 1). It shows the *shite*, the dancer or "doer," the principal actor, standing in the "gallery" (*hashigakari*) after the curtain has been raised. His pose is the Fundamental Subject that is Nothing, emptied of all and about to enter into activity. It symbolizes the calm and still posture of No Mind, which is prior to either moving or not moving, that is, the "body and mind fallen away," about to enter the activity of the liberated mind body.

Zenchiku, in his *Rokurin-ichiro*, a notable treatise on Nō, divides a Nō performance into six cycles, beginning with the entrance and ending with the exit: (1) the cycle of life; (2) the cycle of rising; (3) the abiding cycle; (4) the cycle of the figure; (5) the breaking cycle; (6) the cycle of void. The "Oneness disclosed" (*ichi-ro*) is the Fundamental Subject of the six cycles, and the six cycles are invariably inseparable from this. According to Zenchiku this "Oneness disclosed" means the presence of the eternal, "free from the words emptiness and being, not related to the world of discrimination." This is no other than "body and mind fallen away," that is, the Formless Self.

Coming from behind the curtain to stand on the *hashigakari* is the cycle of life, which Zenchiku says is "the form of heaven and earth yet undivided"; "the primal source of Subtle Profundity." The sixth cycle, of emptiness, is "the return to the original life cycle, after having passed through the other cycles"; it is the stage where the exit is effected. While going through the six stages from entrance to exit, Nō is never once separated from the "Self-nature sword" (*shōken*) of the "Oneness disclosed" (which annihilates both being and emptiness); even in the vehemence of the breaking cycle it does not break away. Zenchiku describes the breaking cycle as "wild movement and action, yet unseparated from the position of sublimity or the pose of quiet."

The disclosure of the One is expressed both in the pose of Plate 28 and in the abandon of Plate 256: all the "poses" point directly to the Oneness disclosed. In Nō, the attitude of body and mind, unseparated from the One in all the changing positions of the six cycles, comprises the Fundamental One; hence without such attitudes there can be no Nō drama. The difference between Nō and other forms of drama revolves upon this point. The movements in Nō are so carried out that this fundamental attitude is never broken. Not only in a negative sense of never breaking, but in a positive sense as well, there must be a fundamental attitude that expresses itself.

Yōkyoku, the Nō chant, is also inseparable from the fundamental attitude in the movements and poses of the performers; it also should emerge from and return to the disclosed One. The instrumental music, employing flute, large and small hand-drums, accompanies the movements of the performers and the recitation of the *yōkyoku*. "An ax rings out. The mountain stillness grows" is a fitting descriptive phrase for Nō. It is dramatic art as the Self-expression of Zen.

35. *Nō masks* (Pls. 259–66)
36. *Nō costumes* (Pls. 267–70)
37. *Nō stage properties* (Pls. 271–76)

In Nō, the masks and costumes are the most important properties. Various masks and costumes have been made in accordance with the character to be portrayed, and a great many of these are extant and preserved as cultural treasures.

While the masks are made to suit the character, insofar as they are masks they cannot match the human face in recording the infinite changes of facial expression that arise. Yet in Nō that very lack of change matches its fundamental attitude. With a bare-faced actor this attitude could never be duplicated, except with rare, veteran performers. Maskless, if the eyes lack the required stability, if they fix on something or focus in the act of conscious looking, it is no longer the unmasked quality of Nō. If a feeling of joy or anger is expressed on the face, as in kabuki or Japanese dance, it cannot be termed the "bare face" of Nō. Because the disclosed One expresses itself in the six cycles, expressions emerge from the surface of the unchanging Nō mask. Therein exists the essential meaning the Nō mask has for the Nō drama.

The costumes are gorgeous and elaborate, yet, just as in the "breaking of the cycle," they evoke Tranquillity. Accordingly, the costumes, because of their color, make all the more clear the Simplicity and Sublime Austerity of Nō.

There are various stage properties used in the Nō performances; the reel and spool utilized in *Kurozuka*; the cut paper hung for exorcism in *Kokaji*; a framework boat for *Kunisu*; a cart for *Yuya*; a shrine for *Itsukushima*; a drum stand for *Fujidaiko*; etc. They are highly symbolic and quite appropriate to Nō.

THE PLATES

1. Liang K'ai • *Śākyamuni Descending the Mountain* (detail of Pl. 37)

2. Mu-ch'i • *Pa-Pa*
Bird on an Old Pine

3. Sesshū • *Winter*, from *Autumn* ▷
and Winter Landscapes

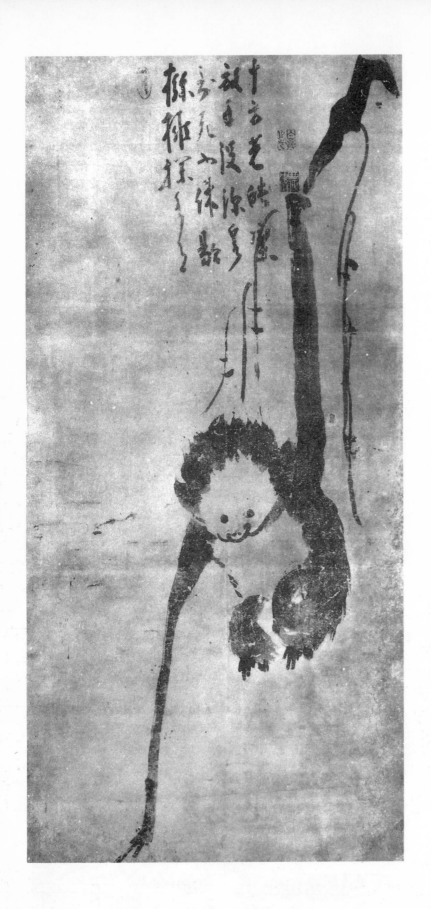

4. Hakuin • *Monkey*

6. Hakuin • The character *Mu* ("No")

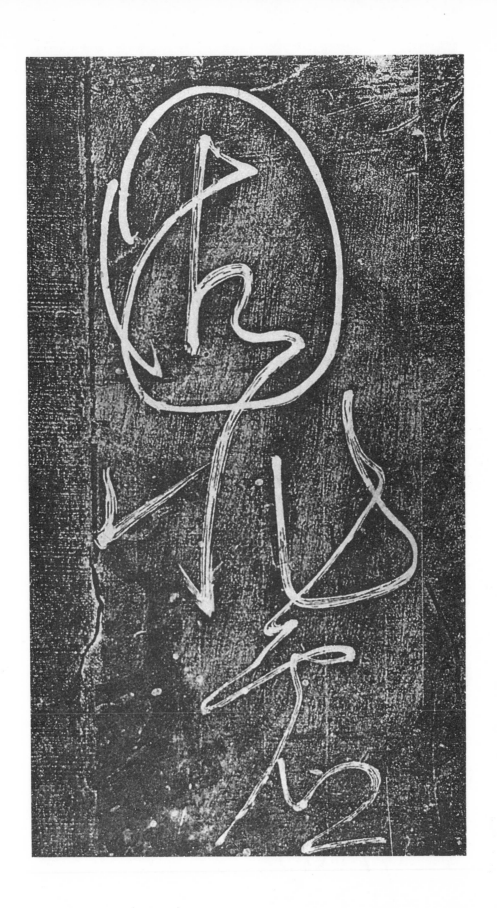

7. Huai-su • Excerpts from *Autobiographical Notes*

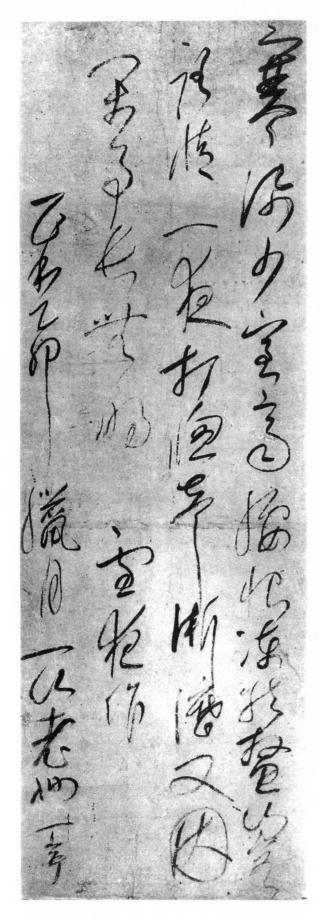

8. I-shan I-ning • *Poem on a Snowy Night*

9. Ryōkan • The characters "Mind, Moon, Circle"

10. Tea room (*shoin* style) of the Zangetsu-tei, Omote Senke, Kyoto

12. *Chabana* • Materials: clematis • Container: black Seto ware vase

13. *Chabana* • Materials: clematis • Container:
Nanban (South Asian) wall vase

14. Stepping-stones below the Tsukimi-dai, Katsura Imperial Villa

15. Path between the Tsukimi-dai and the Gepparō, Katsura Imperial Villa

16. Warikōdai-type teabowl • Yidynasty

17. Goshomaru-type teabowl, named Sekiyō • Yi dynasty

18. Kōetsu • Raku ware teabowl, named Fujisan

19. Cylindrical, Oribe ware teabowl

20. *E*-Shino (painted Shino) ware water container

22. Iron kettle with tortoiseshell pattern

23. attributed to Kōetsu • Inkstone box • Lacquer with metal inlay

25. Pouch for a tea caddy named
Akatsuki • Enshū damask

24. Pouch for a tea caddy named
Yamazakura • Yoshino Kantō fabric

26. Pouch for a cylindrical tea caddy case • Arisugawa pattern brocade

27. Scene from the Nō play *Matsukaze* • Performer: Urada Hosei

29, 30. Ch'an-yüeh • *Arhats*, from *The Sixteen Arhats*

138

31, 32. Ch'an-yüeh • *Arhats*, from *The Sixteen Arhats*

33, 34. attributed to Shih K'o · *The Second Patriarch in Repose*

140

35, 36. Li T'ang • *Landscapes*

37. Liang K'ai • *Śākyamuni*
Descending the Mountain

38. Liang K'ai • *Landscape in Snow*

39. Liang K'ai • *The Sixth Patriarch Cutting Bamboo*

146

40. Liang K'ai • *The Sixth Patriarch Destroying the Sutra*

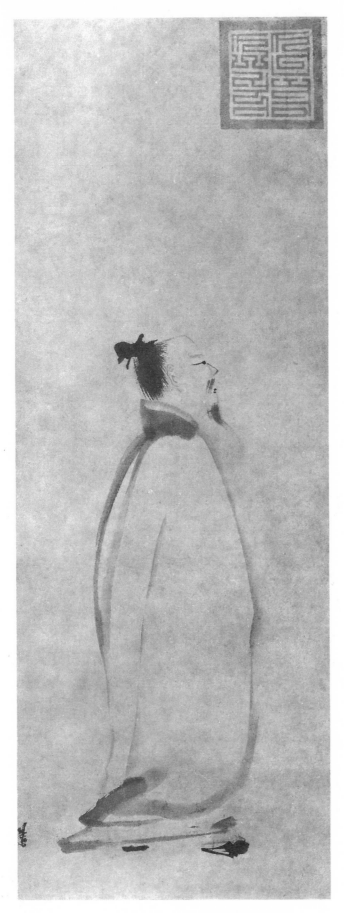

41. Liang K'ai • *Li Po*

42. Liang K'ai • *Dancing Pu-tai*

43. Liang K'ai • *Intoxicated Old Man*

44. Liang K'ai • *Han-shan and Shih-te*

地行不
識名和
姓大戶
高陽一
洞洪雁
兒唾壺
仙宴罷
淋漓樓
袖尚模
糊

45. Liang K'ai • *Sage of Yao-t'ai*

46. attributed to Liang K'ai • *Herons and Swallows in Snow* (detail)

48. artist unknown • *Bodhidharma*

◁ 47. Li Ch'üen • *Pu-tai* (detail), from *Feng-kan, Bodhidharma,* and *Pu-tai* (set of three scrolls)

49. attributed to Ma Yüan • *Fisherman on a River in Winter*

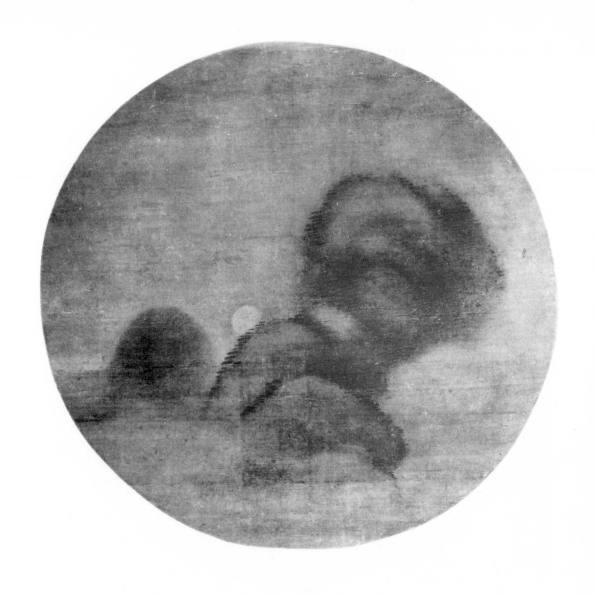

50. attributed to Kao Jan-hui • *Dawn Landscape*

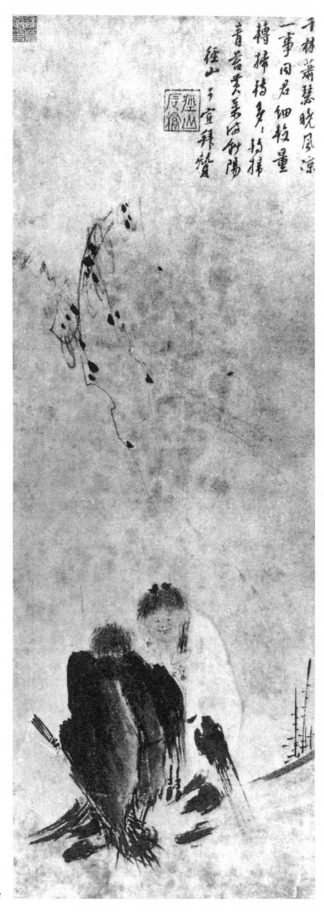

52. Ma Lin • *Han-shan and Shih-te*

56. attributed to Mu-ch'i • *Chestnuts*

163

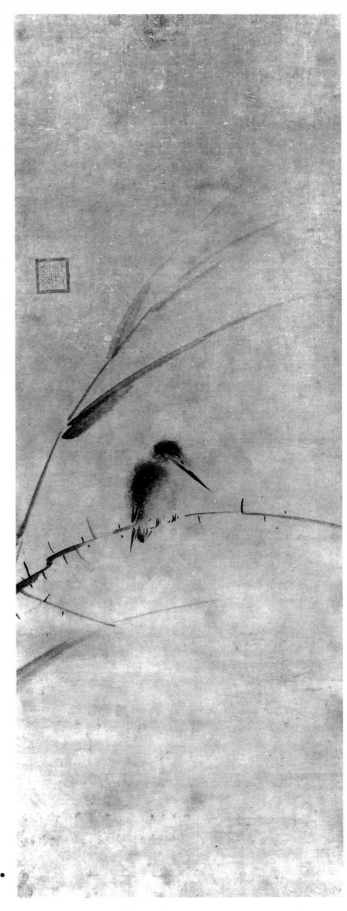

57. attributed to Mu-ch'i •
Kingfisher on a Dry Reed

58. attributed to Mu-ch'i •
Wagtail on a Lotus Leaf

59–61. Mu-ch'i • *Kuan-yin*, *Monkeys*, and *Crane* (set of three scrolls)

62. attributed to Mu-ch'i • *Bodhidharma*

63. attributed to Mu-ch'i • *Lao-tzu*

64. attributed to Mu-ch'i • *Swallow on a Lotus Pod*

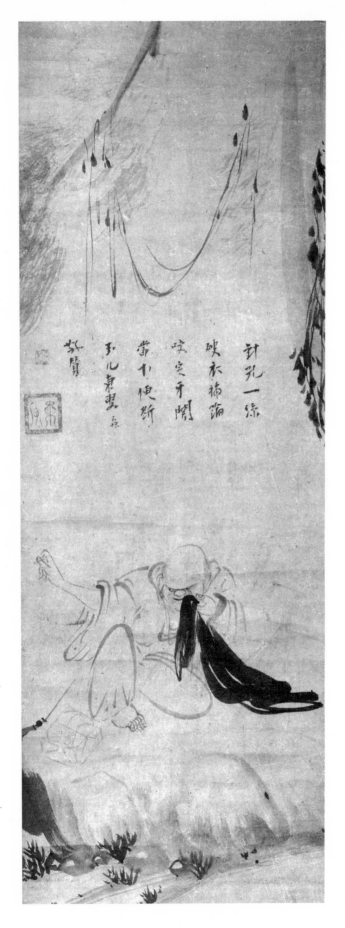

針先一綜
破衣補論
咬定牙閂
當下便新
兀兀東望

65. attributed to Mu-ch'i • *Sunrise*

66. attributed to Mu-ch'i •
Swallows and Willow

67. attributed to Mu-ch'i • *Sunset in a Fishing Village*, from *Eight Views of Hsiao-Hsiang*

68. attributed to Mu-ch'i • *Evening of Snow*, from *Eight Views of Hsiao-Hsiang*

69. attributed to Mu-ch'i • *Autumn Moon over
Lake Tung-t'ing*, from *Eight Views of Hsiao-Hsiang*

70. attributed to Mu-ch'i • *Night Rain at Hsiao-Hsiang*, from *Eight Views of Hsiao-Hsiang*

虎嘯而風烈
武陵□□

178

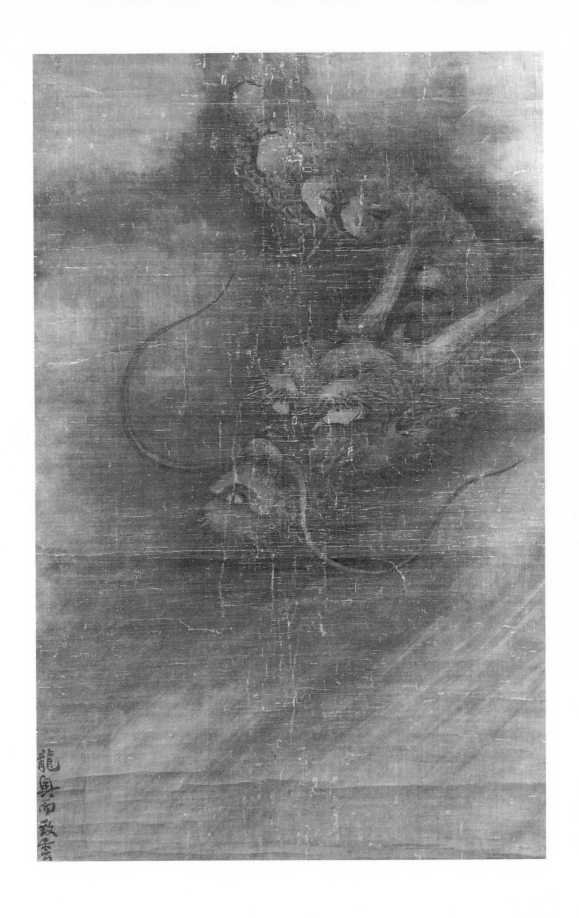

71, 72. attributed to Mu-ch'i • *Dragon* and *Tiger* (pair of scrolls)

179

73. Yü Chien • *Landscape at Lu-shan* (detail)

75. artist unknown • *Yu Shan-chu*,
from *Cheng Huang-nin*, *Bodhidharma*,
and *Yu Shan-chu* (set of three scrolls)

76. Jih-kuan • *Grapes*

77. Chih-weng • *The Sixth Patriarch*

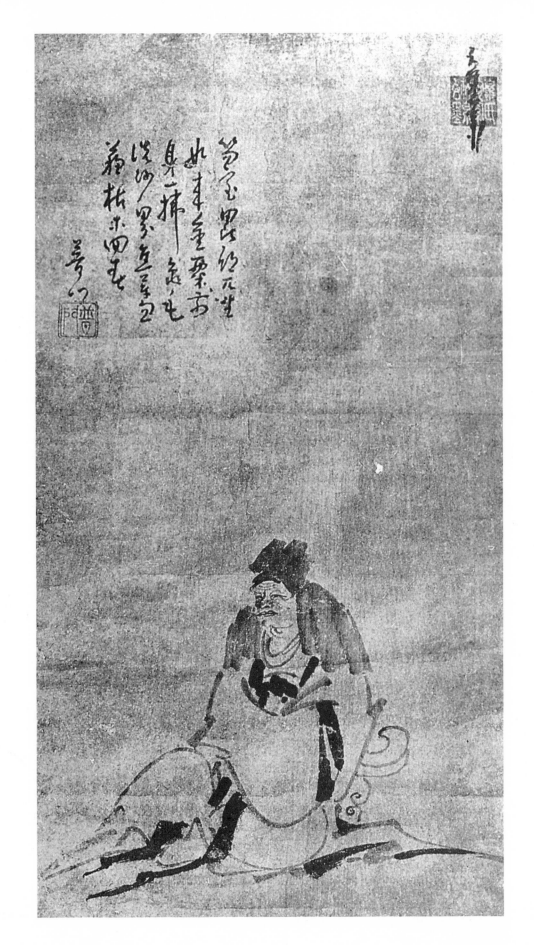

一花衛御街您迎嘆作慈尊又乞魔背上
一具袋栱生眠紫平雲毅蔣摩詰

80. Yin-t'o-lo • *Pu-tai*

187

81, 82. Yin-t'o-lo • *Han-shan* and *Shih-te* (pair of scrolls)

83. Kaō • *Master Hsien-tzu*

84. artist unknown •
Portrait of Daitō Kokushi

85. Mokuan • *The Four Sleepers* (detail)

86. Josetsu • *Catching a Catfish with a Gourd* (detail)

89. Ashikaga Yoshimitsu • *Tu Tzu-mei*

91. Murata Shukō • *Landscape*

92. Sesshū • *Landscape* (detail)

93. Sesshū • *Landscape Scroll of the Four Seasons* (detail)

94, 95. attributed to Sōami • *Landscapes* (from a set of eight paintings)

96, 97. attributed to Sōami • *Landscapes* (from a set of eight paintings)

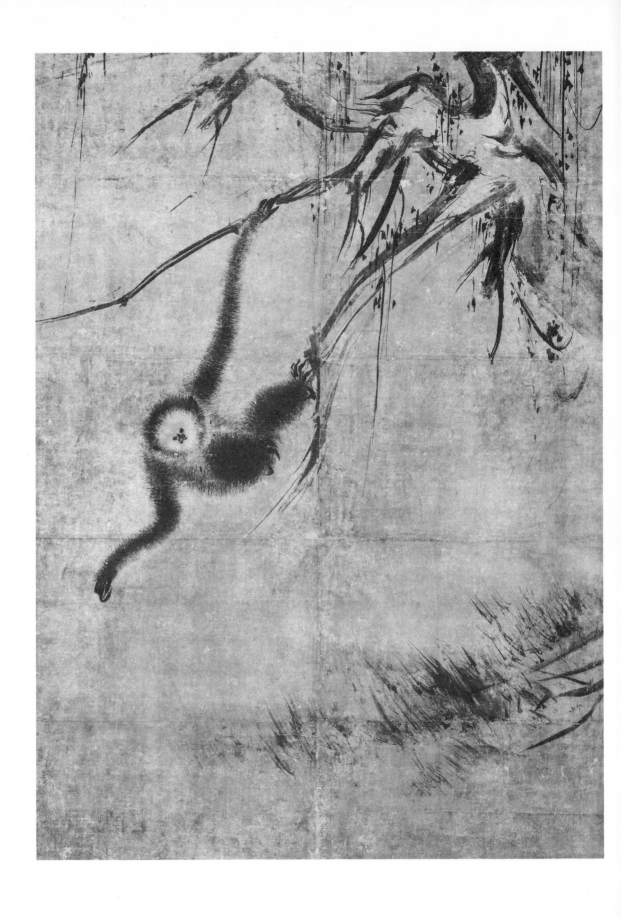

98. Tōhaku • *Monkeys on an Old Tree* (two sliding panels)

99. Tōhaku • *Pine Trees* (pair of six-fold screens)

100. Iwasa Shōi • *Hotei*

101. Iwasa Shōi • *Ki no Tsurayuki*

102. Niten • *Shrike*

103. Niten • *Bodhidharma*

104, 105. Niten • *Wild Geese* (pair of six-fold screens)

106. Niten • *Hotei and Fighting Cocks*

107. Niten • *Rush Leaf Bodhidharma*

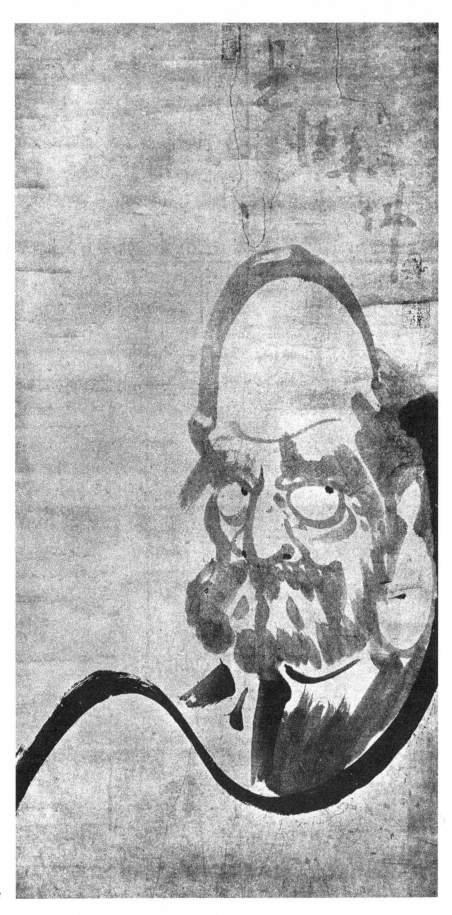

108. Hakuin • *Bodhidharma*

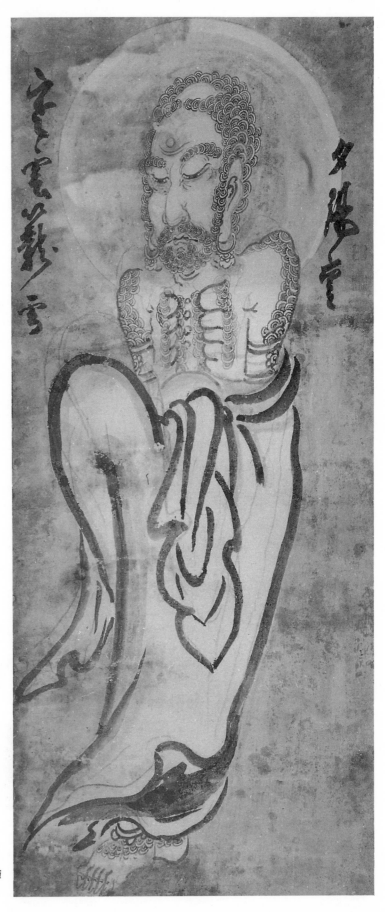

109. Hakuin • *Śākyamuni*
Descending the Mountain

110. Hakuin • *Master Hotei*

111. Hakuin • *Bodhidharma*

112. Hakuin • *Echigo Sanjakubō*

113. Hakuin • *Bodhidharma*

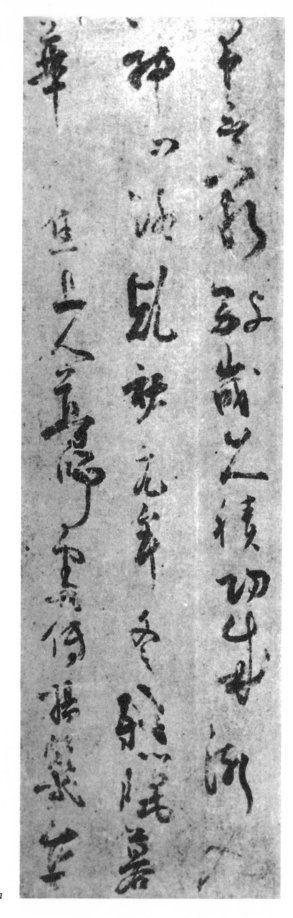

114. Yang Ning-shih • Excerpt from the *Shen-hsien ch'i-chü-fa*

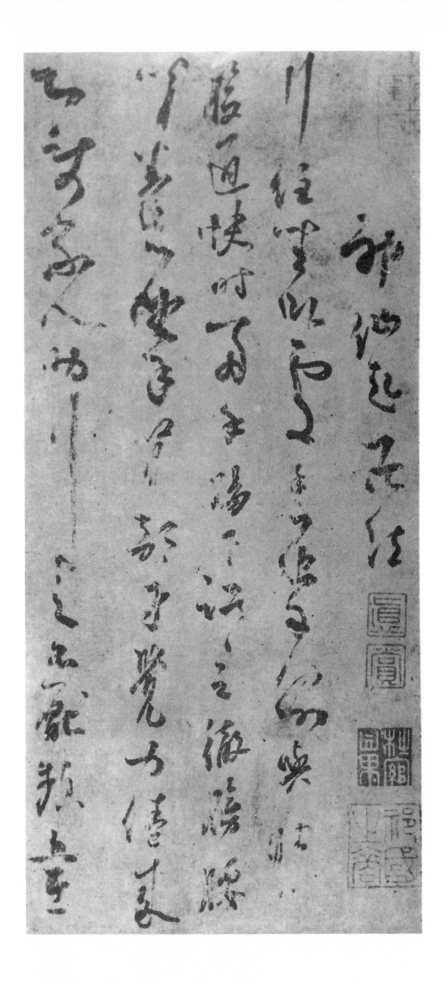

225

115. Yü Chi • Inscription beside Shih K'o's paintings, *The Second Patriarch in Repose* (Pls. 33, 34)

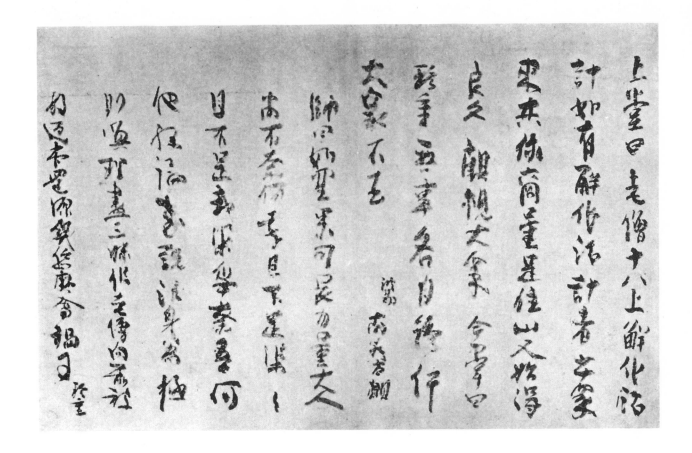

116. attributed to Nan-ch'üan • Excerpt from a Zen lecture

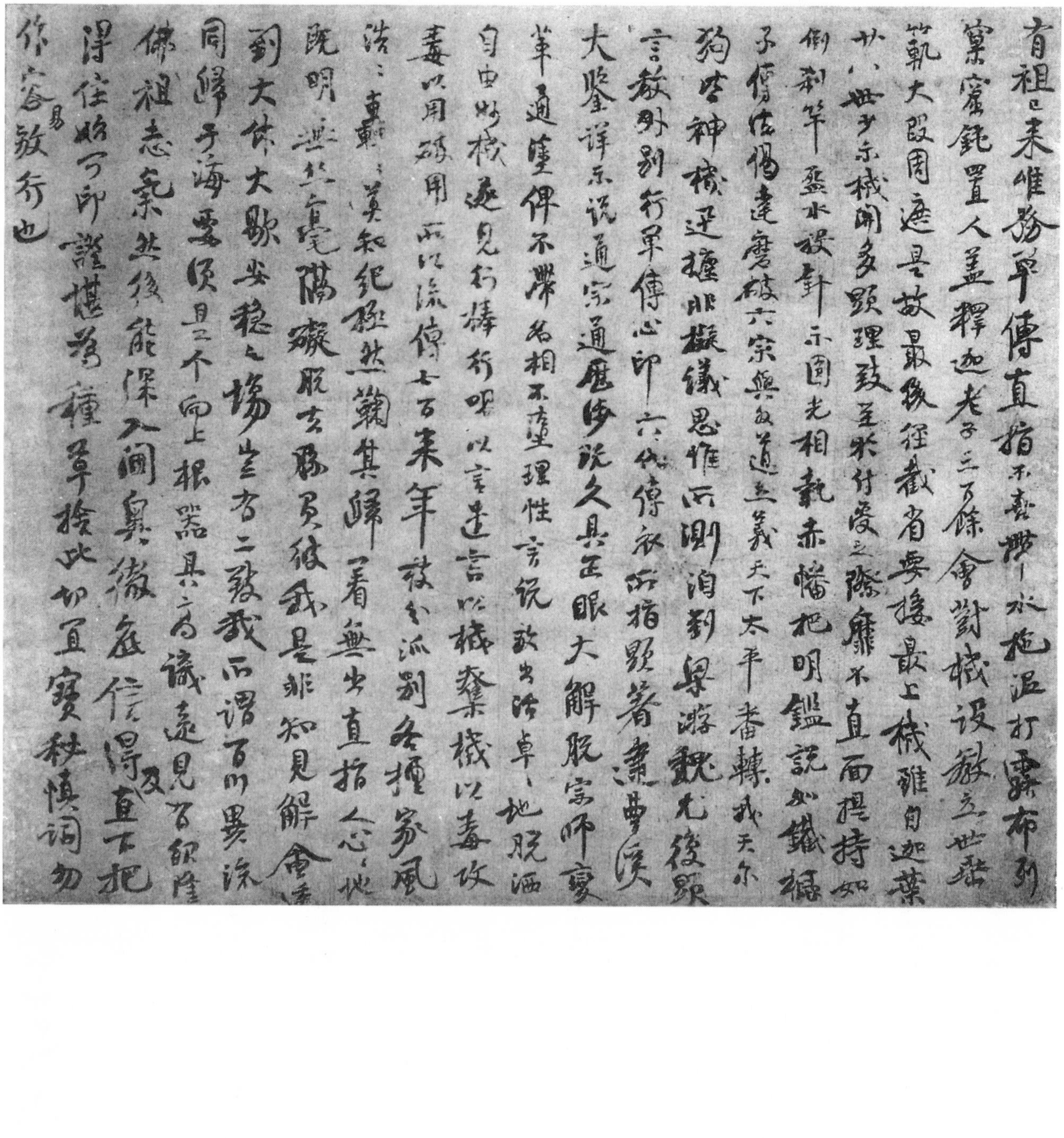

首祖已來唯務單傳直指不立文字以心印心地珝打露布列
窠窟鈍置人蓋釋迦老子三万餘會對機設敎立世諦
執大段周遮是故最後徑截省要揀最上機雖自迦葉
廿八無少示機開多顯理致至米付受之際靡不直而捷持如
倒卻竿盛水致針示圓光相赤幡把明鑑說如鐵橛
子僧佑達磨六宗與敎道五義天下太平番轉我天尔
狗咬神樞遷擇那巖儀思惟示測泪到象游覿光後顯
言敎外別行果傳心印六代傳衣祖指題著淥爭澳
大鑒詳示說通家歷步說久具正眼大解脫家師資
筆通蓬佯不際名相不産坐理性旁說致出活卓地脫洒
自由好機遠見好傳行明以言達言以橛棄機以毒攻
妻以用碍用所以流傳古乀來年致如派別各種家風
浩々重顨莫氣紀然轍其歸一著無出直指人心地
旣明遲其毫隔礙脫玄顯彼我是非知見解金遶
到大徇大歟必穩之場二發我所謂百川異途
同歸于海雲貢且不而上根器具二為識遠見百祖隆
佛祖志氣累然後能深入闡奧徵庶信得真下把
浮住略○所證慎為種草拾此切宜寶秘慎詞勿
作容易敎行也

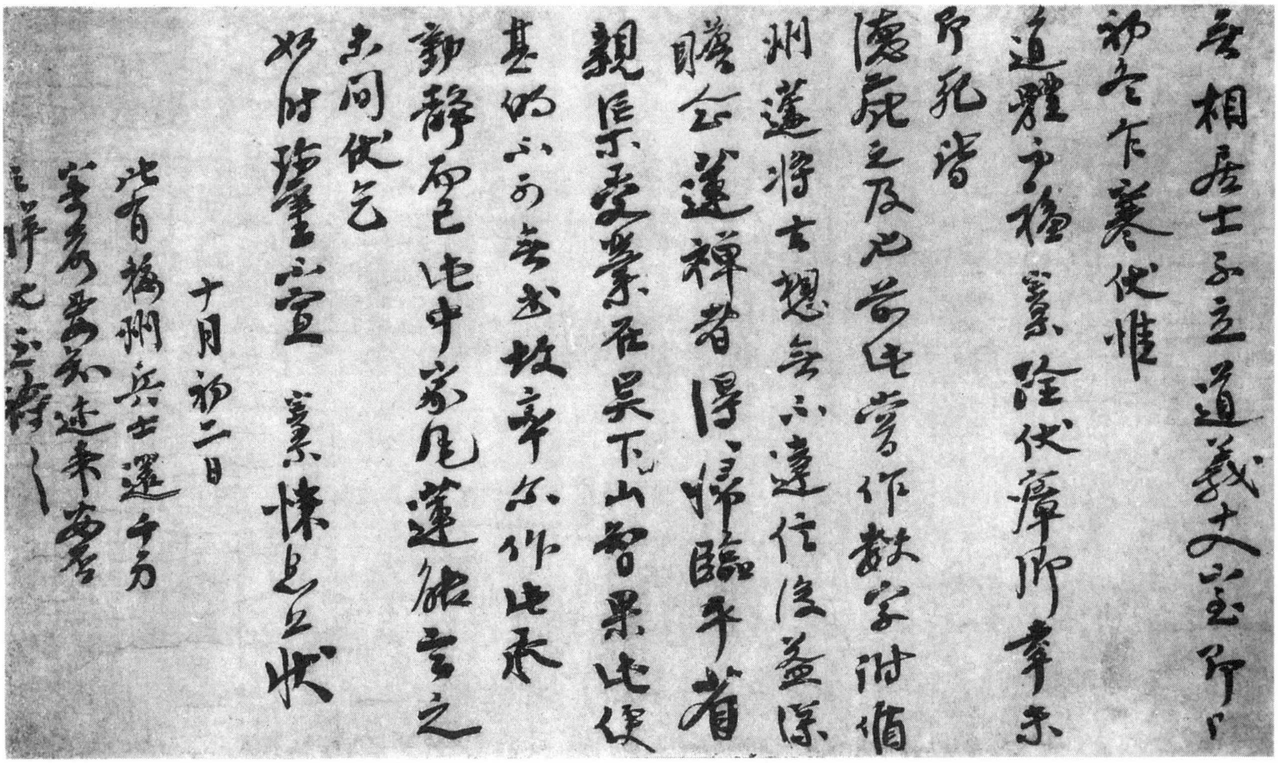

省相居士了立道義士人必至所以
初心乍養他惟
道體安穩業隆伏摩所幸承
所死皆
憂虎之及也嘗屯嘗作敷字附循
州蓬將去想無不達任後益保
瞻公蓬禪者厚歸臨平者
親宗受業在吳下山智果此使
基的不可無去坡辛尓付此承
勤靜堅屯中家尾蓬能言之
去同伏气
妙付瑾童宣業悚上立状

十月初二日
此普梅州兵士選千万
字多要永述乗喬者
尾洋九五将人

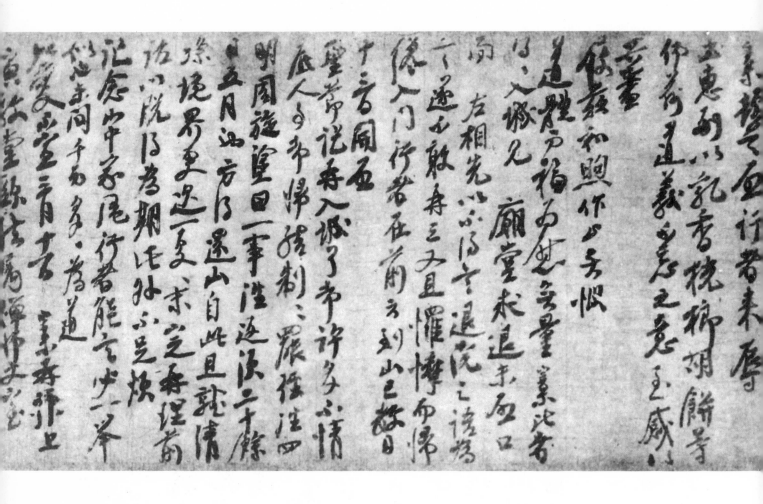

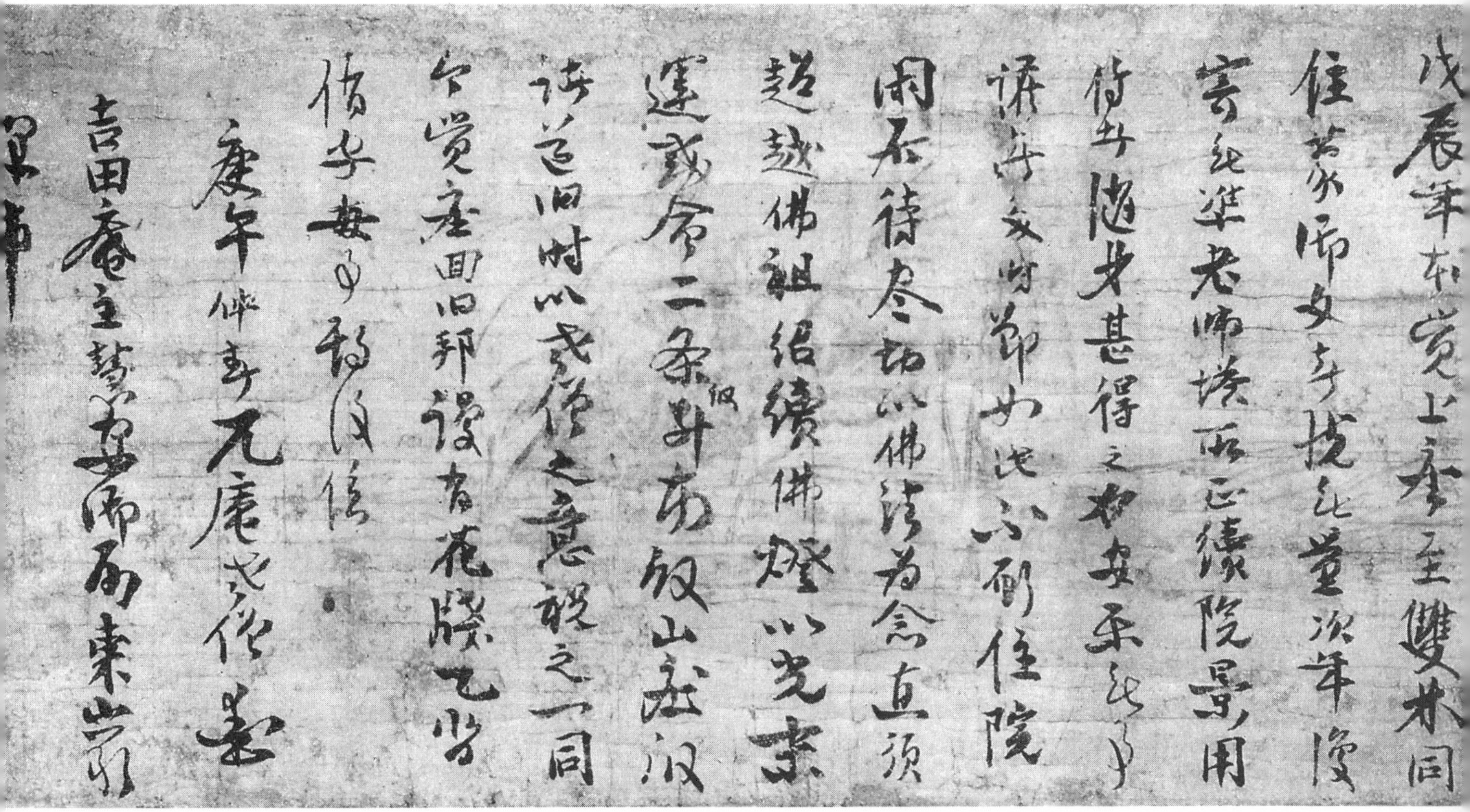

戊辰年布覺上東至雙來同

住蒙師女专拔完童次年侵

寄紀華老師塔正三續院景用

侍母隨步甚得之如妄乐紀乃

诸母女吶節如此以卻佳院

問吞待參切以佛洁為念直須

超越佛祖紹續佛燈以光宗

運惑念二條斗南叙山庄沒

诗道旧时以光修之意祝之一同

今覺產田旧邦諸方花膝乙少

條子每々稠日信

庚年体事无庵光作畫

吉田庵主藝軒師勛東山叫

231

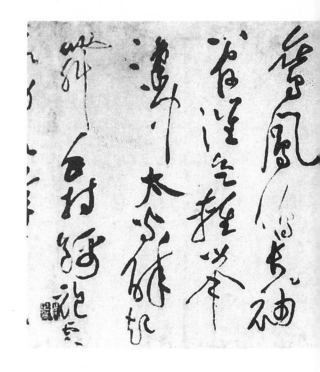

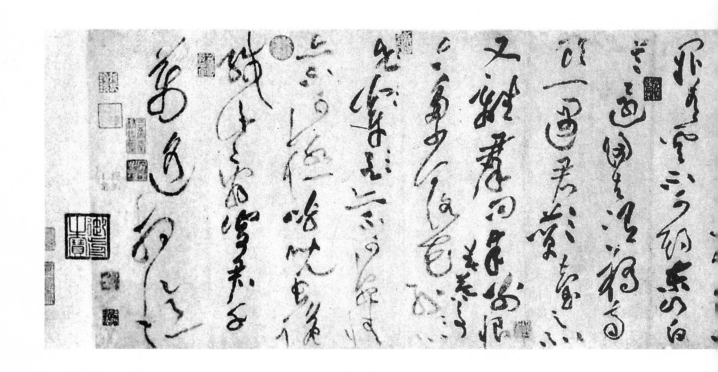

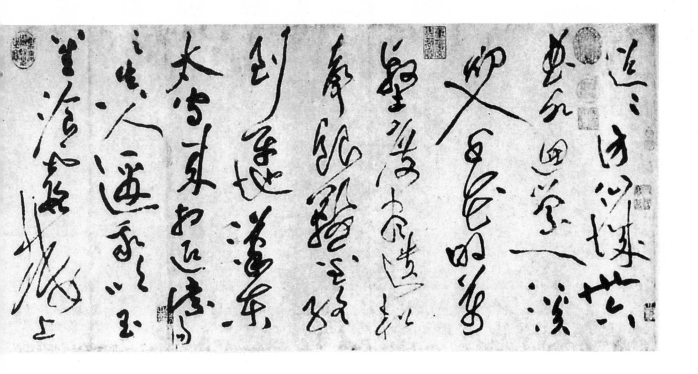

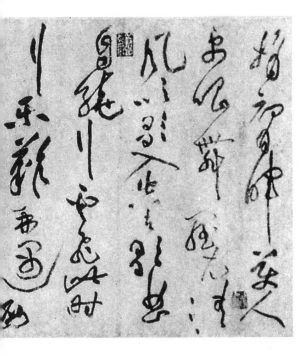

121. Huang T'ing-chien • Excerpt from Li Po's poem *I-chin-yu*

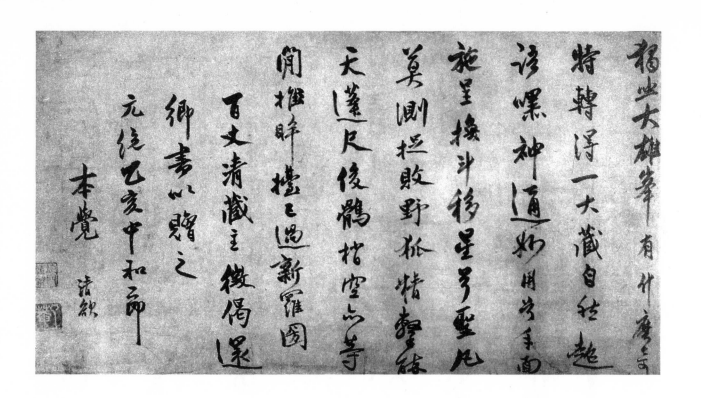

福業大雄峰有什麼事
特轉浮一大藏自結趣
諮課神通釡用盡手面
施呈擡斗移星弄靈凡
莫測挫敗野狐精擎經
天連尺俊鶻楷空品等
開榷睟擡之過新羅國
百丈清藏之微偈還
卿壽以贈之
元統乙亥中和再
本覺 清欲

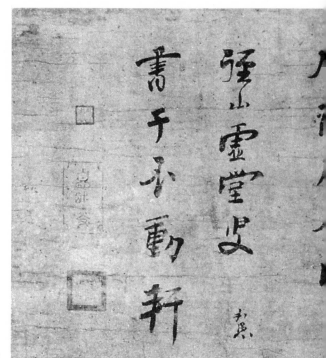

彊山靈堂史
書干丞勷軒

123. Hsü-t'ang Chih-yü ● Poem

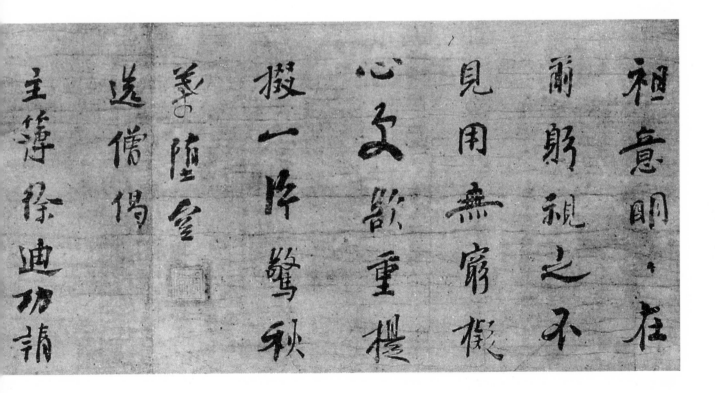

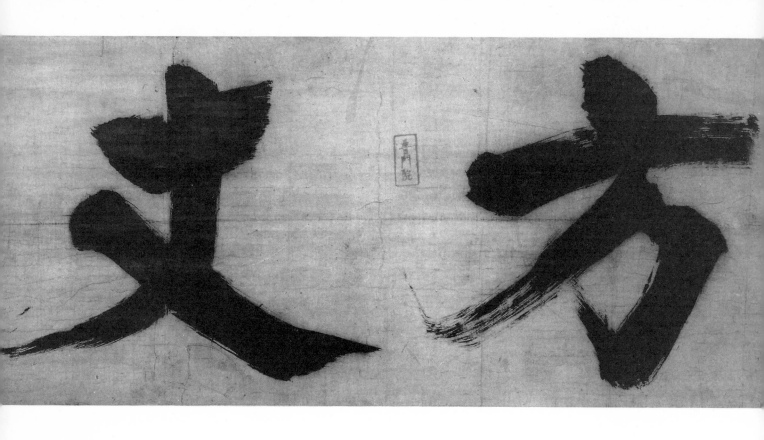

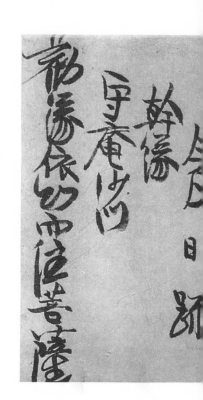

236

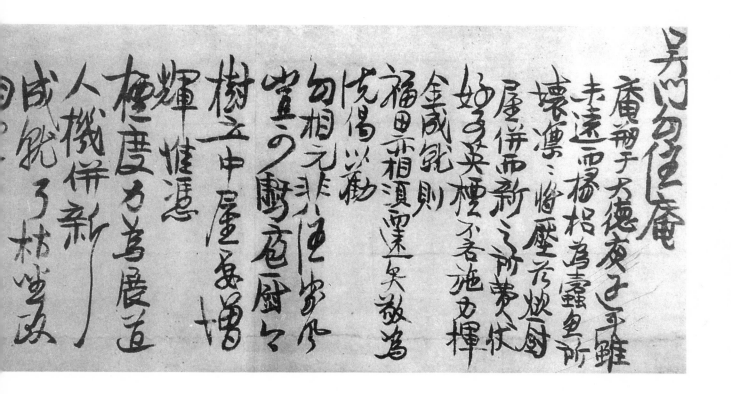

125. Chung-feng Ming-pen • Letter soliciting contributions to build the Huan-chu-an

一層樓看春

求人雪更

宵花發善

柟樹

大法百祇存

員千寫法道

佛祖授受前

不容髮出帝

宗書因書此

以示將來之時

弘安三年中夏

善字宙元書

賦云山昌

承建四年二月至

金陵鳳基

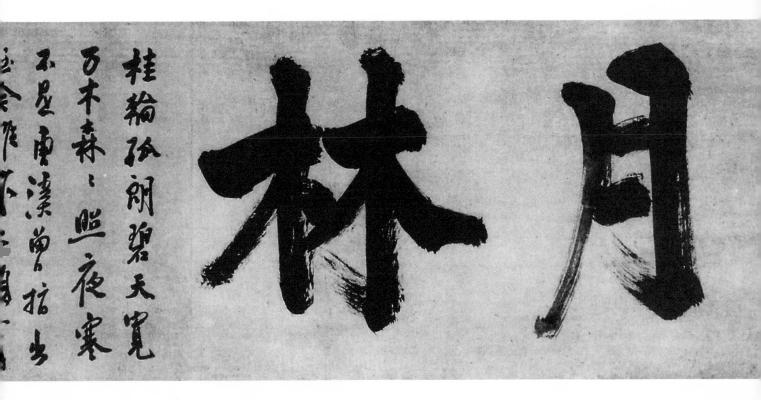

127. Ku-lin Ch'ing-mao • Certificate of the title Yüeh-lin given to a disciple

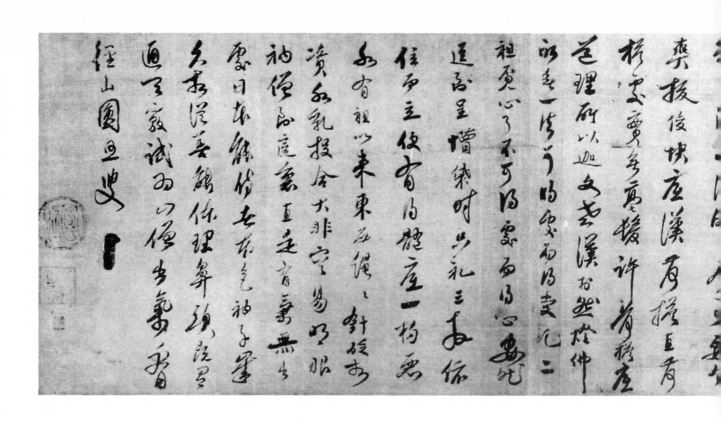

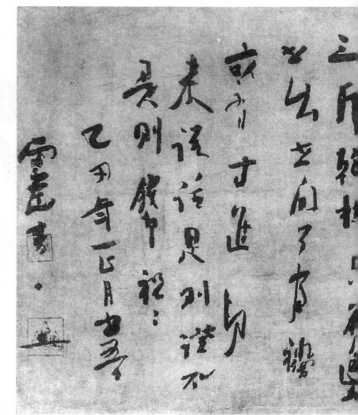

129. Ling-shan Tao-yin • Religious text

128. Wu-chun Shih-fan • Certificate of a disciple's Awakening

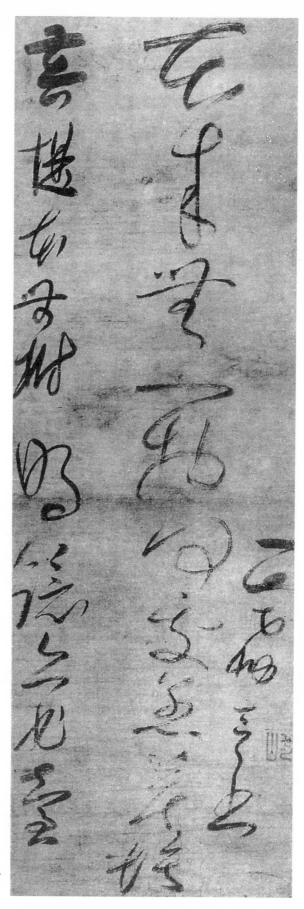

130. I-shan I-ning • The poem of Hui-
neng, the Sixth Patriarch

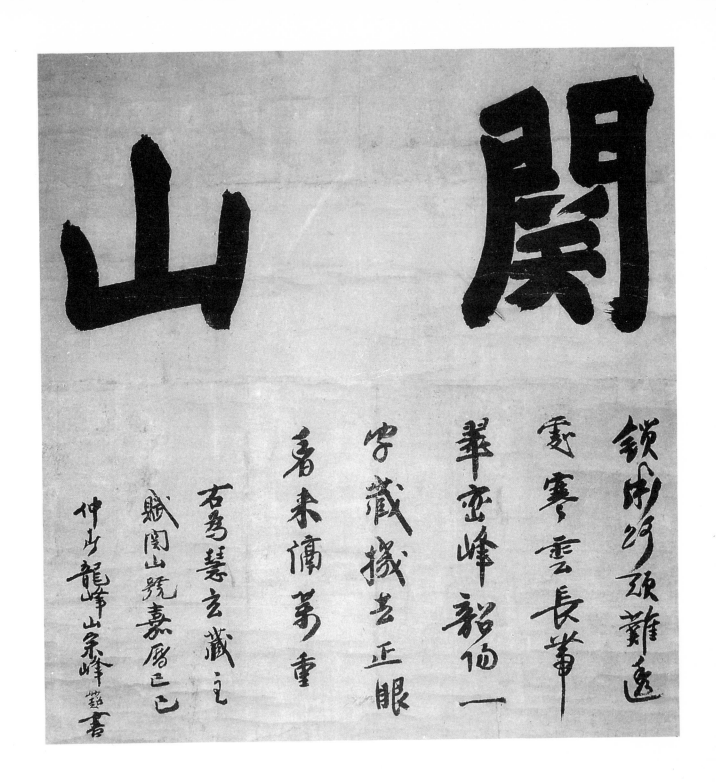

131. Daitō Kokushi • Certificate of the title Kanzan given to a disciple

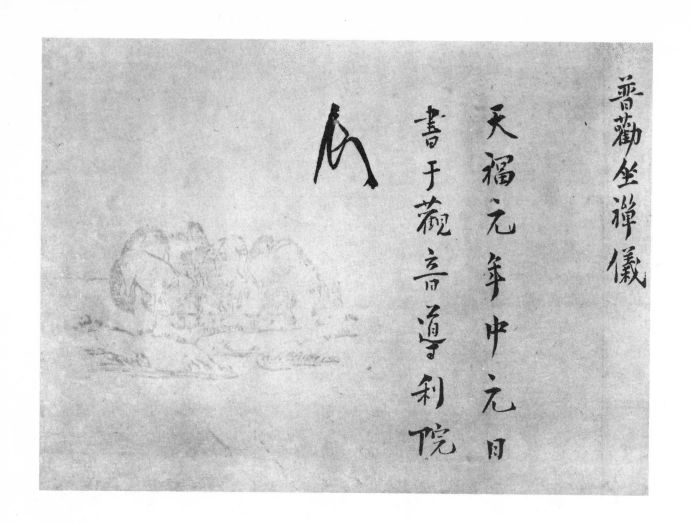

132. Dōgen • Excerpt from the original manuscript of the *Fukan Zazengi*

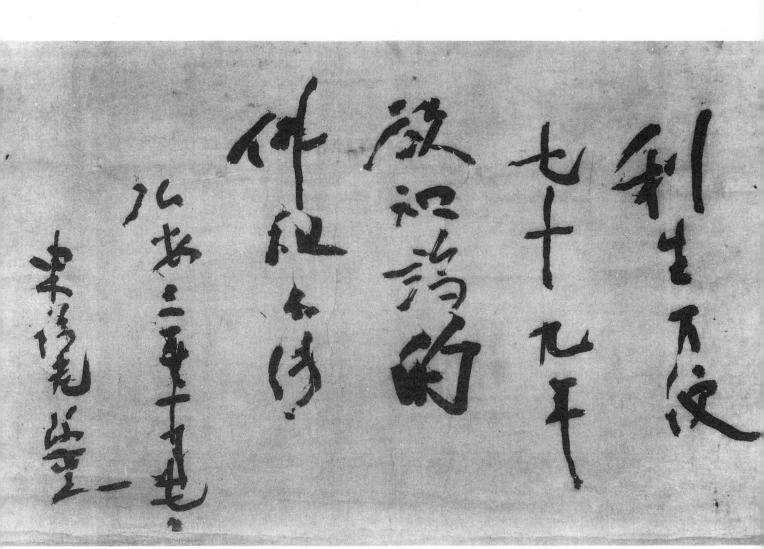

133. Shōitsu Kokushi • *Last Poem*

134. Musō Soseki •
Religious aphorism

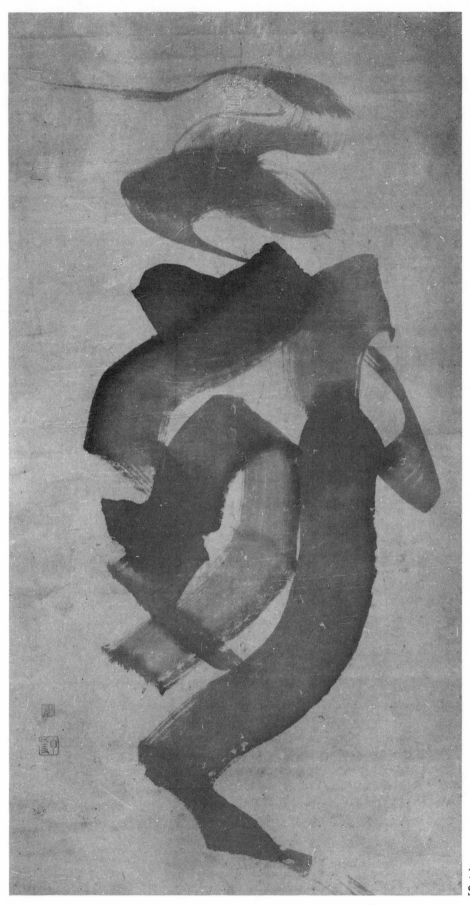

136. Hakuin •
Sanskrit character

137. Jiun • Religious aphorism

138. Jiun • The character "Buddha"

139. Jiun • The character "Man"

140. Jiun • The characters *Ai-zan* ("Love of Mountains")

141. Jiun • The characters *Kan-gin* ("Reciting Poetry Quietly")

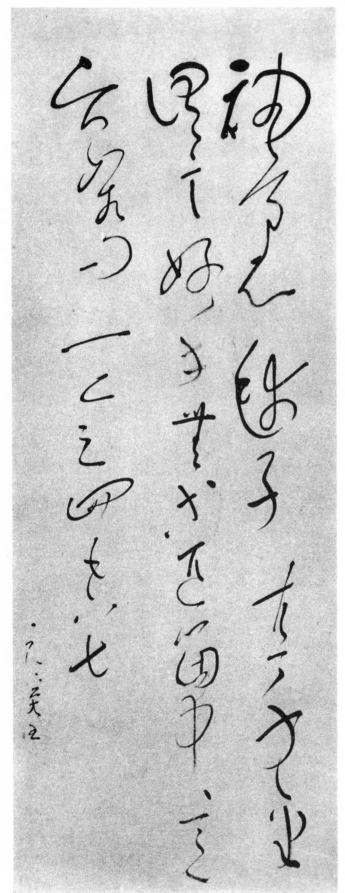

142. Ryōkan • Poem

254

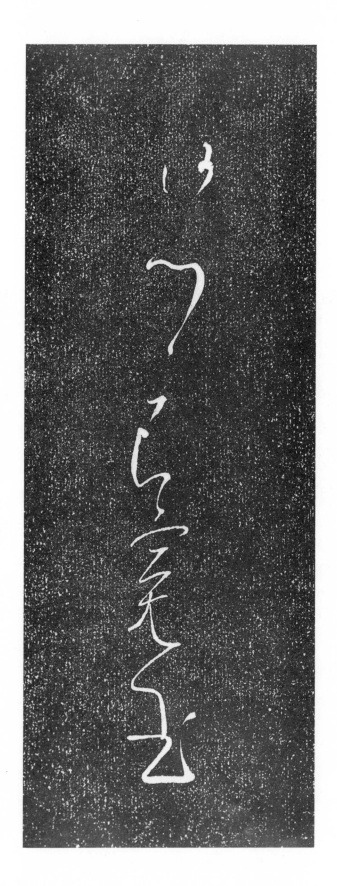

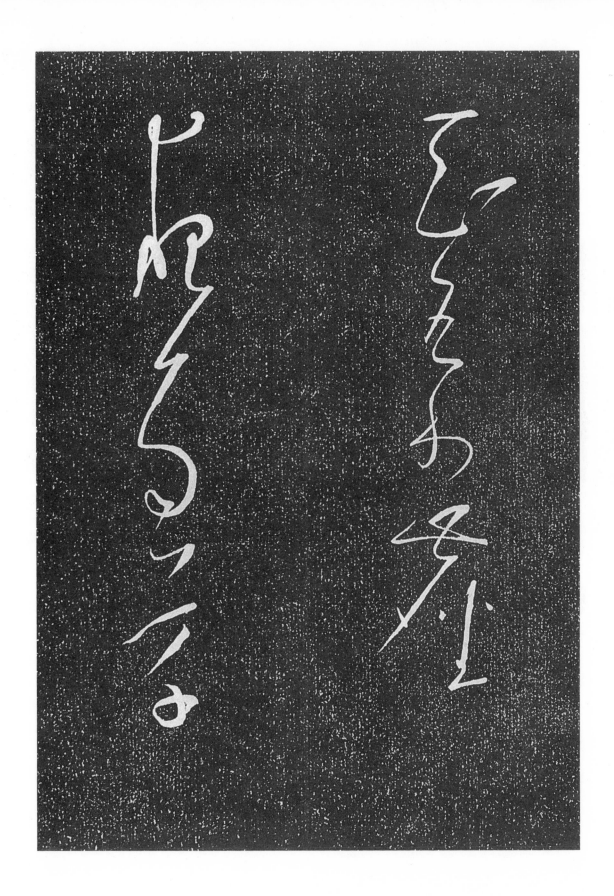

144. Ryōkan • Excerpt from an ink rubbing of the manuscript of *Tenshinchō*

145. The Hiun-kaku Pavilion, Nishi Hongan-ji, Kyoto

147. Gakki-no-ma ("Musical Instrument Room"), Katsura Imperial Villa

148. Desk and shelves (Katsura-dana) in the New Goten, Katsura Imperial Villa

149. The Ryōkaku-tei tea house, Ninna-ji, Kyoto

150. Interior of the Ryōkaku-tei tea house, Ninna-ji, Kyoto

151. Tokonoma alcove and entrance to the Sa-an tea room, Gyokurin-in temple, Kyoto

153. Tea room of the Teigyoku-ken, Shinju-an temple, Kyoto

154. The Hassō-no-seki tea room, Konchi-in temple, Kyoto

155. *Chabana* • Materials: Rose of Sharon, begonia • Container: basket

157. *Chabana* • Materials: Rose of Sharon • Container: one-windowed bamboo vase

158. *Chabana* • Materials:
clematis • Container: basket

159. Front gate and fence, Katsura Imperial Villa

160. Entrance of the Old Shoin and stepping-stones, Katsura Imperial Villa

161. Inner gate, Katsura Imperial Villa

162. Stepping-stones before the entrance of the Old Shoin, Katsura Imperial Villa

163. The Gepparō seen from the Miyuki Path, Katsura Imperial Villa

164. The west side of the Middle Shoin seen from the New Goten, Katsura Imperial Villa

165. Stone composition with basin, Shōi-ken, Katsura Imperial Villa

167. Takasago Beach and stone lantern, Katsura Imperial Villa

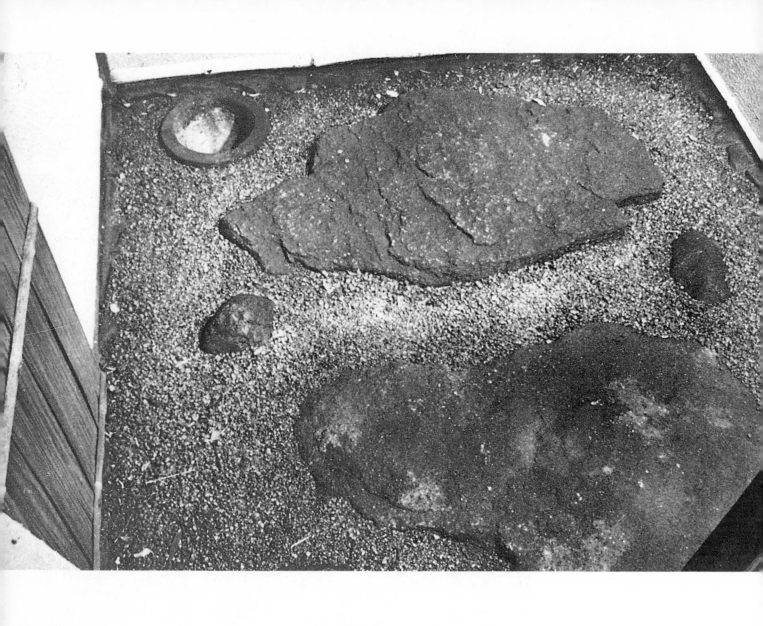

169. Toilet, Fushin-an tea house, Omote Senke, Kyoto

171. Stone composition with basin, Teigyoku-ken, Shinju-an temple, Kyoto

172. Shoe-removing stones, Shōseien Detached Villa, belonging to the Higashi Hongan-ji, Kyoto

173, 174. Stone Garden, Ryōan-ji, Kyoto

175. Stone Garden, Ryōan-ji, Kyoto

176. "Tortoiseshell" *temmoku* teabowl with phoenix design • Sung dynasty

177. Ido-type teabowl, named Tsutsu-izutsu • Yi dynasty ▷

178. Ido-type teabowl, named Kizaemon • Yi dynasty

179. Kugibori Irabo-type teabowl, named Miyamaji • Yi dynasty

180. Goshomaru-type teabowl (inverted), named Furuta Kōrai • Yi dynasty

181. Goshomaru-type, black brushmarked teabowl, named Hibakama • Yi dynasty

182. Komogai-type teabowl, named Kagamurasaki • Yi dynasty

183. Sohaku-type teabowl • Yi dynasty

184. Warikōdai-type, Hagi ware teabowl, named Zegaibō

185. Old Hagi ware teabowl in the shape of a bowl for washing brushes

186. Yellow Seto ware teabowl, named **Asahina**

187. Cylindrical, black Seto ware teabowl, named Hi-no-matsu

189. Hakuan-type teabowl, named Fuyuki

190. Gray Shino ware teabowl, named Mine-no-momiji

191. Shino ware teabowl, named U-no-hanagaki

192. Neriage-type, Shino ware teabowl

193. Shino ware teabowl, named Yama-no-ha

194. Hori-Mishima type, gray Shino ware teabowl, named Sazanami

195. Karatsu ware teabowl with *ishihaze* ("burst pebbles") effect

196. Black Oribe ware teabowl, named Matsukaze

197. Cylindrical, black Oribe ware teabowl

198. Shinbei • Shigaraki ware teabowl,
named Fugen

199. Chōjirō • Red Raku ware teabowl, named Muichimotsu

200. Chōjirō • Black Raku ware teabowl, named Tōyōbō

201. Chōjirō • Black Raku ware teabowl, named Hinsō

202. Chōjirō • Red Raku ware teabowl, named Kokeshimizu

203. Nonkō • Black Raku ware teabowl, named Chidori

204. Nonkō • Black Raku ware teabowl, named Masu

205. Nonkō • Black Raku ware teabowl, named Imaeda

206. Nonkō • Black Raku ware teabowl, named Jurōjin

207. Kōetsu • Red Raku ware teabowl, named Kaga-Kōetsu

208. Kōetsu • Red Raku ware teabowl, named Otogoze

209. Kōetsu • Black Raku ware teabowl, named Amagumo

210. Kūchū • Cylindrical, black Raku ware teabowl, named Kangetsu

211. Kenzan • Teabowl with waterfall design

212. Asahi ware teabowl, named Kawagiri

213. Ido-type incense burner,
named Konoyo • Yi dynasty

214. Three-footed, Oribe ware incense container

215. Oribe ware tea caddy, named Miotsukushi

217. Flat-shouldered, old Seto ware tea caddy, named Yari-no-saya

218. Seto ware tea caddy, named Tengō-an

219. Flat-shouldered tea caddy,
named Matsuya • Sung dynasty

220. Flat-shouldered, old Bizen ware tea caddy, named Sabisuke

221. *E*-Shino (painted Shino) ware water container, named Kogan

222. Bizen ware water container

223. Iga ware vase, named Jurōjin

225. Mino-Iga ware water container

226. Tamba ware vase

339

229. Mottled, Karatsu ware bowl

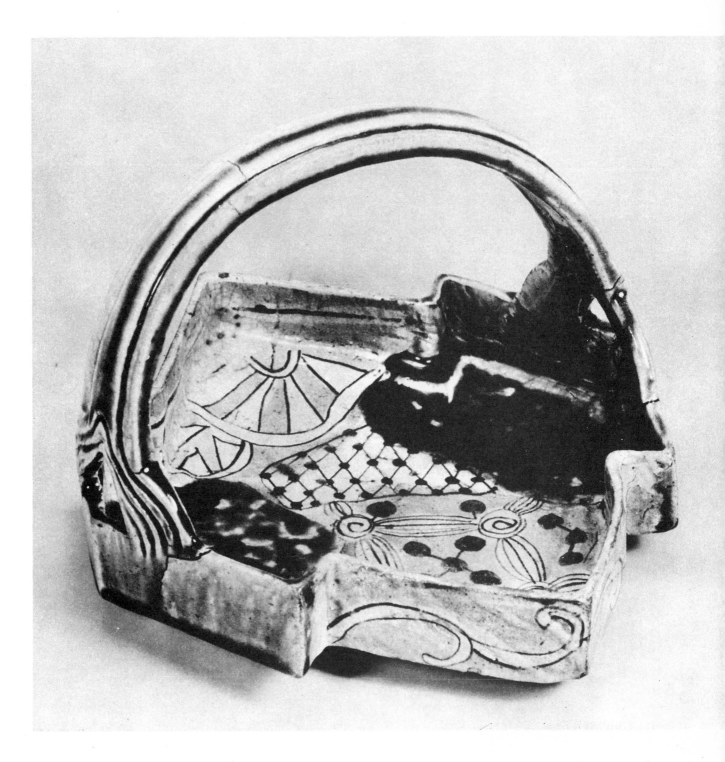

230. Handled, Oribe ware bowl, Matsukawabishi shape

231. Handled, Oribe ware bowl

232. Kenzan • Ceramic bowl • Decorated by Kōrin with figure of Han-shan

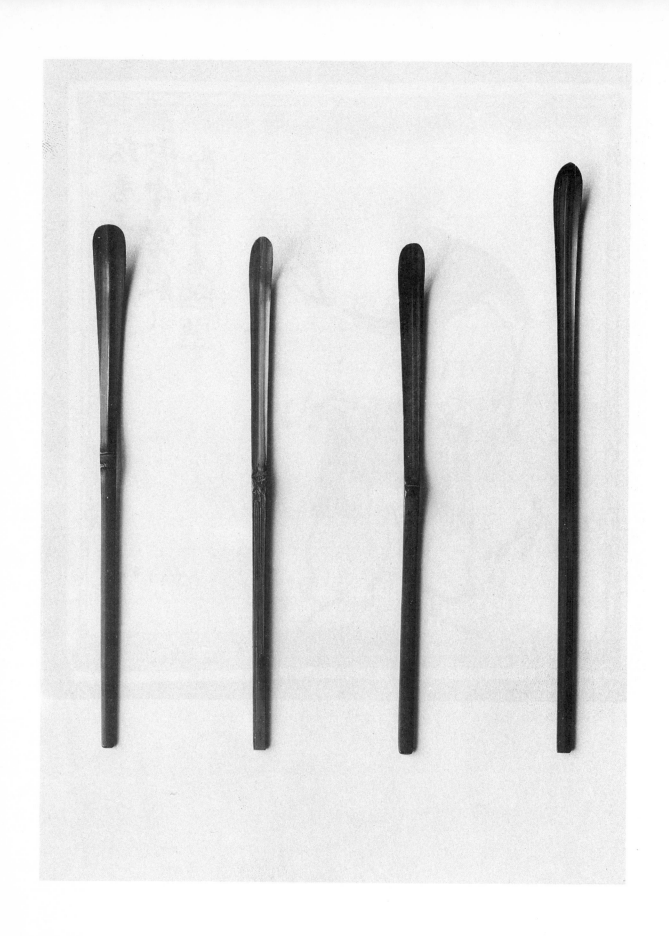

233–236. (from left) Seta Kamon, Kūchū, Furuta Oribe, Shutoku • Bamboo tea spoons

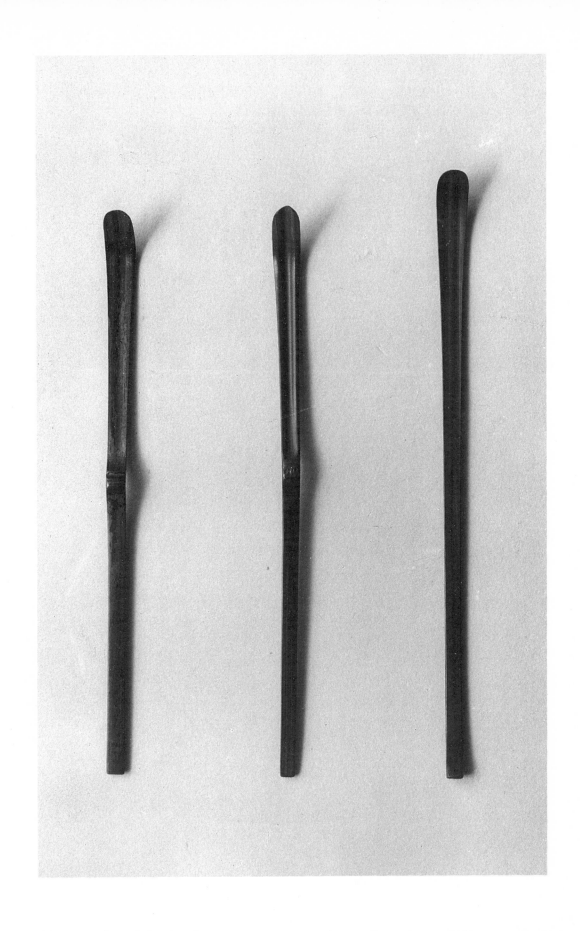

237–239. (from left) Hosokawa Sansai, Sen no Rikyū, Takeno Jōō • Bamboo tea spoons

240. Kobori Enshū • One-windowed bamboo flower container, named Fujinami

242. Grained wood tea container (*natsume*) with chrysanthemum relief on lid

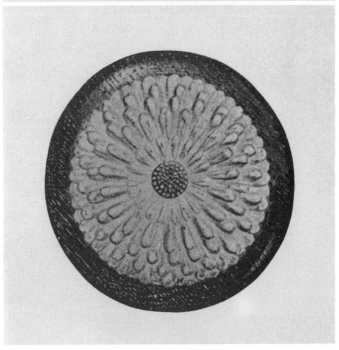

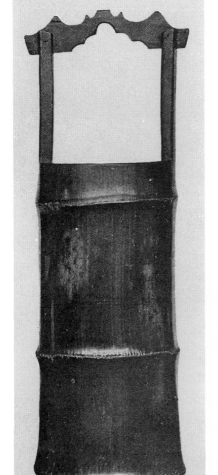

241. Sen no Rikyū • Bamboo flower container

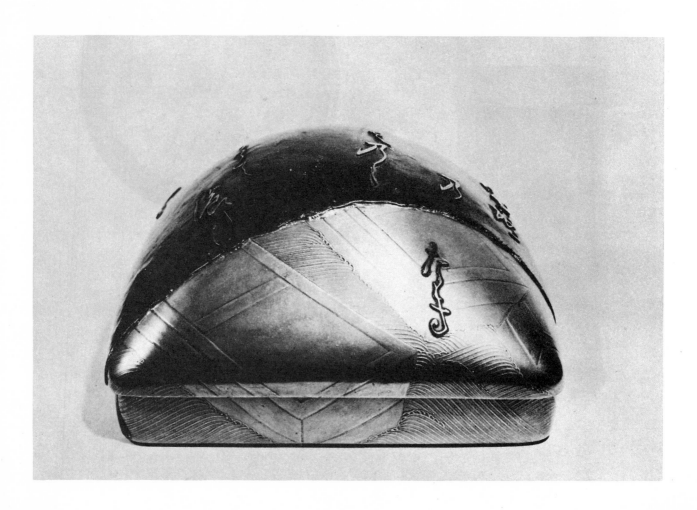

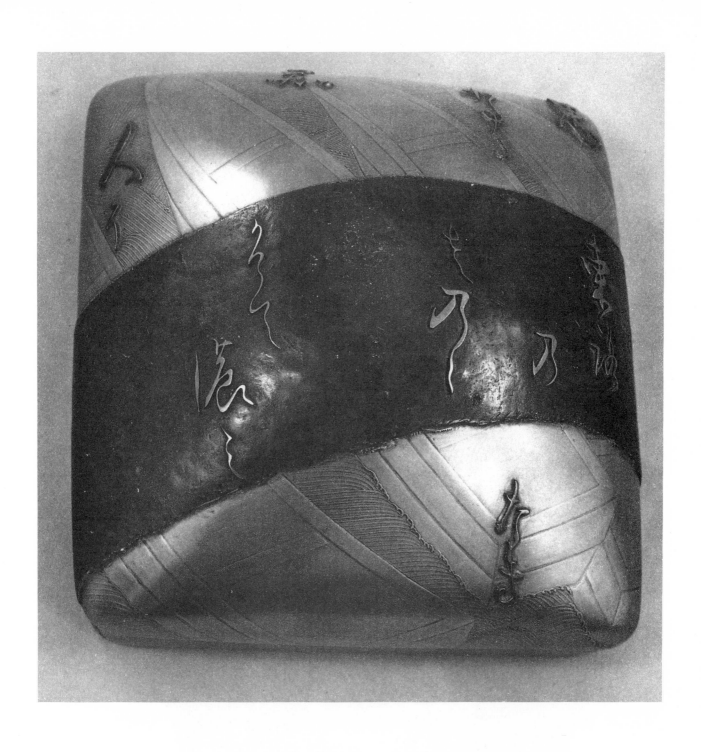

243. Kōetsu • Inkstone box • Lacquer with metal inlay

244. Iron kettle with "hailstone" surface and *tanzaku* (paper slips for writing poetry) designs

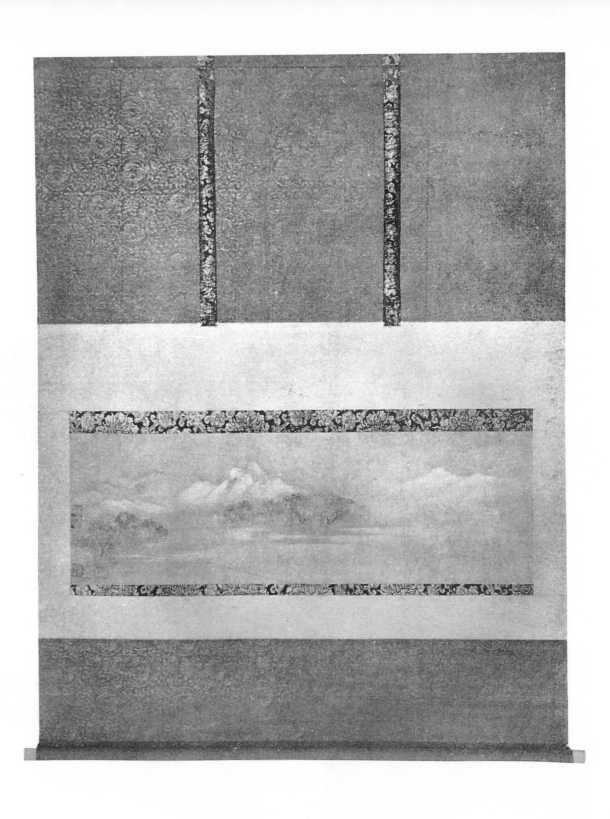

245. Mounting of Mu-ch'i's *Evening of Snow* (Pl. 68)

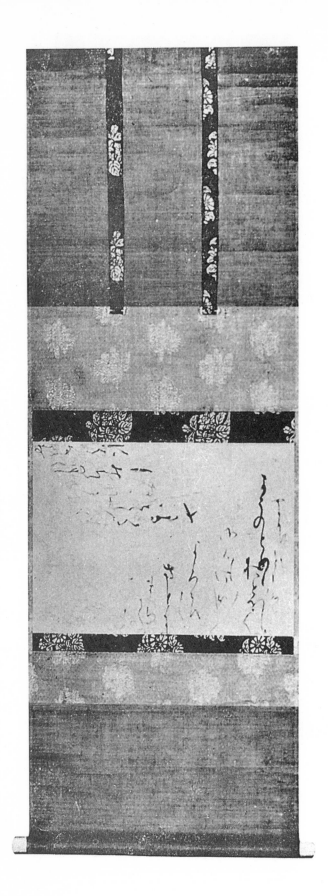

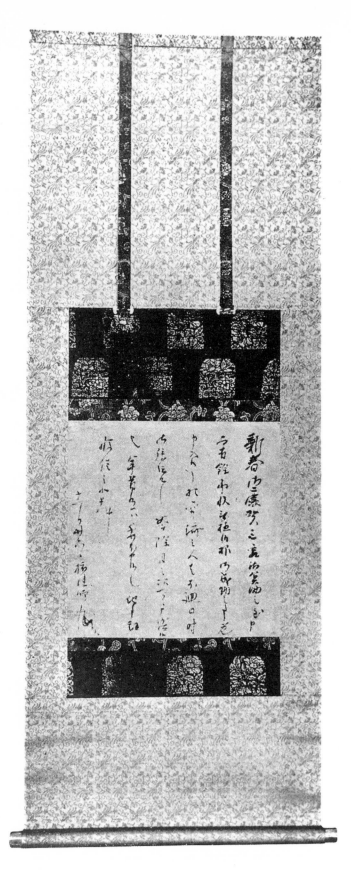

246. Mounting of calligraphy by Saigyō Hōshi

247. Mounting of calligraphy by Eisai Zenji

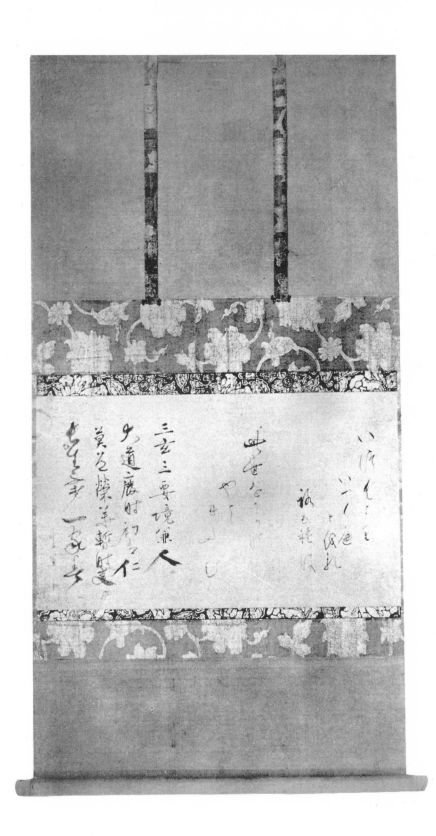

250. Pouch for a cylindrical tea caddy case • Wan-li damask

354

251. Pouch for a wooden tea container (*natsume*) • White silk and silver brocade

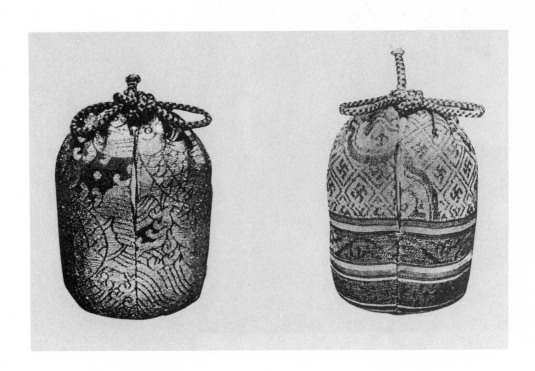

252. Pouches for a tea caddy named Takitsuse • Left: Araiso pattern damask;
Right: Tawaraya pattern brocade

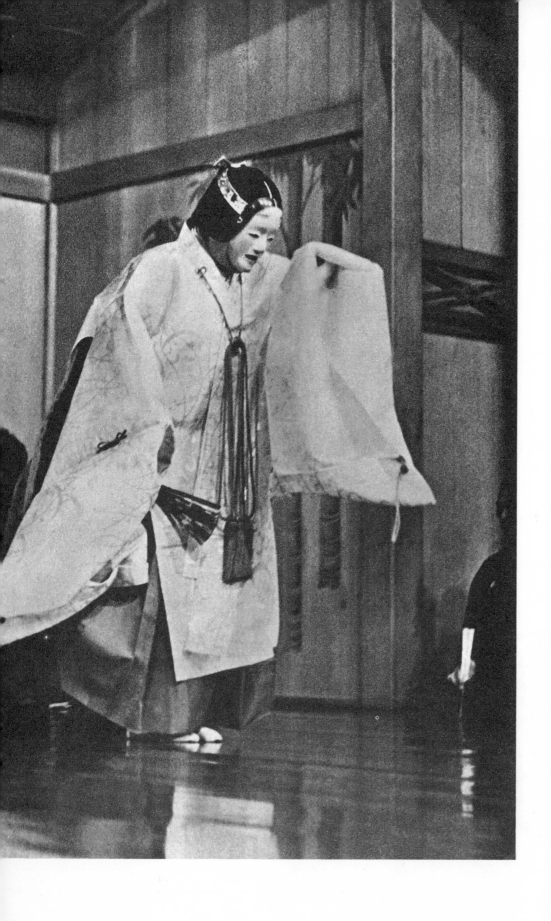

253. Scene from the Nō play *Hajitomi* • Performer: Kanze Kasetsu

254. Scene from the Nō play *Seigan-ji* • Performer: Yoshii Shirō

255. Scene from the Nō play *Tōru* • Performer: Umewaka Manzaburō

256. Scene from the Nō play *Dōjō-ji* • Performer: Kawamura Takashi ▷

258. Scene from the Nō play *Matsukaze* • Performer: Takaoka Saishi

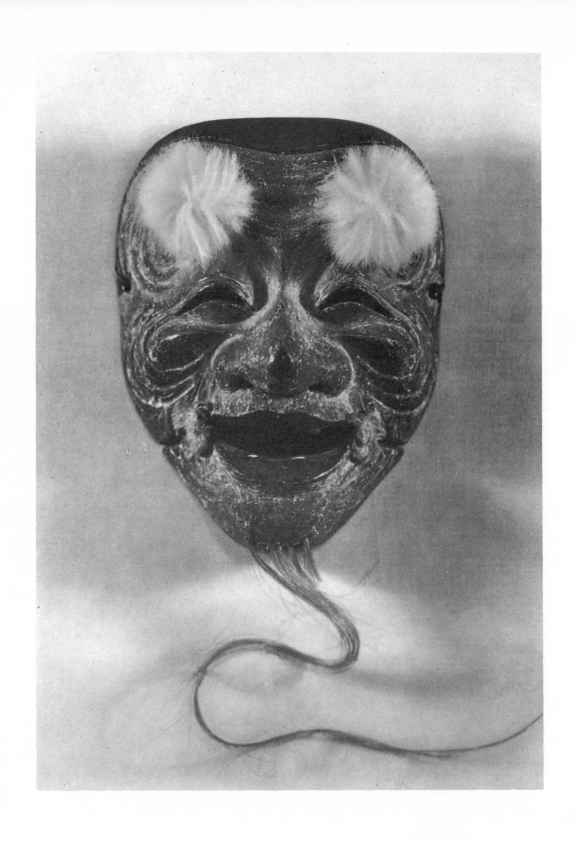

259. Nō mask • Okina

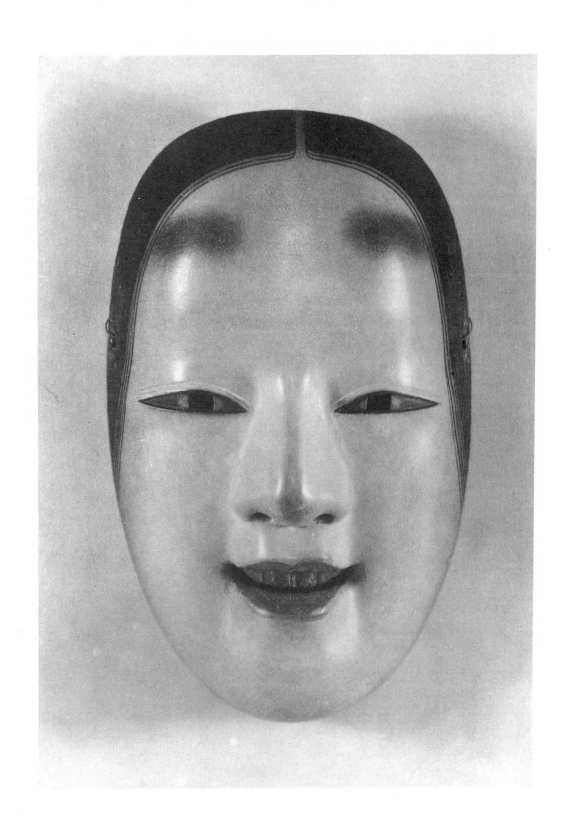

260. Nō mask • Magojirō

261. Nō mask • Hannya

262. Nō mask • Emmeikaja

264. Nō mask • Yaseotoko

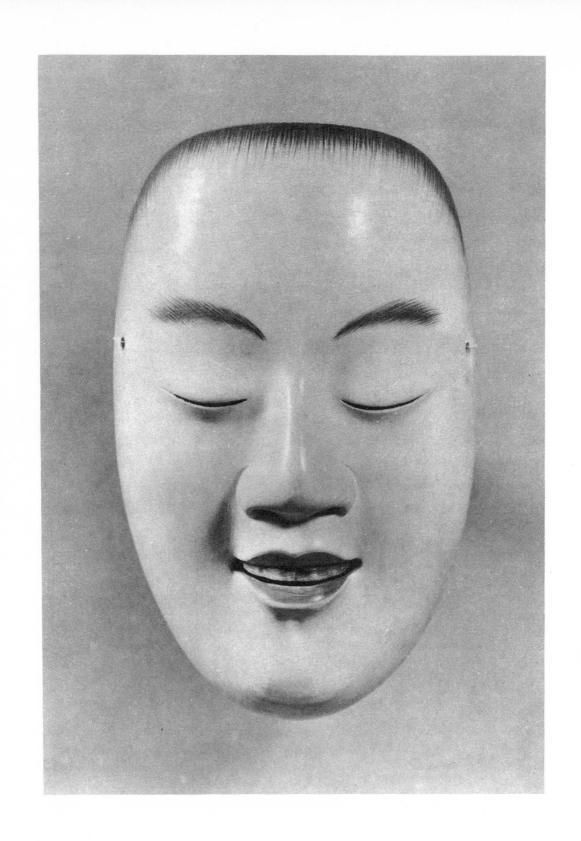

265. Nō mask · Yorōboshi

266. Nō mask · Ōbeshimi

267. Nō costume • *Tsujigahana* dyeing

268. Nō costume • *Surihaku* (applied gold dust) design

269. Nō costume • *Kara-ori* brocade

270. Nō costume • *Kara-ori* brocade

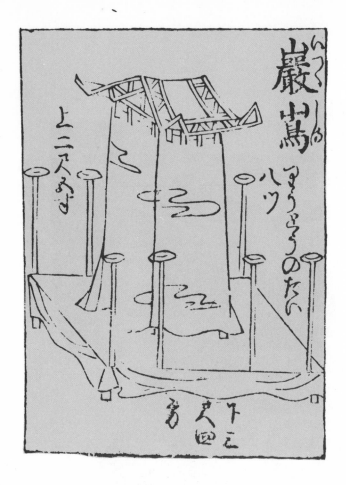

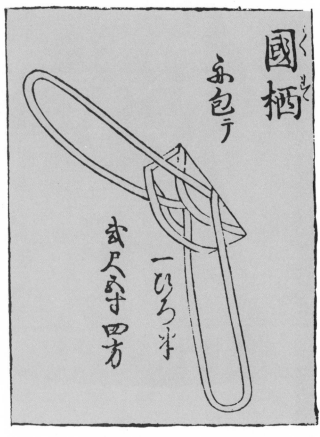

271. Nō stage property • Shrine

272. Nō stage property • Boat

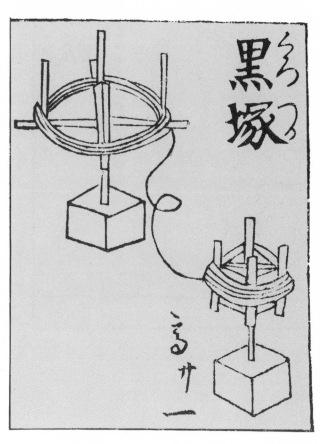

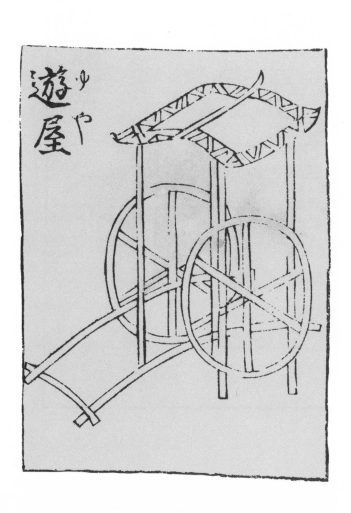

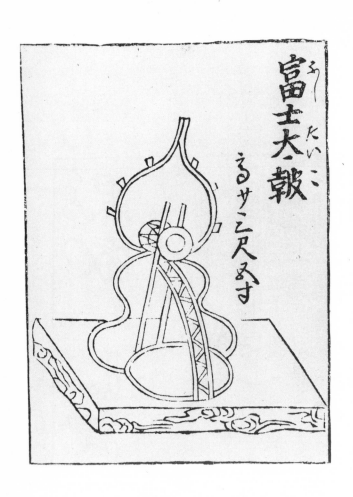

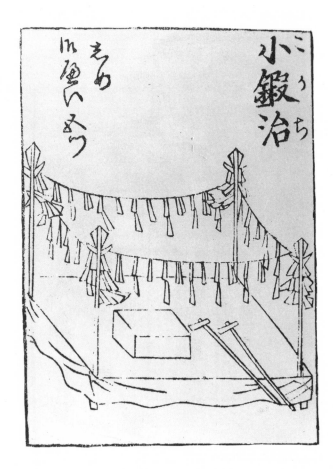

275. Nō stage property • Drum stand

276. Nō stage property • Swordsmith's shop

NOTES TO THE PLATES

1. Liang K'ai • *Śākyamuni Descending the Mountain* (see Pl. 37).

2. Mu-ch'i • *Pa-Pa Bird on an Old Pine* (老松叭々鳥) • Southern Sung dynasty (late thirteenth century) • ink on paper • 79.0 × 39.0 cm.

3. Sesshū • *Winter,* from *Autumn and Winter Landscapes* (秋冬山水) • Muromachi period (end of fifteenth century) • ink on paper • 46.9 × 29.2 cm.

4. Hakuin • *Monkey* (猿猴) • Edo period (mid-eighteenth century) • ink on paper

5, Fig. 8. Tōhaku • *Maple* (楓) • Momoyama period (end of sixteenth century) color on paper • 177.0 × 138.0 cm.

6. Hakuin • The character *Mu* (無) ("No") • Edo period (mid-eighteenth century) • ink on paper • 43.6 × 42.2 cm.

7. Huai-su • excerpts from *Autobiographical Notes* (自叙帖) • T'ang dynasty (dated 777) • detail of ink-rubbing copy • original handscroll: 28.3 × 755 cm.

8. I-shan I-ning • *Poem on a Snowy Night* (雪夜作) • Muromachi period (dated 1315) • ink on paper • Kennin-ji, Kyoto

9. Ryōkan • The characters "Mind, Moon, Circle" (心月輪) (Japanese: *shin-gachi-rin*) •

late Edo period (early nineteenth century) • limed engraving on the underside of a cedar-wood kettle lid • These three characters are an expression of the likening, in Buddhism, of the heart and mind to the full moon, an image reinforced by the round kettle lid.

10. Tea room (*shoin* style) of the Zangetsu-tei (残月亭) • Momoyama period (late sixteenth century) • Omote Senke, Kyoto

11. Shōkin-tei (松琴亭) tea house • early Edo period (early seventeenth century) • Katsura Imperial Villa

14. Stepping-stones below the Tsukimi-dai (Moon-Viewing Platform) of the Old Shoin • early Edo period • Katsura Imperial Villa

15. Path between the Tsukimi-dai and the Gepparō (Moon Wave Pavilion) • early Edo period • Katsura Imperial Villa

16, Fig. 9. Warikōdai-type (割高台) (notched foot) teabowl • Yi dynasty (Korea) (*ca.* sixteenth century) • height : 9.7 – 10.6 cm.; mouth: 13.4 × 11.8 cm.; foot: 7.6 × 7.9 cm.

17. Goshomaru-type teabowl, named Sekiyō (夕陽) (Sunset) • Yi dynasty (Korea) (*ca.* sixteenth century) • height: 6.6 cm.; mouth: 13.2 × 10.0 cm. • Fujita Museum of Art, Osaka

18, Fig. 10. Hon'ami Kōetsu • Raku ware teabowl, named Fujisan (不二山) (Mount Fuji) • Edo period (early seventeenth century) • height: 8.5 cm.; mouth: 11.5 cm.; foot: 5.4 cm. • Kōetsu employed a homonym for the famous mountain in naming this bowl: the characters used literally translate "no two mountains," referring, obviously, to the One Mountain in Japan, Fuji.

19. Cylindrical, Oribe ware teabowl • Momoyama period (end of sixteenth century) • height: 8.8 cm.; mouth: 10.6 cm.

20. E-Shino (painted Shino) ware water container • Momoyama period (end of sixteenth century) • height: 17.7 cm.; mouth: 18.2 cm.

21. Kobori Enshū • bamboo flower container, named Sairai (再來) (to come again or be born again) • Edo period (early seventeenth century) • height: 29.3 cm.; mouth: 10.6 • Nezu Art Museum, Tokyo

22. Iron kettle with tortoiseshell pattern • Momoyama period (sixteenth century) • height: 14.9 cm.; mouth: 12.3 cm.; body: 26.8 cm.

23. attributed to Hon'ami Kōetsu • inkstone box • lacquer with metal inlay, design of cranes and paddy field • 23.7 × 21.3 cm.

24. Pouch for a tea caddy named Yamazakura (山櫻) (Mountain Cherry) • Yoshino kantō fabric • This type of kantō fabric was named after Yoshino Tayū, a famous courtesan of the seventeenth century, who was known to favor this kind of stripped weave.

25. Pouch for an old Seto ware tea caddy named Akatsuki (暁) (Dawn) • Enshū damask (named after Kobori Enshū)

26. Pouch for a cylindrical tea caddy case (hikiya) • Arisugawa pattern brocade

29–32. Ch'an-yüeh • Arhats, from The Sixteen Arhats (十六羅漢像) • Five Dynasties (tenth century) • color on silk • all 91.8 ×

45.1 cm. • Imperial Household Collection

33, 34. attributed to Shih K'o • The Second Patriarch in Repose (二祖調心) • Five Dynasties (tenth century) • ink on paper • both 35.5 × 64.5 cm. • Tokyo National Museum

35, 36. Li T'ang • Landscapes (山水) • Southern Sung dynasty (early twelfth century) • ink on silk • both 98.5 × 43.6 cm • Kōtōin, Kyoto

37. Liang K'ai • Śākyamuni Descending the Mountain (出山釋迦) • Southern Sung dynasty (early thirteenth century) • ink and color on silk • 119.0 × 52.0 cm.

38. Liang K'ai • Landscape in Snow (雪景山水) • Southern Sung dynasty (early thirteenth century) • ink and color on silk • 111.0 × 50.0 cm. • Tokyo National Museum

39. Liang K'ai • The Sixth Patriarch Cutting Bamboo (六祖截竹) • Southern Sung dynasty • ink on paper • 72.7 × 31.5 cm. • Tokyo National Museum

40. Liang K'ai • The Sixth Patriarch Destroying the Sutra (六祖破經) • Southern Sung dynasty • ink on paper • 74.0 × 32.0 cm.

41. Liang K'ai • Li Po (李白) • Southern Sung dynasty • ink on paper • 80.9 × 32.7 cm. • Tokyo National Museum

42. Liang K'ai • Dancing Pu-tai (布袋) • Southern Sung dynasty • ink on paper • 80.9 × 32.7 cm.

43. Liang K'ai • Intoxicated Old Man (醉翁) • Southern Sung dynasty • ink on silk • 21.0 × 18.8 cm.

44. Liang K'ai • Han-shan and Shih-te (寒山拾得) • Southern Sung dynasty • ink on paper • 81.2 × 33.9 cm. • Atami Art Museum, Atami

45. Liang K'ai • Sage of Yao-t'ai (瑤臺仙) (album leaf) • Southern Sung dynasty • ink on paper • 48.6 × 27.7 cm.

46. attributed to Liang K'ai • Herons and

Swallows in Snow (雪中鷺雀) (detail) • Southern Sung dynasty • Fogg Art Museum

47. Li Ch'üen • *Pu-tai, from Feng-kan, Bodhidharma,* and *Pu-tai* (佛鑑, 達磨, 布袋図) (set of three scrolls) • Southern Sung dynasty • ink on paper • 104.8 × 32.1 cm. • Myōshin-ji, Kyōto

48. artist unknown • *Bodhidharma* (達磨) • Southern Sung or Yüan dynasty (thirteenth or fourteenth century) • ink and color on silk • 124.0 × 61.2 cm.

49. attributed to Ma Yüan • *Fisherman on a River in Winter* (寒江独釣) • Southern Sung dynasty (late twelfth century) • ink on silk • 26.9 × 50.3 cm. • Tokyo National Museum

50. attributed to Kao Jan-hui • *Dawn Landscape* (朝陽山水) • Yüan dynasty (fourteenth century) • ink on silk • 50.8 × 52.6 cm.

51. attributed to Hsia Kuei • *Landscape in Rain* (風雨山水) • Southern Sung dynasty (late twelfth century) • ink on paper • 79.0 × 33.0 cm.

52. Ma Lin • *Han-shan and Shih-te* (寒山拾得) • Southern Sung dynasty (early thirteenth century) • ink on paper

53. artist unknown • *Waterfall* (瀑布) • Southern Sung dynasty (*ca.* thirteenth century) • ink and wash on paper • 64.2 × 10.3 cm. • Chishaku-in, Kyoto

54. Ma Lin • *Sunset Landscape* (夕陽山水) (detail) • Southern Sung dynasty (dated 1254) • ink and wash on silk • full size: 52.0 × 27.0 cm. • Nezu Art Museum, Tokyo

55. attributed to Mu-ch'i • *Persimmons* (柿) • Southern Sung dynasty (late thirteenth century) • ink on paper • 35.0 × 33.6 cm. • Ryōkō-in, Daitoku-ji, Kyoto

56. attributed to Mu-ch'i • *Chestnuts* (栗) • Southern Sung dynasty (late thirteenth century) • ink on paper • 35.1 × 29.1 cm. • Ryōkō-in, Daitoku-ji, Kyoto

57. attributed to Mu-ch'i • *Kingfisher on a*

Dry Reed (枯蘆翡翠) • Southern Sung dynasty • ink on paper • 79.4 × 30.9 cm.

58. attributed to Mu-ch'i • *Wagtail on a Lotus Leaf* (敗荷鶺鴒) • Southern Sung dynasty • ink on paper • 79.4 × 30.9 cm. • Atami Art Museum, Atami

59–61. Mu-ch'i *Kuan-yin, Monkeys,* and *Crane* (観音猿鶴) (set of three scrolls) • Southern Sung dynasty • ink on silk • *Kuan-yin*: 173.0 × 97.8 cm.; *Monkeys*: 174.5 × 98.7 cm.; *Crane*: 174.5 × 99.0 cm. • Daitoku-ji, Kyoto

62. attributed to Mu-ch'i • *Bodhidharma* (達磨) • Southern Sung dynasty • ink on paper • 96.4 × 34.2 cm.

63. attributed to Mu-ch'i • *Lao-tzu* (老子) • Southern Sung dynasty • ink on paper • 89.0 × 33.0 cm.

64. attributed to Mu-ch'i • *Swallow on a Lotus Pod* (蓮燕) • Southern Sung dynasty • ink on paper • 72.1 × 30.3 cm.

65. attributed to Mu-ch'i • *Sunrise* (朝陽) • Southern Sung dynasty • ink on paper • 83.9 × 30.3 cm.

66. attributed to Mu-ch'i • *Swallows and Willow* (柳燕) • Southern Sung dynasty • ink on silk • 87.8 × 44.2 cm. • Tokugawa Art Museum, Nagoya

67. attributed to Mu-ch'i • *Sunset in a Fishing Village* (漁村夕照), from *Eight Views of Hsiao-Hsiang* (瀟湘八景) • Southern Sung dynasty • ink on paper • 33.1 × 113.3 cm. • Nezu Art Museum, Tokyo

68. attributed to Mu-ch'i • *Evening of Snow* (江天暮雪), from *Eight Views of Hsiao-Hsiang* • Southern Sung dynasty • ink on paper • 29.5 × 95.5 cm.

69. attributed to Mu-ch'i • *Autumn Moon over Lake Tung-t'ing* (洞庭秋月) • Southern Sung dynasty • ink on paper • 27.2 × 86.4 cm. • Tokugawa Art Museum, Nagoya

70. attributed to Mu-ch'i • *Night Rain at Hsiao-Hsiang* (瀟湘夜雨) • Southern Sung dynasty • ink on paper

71, 72. attributed to Mu-ch'i • *Dragon* and *Tiger* (龍虎) (pair of scrolls) • Southern Sung dynasty • ink on silk • both 148.4×93.9 cm. • Daitoku-ji, Kyoto

73. Yü Chien • *Landscape at Lu-shan* (盧山瀑布) (detail) • Southern Sung dynasty • ink on silk • 35.0×62.5 cm. • This painting, originally titled *Waterfall at Lu-shan*, was cut to accomodate the width of a connoisseur's *tokonoma* alcove; the waterfall section is still extant.

74. Yü Chien • *Clear Mourning in a Mountain Village* (山市晴嵐) (detail), from *Eight Views of Hsiao-Hsiang* • Southern Sung dynasty (mid-thirteenth century) • ink on paper • 30.3×84.0 cm.

75. artist unknown • *Yu Shan-chu*, from *Cheng Huang-nin, Bodhidharma*, and *Yu Shan-chu* (郁山主政黃牛) (set of three scrolls) • Southern Sung dynasty (twelfth or thirteenth century) • ink on paper • 84.8×30.3 cm. • Tokugawa Art Museum, Nagoya

76. Jih-kuan • *Grapes* (葡萄) • Yüan dynasty (late thirteenth century) • ink on silk • 102.8×34.3 cm. • Nezu Art Museum, Tokyo

77. Chih-weng • *The Sixth Patriarch* (六祖挾担) • Southern Sung dynasty (late thirteenth century) • ink on paper • 90.0×36.4 cm. • Dai-Tokyū Memorial Library, Tokyo

78. Yin-t'o-lo • *Vimalakīrti* (維摩) • Yüan dynasty (mid-fourteenth century) • ink on paper • 92.0×28.0 cm.

79. attributed to Yin-t'o-lo • *Tan-hsia Burning a Buddha Image* (丹霞燒佛) • Yüan dynasty • ink on paper • 35.1×36.6 cm.

80. Yin-t'o-lo • *Pu-tai* (布袋) • Yüan dynasty • ink on paper • 35.7×48.8 cm. • Nezu Art Museum, Tokyo

81, 82. Yin-t'o-lo • *Han-shan* and *Shih-te* (寒山拾得) (pair of scrolls) • Yüan dynasty • ink on paper • each scroll: 68.0×63.0 cm.

83. Kaō • *Master Hsien-tzu* (蜆子和尚) • Muromachi period (fourteenth century) • ink on silk • 86.6×31.5 cm. • Tokyo National Museum

84. artist unknown • *Portrait of Daitō Kokushe* (大燈國師) • end of Kamakura period (inscription by Daitō Kokushi dated 1334) • color on silk • 113.7×56.7 cm. • Daitoku-ji, Kyoto

85. Mokuan • *The Four Sleepers* (四睡) (detail) • Muromachi period (mid-fourteenth century) • ink on paper • full size: 70.0×36.0 cm. • Maeda Ikutokukai Foundation, Tokyo

86. Josetsu • *Catching a Catfish with a Gourd* (瓢鮎) (detail) • Muromachi period (late fourteenth century) • ink and wash on paper • full size; 11.5×75.8 cm. • Taizō-in, Myōshin-ji, Kyoto

87. Josetsu • *Three Sages* (三教) (detail) • Muromachi period • ink on paper

88. Tan'an • *Heron* (鷺) • Momoyama period (sixteenth century) • ink on paper • 32.9×49.1 cm. • Tokyo National Museum

89. Ashikaga Yoshimitsu • *Tu Tzu-mei* (杜子美) • Muromachi period (late fourteenth century) • ink on paper

90. Soga Dasoku • *Lin-chi* (臨済) (detail) • Muromachi period (late fifteenth century) • ink on paper • Yōtoku-in, Daitoku-ji, Kyoto

91. Murata Shukō • *Landscape* (山水) • Muromachi period (late fifteenth century) • ink on paper • 41.8×21.8 cm.

92. Sesshū • *Landscape* (山水) (detail) • Muromachi period (late fifteenth century) • ink on paper • full size: 147.9×32.7 cm. • Tokyo National Museum

93. Sesshū • *Landscape Scroll of the Four Seasons* (四季山水) (detail) • Muromachi period (dated 1495) • ink on paper • full size: 40.0×1807.5 cm.

94–97. attributed to Sōami • *Landscapes* (山水) (from a set of eight paintings) • Muromachi period (early sixteenth century)

• ink on paper • all 86.7 × 46.7 cm. • Daisen-in, Daitoku-ji, Kyoto

98. Tōhaku • *Monkeys on an Old Tree* (枯木猿猴) (two sliding panels) • Momoyama period (end of sixteenth century) • ink on paper • each panel: 155.6 × 116.1 cm. • Ryōsen-an, Kyoto

99. Tōhaku • *Pine Trees* (松林) (pair of six-fold screens) • Momoyama period • ink on paper • each screen: 155.8 × 346.7 cm. • Tokyo National Museum

100. Iwasa Shōi • *Hotei* (布袋) • early Edo period (early seventeenth century) • ink on paper • 101.2 × 33.6 cm.

101. Iwasa Shōi • *Ki no Tsurayuki* (紀貫之) • early Edo period • ink on paper • 94.0 × 35.5 cm. • Atami Art Museum, Atami

102. Niten • *Shrike* (枯木鳴鵙) • early Edo period • ink on paper • 125.6 × 54.3 cm.

103. Niten • *Bodhidharma* (達磨) • early Edo period • ink on paper

104, 105. Niten • *Wild Geese* (蘆雁) (pair of six-fold screens) • early Edo period (seventeenth century) • ink on paper • each screen: 162.1 × 327.3 cm.

106. Niten • *Hotei and Fighting Cocks* (布袋見闘) • early Edo period • ink on paper • 70.3 × 31.3 cm. • Matsunaga Memorial Museum, Kanagawa

107. Niten • *Rush Leaf Bodhidharma* (蘆葉達磨) • early Edo period • ink on paper • 112.7 × 28.3 cm.

108. Hakuin • *Bodhidharma* (達磨) • middle Edo period (mid-eighteenth century) • ink on paper • Senbutsu-ji, Kyoto

109. Hakuin • *Śākyamuni Descending the Mountain* (出山釋迦) • middle Edo period • ink on paper

110. Hakuin • *Master Hotei* (布袋和尚) • middle Edo period • ink on paper

111. Hakuin • *Bodhidharma* (達磨) • middle Edo period • ink on paper

112. Hakuin • *Echigo Sanjakubō* (越後三尺坊)

• middle Edo period • ink on paper • This painting would seem to portray a monk named Sanjakubō of Echigo Province in the guise of Fudō Myōō (Acala).

113. Hakuin • *Bodhidharma* (達磨) • middle Edo period • ink on paper

114. Yang Ning-shih • excerpt from the *Shen-hsien ch'i-chü-fa* (神仙起居法) • Five Dynasties (dated 948) • ink on paper • height: 28.2 cm. • Museum of Calligraphy, Tokyo

115. Yü Chi • inscription beside Shih K'o's paintings, *The Second Patriarch in Repose* (二祖調心) • Yüan dynasty (early fourteenth century) • ink on paper

116. attributed to Nan-ch'üan • excerpt from a Zen lecture (上堂語) • T'ang dynasty • ink on paper • 33.5 × 53.1 cm.

117. Yuan-wu K'o-ch'in • certificate of a disciple's Awakening (印可狀) • Sung dynasty (early twelfth century) • ink on paper • 52.1 × 43.9 cm. • Tokyo National Museum

118. Ta-hui Tsung-kao • letter (尺牘) • Southern Sung dynasty (early twelfth century) • ink on paper • 38.2 × 56.8 cm. • Tokyo National Museum

119. Ta-hui Tsung-kao • letter (尺牘) • Southern Sung dynasty • ink on paper • 38.2 × 73.6 cm. • Tokyo National Museum

120. Wu-an P'u-ning • letter (尺牘) • Southern Sung dynasty (mid-thirteenth century) • ink on paper • 29.1 × 58.8 cm.

121. Huang T'ing-chien • excerpt from Li Po's poem *I-chin-yu* (李白憶舊遊詩) • Sung dynasty (end of eleventh century) • ink on paper • full size: 37.0 × 391.8 cm. • Tō-fuku-ji, Kyoto

122. Liao-an Ch'ing-yü • *Farewell Poem* (送別偈) • Yüan dynasty (early fourteenth century) • ink on paper • 33.0 × 61.5 cm.

123. Hsü-t'ang Chih-yü • poem (偈頌) • Southern Sung dynasty (early thirteenth century) • ink on paper • 27.9 × 85.5 cm.

124. Chang Chi-chih • the characters *Fang-chang* (方丈) ("Main Temple Hall") • Southern Sung (early thirteenth century) • 27.9 × 85.5 cm. • Tōfuku-ji, Kyoto

125. Chung-feng Ming-pen • letter soliciting contributions to build the Huan-chu-an (幻住庵勧縁疏) • Yüan dynasty (early fourteenth century) • ink on paper • 32.4 × 87.6 cm.

126. Wu-hsüeh Tsu-yüan • poem (偈頌) • Southern Sung dynasty (mid-thirteenth century) • ink on paper • 36.7 × 107.0 cm. • Nezu Art Museum, Tokyo

127. Ku-lin Ch'ing-mao • certificate of the title Yüeh-lin given to a disciple (月林頌号) • Yüan dynasty • ink on paper • 36.7 × 120.3 cm. • Chōfuku-ji, Kyoto

128. Wu-chun Shih-fan • certificate of a disciple's Awakening (印可状) • Southern Sung dynasty (early thirteenth century) • ink on silk • 38.8 × 110.9 cm.

129. Ling-shan Tao-yin • religious text (法語) • Yüan dynasty (early fourteenth century) • ink on paper • 31.1 × 81.5 cm. • Tokyo National Museum

130. I-shan I-ning • the poem of Hui-neng, the Sixth Patriarch (六祖偈) • Yüan dynasty (early fourteenth century) • ink on paper • 87.9 × 29.8 cm.

131. Daitō Kokushi • certificate of the title Kanzan given to a disciple (関山頌号) • end of Kamakura period (early fourteenth century) • ink on paper • 66.7 × 61.8 cm. • Myōshin-ji, Kyoto

132. Dōgen • excerpt from the original manuscript of the *Fukan Zazengi* (普勧坐禅儀) • Kamakura period (thirteenth century) • ink on paper • full size: 28.8 × 319.1 cm. • Eihei-ji, Fukui Prefecture

133. Shoitsu Kokushi • *Last Poem* (遺偈) • Kamakura period (ca. 1280) • ink on paper • 33.9 × 77.6 cm. • Tōfuku-ji, Kyoto

134. Musō Soseki • religious aphorism (法語) • end of Kamakura period (early fourteenth century) • ink on paper • 106.7 × 29.4 cm. • Hakone Art Museum, Kanagawa Prefecture

135. Ikkyū • religious aphorism (法語) • Muromachi period (mid-fifteenth century) • ink on paper • 133.3 × 41.8 cm. • Shinju-an, Daitoku-ji, Kyoto

136. Hakuin • Sanskrit character (梵字) • Edo period (mid-eighteenth century) • ink on paper • 107.8 × 56.7 cm.

137. Jiun • religious aphoism (常在靈鷲山) • Edo period (late eighteenth century) • ink on paper • 116.0 × 53.7 cm.

138. Jiun • the character "Buddha" (佛) • Edo period • ink on paper • height: 29.4 cm.

139. Jiun • the character "Man" (人) • Edo period • ink on paper • 42.2 × 57.5 cm.

140. Jiun • the characters *Ai-zan* (愛山) ("Love of Mountains") • Edo period • ink on paper • 49.4 × 62.4 cm.

141. Jiun • the characters *Kan-gin* (閑吟) ("Reciting Poetry Quietly") • Edo period • ink on paper

142. Ryōkan • poem (七絶一首) • Edo period (early nineteenth century) • ink on paper

143. Ryōkan • religious aphorism (人間是非一夢中) • Edo period • limed engraving on wood

144. Ryōkan • excerpt from an ink rubbing of the manuscript of *Tenshinchō* (天眞帖) • Edo period

145–154, 159–175. The approximate dates for the structures and gardens listed are as follows: Katsura Imperial Villa, first half of seventeenth century; Hiun-kaku, late sixteenth century; Ryōkaku-tei, late seventeenth to early eighteenth centuries; Teigyoku-ken, mid-seventeenth century; Sa-an, mid-eighteenth century; Fushin-an, late sixteenth century; Shōseien, mid-seventeenth century, Stone Garden (Ryōan-ji), early sixteenth century.

176. "Tortoiseshell' *temmoku* teabowl with phoenix design (玳玻天目) • Chi-chou ware • Sung dynasty • mouth: 12.7 cm.

177. Ido-type teabowl, named Tsutsu-izutsu (筒井筒) • Yi dynasty • height: 9.4 cm.; mouth: 15.5 cm.; foot: 5.6 cm. • "Tsutsu-izutsu" comes from a line in the *Tales of Ise*, and refers to the name of the bowl's first owner, Tsutsui Junkei (1549–84).

178. Ido-type teabowl, named Kizaemon (喜左衛門) • Yi dynasty • height: 9.1 cm.; mouth: 15.5 cm.; foot: 4.9 cm. • Kohō-an, Daitoku-ji, Kyoto • Named after its owner, Takeda Kizaemon (early seventeenth century), a famous tea master

179. Kugibori Irabo-type teabowl, named Miyamaji (深山路) (Mountain Path) • Yi dynasty • height: 7.6 cm.; mouth: 14.3 cm.; foot: 6.2 cm.

180. Goshomaru-type teabowl, named Furuta Kōrai (古田高麗) • Yi dynasty • height: 7.6 cm.; mouth: 13.0 × 9.7 cm.; pentagonal foot • Named after its owner, Furuta Oribe; *kōrai* is a general term or Korean ware.

181. Goshomaru-type, black brushmarked teabowl, named Hibakama (緋袴) • Yi dynasty • height: 7.4 cm.; mouth: 13.3 × 10.0 cm.; foot: 6.4 cm. • Fujita Art Museum, Osaka • The name means "Scarlet *Hakama*"; *hakama* is a full, divided, skirtlike garment.

182. Komogai-type teabowl, named Kaga-murasaki (加賀紫) • Yi dynasty • height: 7.3–7.6 cm.; mouth: 13.1 × 12.8 cm.; foot: 5.5 cm. • The name, "Kaga Purple," was given because the bowl is purplish and was found in Kaga Province.

183. Sohaku-type teabowl • Yi dynasty • height: 7.0–7.7 cm.; mouth: 8.5 × 9.4 cm.; foot: 5.2 cm.

184. Warikōdai-type, Hagi ware teabowl, named Zegaibō (是界坊) • seventeenth century • height: 9.1–9.4 cm.; mouth: 12.2 ×

15.2 cm.; foot: 7.0 × 8.2 cm. • Zegaibō is the main character, a demon called a *tengu*, in the Nō play *Zegai*.

185. Hagi ware teabowl in the shape of a bowl for washing brushes • seventeenth century • height: 7.9 cm.; mouth: 11.5 × 12.4 cm.; foot: 5.2 cm. • Fujita Art Museum, Osaka

186. Yellow Seto ware teabowl, named Asahina (朝比奈) • end of sixteenth or beginning of seventeenth century • height: 7.5–7.8 cm.; mouth: 12.2 × 13.1 cm.; foot: 6.1 × 6.4 cm.

187. Cylindrical, black Seto ware teabowl, named Hi-no-matsu (日松) • late sixteenth century • height: 11.1 cm.; mouth: 10.6 × 10.9 cm.; foot: 4.9 cm.

188. Cylindrical, old Iga ware teabowl • sixteenth century • height: 11.4 cm.; mouth: 11.4 cm.

189. Hakuan-type teabowl, named Fuyuki (冬木) (Winter Tree) • *ca.* sixteenth or seventeenth centuries • height: 8.8 cm.; mouth: 16.1 cm.; foot: 6.8 cm.

190. Gray Shino ware teabowl, named Mine-no-momiji (峰紅葉) (Mountain Peak Maple) • end of sixteenth century • height: 8.7 cm.; mouth: 14.0 cm.; foot: 62. cm. • Gotō Art Museum, Tokyo

191. Shino ware teabowl, named U-no-hanagaki (卯の花墻) • end of sixteenth century • height: 9.3 cm.; mouth: 11.8 cm.; foot: 6.2 cm. • The name means a fence of white deutzia flowers, referring to the white of the glaze and the fencelike design.

192. Neriage-type, Shino ware teabowl • seventeenth century • height: 8.1 cm.; mouth: 13.4 cm.; foot: 6.5 cm.

193. Shino ware teabowl, named Yama-no-ha (山端) (Mountain Silhouette) • end of sixteenth century • height: 8.5–9.0 cm.; mouth: 13.7 cm.; foot: 5.5–5.8 cm. • Nezu Art Museum, Tokyo

194. Hori-Mishima-type, gray Shino ware teabowl, named Sazanami (さざ波) (Ripples) • end of sixteenth century • height: 8.7 cm.; mouth: 13.0 cm.; foot: 6.5 cm.

195. Karatsu ware teabowl with *ishihaze* effect • seventeenth century • height: 7.3 cm.; mouth: 10.3 × 10.6 cm.; foot: 4.0 cm. • *Ishihaze* refers to the surface effect resulting from pebbles in the clay bursting or expanding during firing

196. Black Oribe ware teabowl, named Matsukaze (松風)(Pine Wind) • end of sixteenth century • height: 6.5 cm.; mouth: 15.7 × 10.3 cm. • Museum Yamato Bunkakan, Nara Prefecture

197. Cylindrical, black Oribe ware teabowl • end of sixteenth century

198. Shinbei • Shigaraki ware teabowl, named Fugen (不言) (No Words) • mid-seventeenth century • height: 6.8–7.2 cm.; mouth: 14.3 × 9.8 cm.; foot: 7.6 × 6.4 cm.

199. Chōjirō • red Raku ware teabowl, named Muichimotsu (無一物) (Not One Thing) • late sixteenth century • height: 8.4 cm.; mouth: 10.6 × 11.2 cm.; foot: 5.0 cm.

200. Chōjirō • black Raku ware teabowl, named Tōyōbō (東陽坊) • height: 8.5 cm.; mouth: 12.2 cm.; foot: 4.9 cm. • This teabowl was owned by a disciple of Rikyū who was abbot of the Tōyō-bō Temple in Kyoto.

201. Chōjirō • black Raku ware teabowl, named Hinsō (貧僧) (Poor Monk) • height: 9.7 cm; mouth: 8.5 cm.; foot: 5.5 × 5.8 cm.

202. Chōjirō • red Raku ware teabowl, named Kokeshimizu (苔清水) • height: 10.0 cm.; mouth: 9.1 m.; foot: 4.5 × 4.9 cm. • The name means the pure water flowing between mossy stones or banks, and was taken from a poem by Saigyō Hōshi (1118–90).

203. Nonkō • black Raku ware teabowl, named Chidori (千鳥) (Plover) • early seventeenth century • height: 7.6–7.9 cm.; mouth; 12.5 × 12.2 cm.; foot: 5.5 × 5.2 cm. • Fujita Art Museum, Osaka

204. Nonkō • black Raku ware teabowl, named Masu (升) • height: 7.6 cm.; mouth: 11.2 × 11.7 cm.; foot: 5.5 cm. • A *masu* is a square box of standard size used as a volume measure for grain, etc.

205. Nonkō • black Raku ware teabowl, named Imaeda (今枝) (named after the owner) • height: 9.3 cm.; mouth: 11.1 × 11.5 cm.; foot: 5.2 × 5.0 cm.

206. Nonkō • black Raku ware teabowl, named Jurōjin (壽老人) • height: 8.8 cm.; mouth: 11.0 × 11.3 cm.; foot: 5.2 cm. • Jurōjin, the Taoist God of Longevity, is characterized by his towering, bald head.

207. Kōetsu • red Raku ware teabowl, named Kaga-Kōetsu (加賀光悦) • early seventeenth century • height: 9.7–8.8 cm.; mouth: 12.7 × 11.2 cm.; foot: 6.8 cm. • Named after Kōetsu and the fact that it was found in Kaga Province.

208. Kōetsu • red Raku ware teabowl, named Otogoze (乙御前) • height: 8.8 cm. mouth: 11.5 × 10.0 cm; foot: 3.8 cm. • *Otogoze* is a moon-faced, puff-cheeked, comic female figure.

209. Kōetsu • black ware teabowl, named Amagumo (雨雲) (Rain Cloud) • height: 8.6–9.3 cm.; mouth: 11.6 × 12.4 cm.; foot: 3.1 cm.

210. Hon'ami Kūchū • cylindrical, black Raku ware teabowl, named Kangetsu (寒月) (Cold Moon) • late seventeenth century • height: 10.5–10.8 cm.; mouth: 8.8 × 8.1 cm.; foot: 5.4 × 4.8 cm.

211. Kenzan • teabowl with waterfall design • end of seventeenth century • height: 7.0 cm.; mouth: 9.5 cm.; foot: 4.0 cm.

212. Asahi ware teabowl, named Kawagiri (河霧) (River Mist) • seventeenth century •

height: 8.3 cm.; mouth: 11.3 cm.; foot: 6.6 cm.

213. Ido-type incense burner, named Kono-yo (この世) (This World) • Yi dynasty • height: 7.6 cm.; mouth: 7.6 cm.; foot: 8.8 cm. • Nezu Art Museum, Tokyo • The name was inspired by a line from a love poem by the middle Heian period poetess Izumi Shikibu.

214. Three-footed, Oribe ware incense container • early seventeenth century • The beadlike design is derived from the shape of round, skewered rice cakes.

215. Oribe ware tea caddy, named Mio-tsukushi (澪標) • late sixteenth or early seventeenth century • height: 9.0 cm.; mouth: 4.8 cm.; foot: 4.2 cm. • *Miotsuku-shi* has many meanings, but here it refers to the kind of buoy used to indicate ship channels.

216. Wide-mouthed, old Seto ware tea caddy, named Shikishima (敷島) • late sixteenth century • height: 5.9 cm.; mouth: 7.3 cm.; body: 10.8 m.; foot: 4.3 cm. • Nezu Art Museum, Tokyo • Shikishima is an old name for Yamato, and thus another term for Japan.

217. Flat-shouldered, old Seto ware tea caddy, named Yari-no-saya (鎗の鞘) (Spear Sheath) • late sixteenth century • height: 9.4 cm.; mouth: 3.3 cm.; body: 5.8 cm.; foot: 4.5 cm.

218. Seto ware tea caddy, named Tengō-an (轉合庵) (after Kobori Enshū's tea room) • sixteenth century • height: 7.4 cm.; mouth: 4.1 cm.; body: 10.6 cm.; foot: 7.0 cm.

219. Flat-shouldered tea caddy, named Matsuya (松屋) • Sung dynasty • height: 7.8 cm.; mouth: 4.7 cm.; foot: 4.9 cm. • Nezu Art Museum, Tokyo

220. Flat-shouldered, old Bizen ware tea caddy, named Sabisuke (さび助) • end of sixteenth century • height: 7.5–7.1 cm.; mouth: 3.7 × 3.4 cm.

221. Painted Shino ware water container, named Kogan (古岸) • end of sixteenth century • height: 18.0 cm.; mouth: 19.2 cm.; foot: 20.2 cm.

222. Bizen ware water container • end of sixteenth century • height: 18.0 cm.; mouth: 18.3 cm.

223. Iga ware vase, named Jorōjin (壽老人) (see Pl. 206) • seventeenth century • height: 28.1 cm.; mouth: 13.0 cm.; body: 13.4 cm.; foot: 11.9 cm. • Nezu Art Museum, Tokyo

224. Shigaraki ware jar with natural ash glaze • Muromachi period

225. Mino-Iga ware water container • end of sixteenth century • height: 18.4 cm.; mouth: 20.5 cm.;

226. Tamba ware vase • late sixteenth century • height: 25.7 cm.; mouth: 7.0 cm.; foot: 11.8 cm.

227. Old Bizen ware vase • late sixteenth century • height: 22.9 cm.; mouth: 13.0 cm.

228. Oribe ware vase • late sixteenth century • height: 30.4 cm.; mouth: 9.6 cm.; foot: 9.8 cm.

229. Mottled, Karatsu ware bowl. • early seventeenth century • height: 8.2 cm.; mouth: 15.0 cm.; foot: 6.6 cm.

230. Handled, Oribe ware bowl. Matsu-kawabishi shape • end of sixteenth ecntury • height: 17.5 cm.; width: 26.3 × 24.4 cm.

231. Handled, Oribe ware bowl • end of sixteenth century

232. Kenzan • ceramic bowl • decorated by Kōrin with figure of Han-shan • end of seventeenth century • height: 2.8–3.0 cm.; mouth: 21.8 cm.; foot: 21.2 × 20.2 cm.

233. Seta Kamon • bamboo tea spoon • late sixteenth century • length: 18.5 cm. • Yōmei Library, Kyoto

234. Hon'ami Kūchū • bamboo tea spoon •

late seventeenth century • length: 17.6 cm. • Yōmei Library, Kyoto

235. Furuta Oribe • bamboo tea spoon • end of sixteenth century • length: 17.5 cm. • Yōmei Library, Kyoto

236. Shutoku • bamboo tea spoon • end of fifteenth century • length: 20.5 cm. • Yōmei Library, Kyoto

237. Hosokawa Sansai • bamboo tea spoon • early seventeenth century • Yōmei Library, Kyoto

238. Sen no Rikyū • bamboo tea spoon • late sixteenth century • length: 17.9 cm. • Yōmei Library, Kyoto

239. Takeno Jōō • bamboo tea spoon • early sixteenth century • length: 19.1 cm. • Yōmei Library, Kyoto

240. Kobori Enshū • one-windowed bamboo flower container, named Fujinami (藤浪) (Wisteria Waves) • early seventeenth century • height: 30.3 cm.; mouth: 14.0 cm.; height of window: 4.4 cm. • Nezu Art Museum, Tokyo

241. Sen no Rikyū • bamboo flower container • late sixteenth century

242. Grained wood tea container (*natsume*) with chrysanthemum relief on lid • late sixteenth century

243. Kōetsu • inkstone box • lacquer with metal inlay, design of bridge and boats • end of sixteenth or early seventeenth century • height: 12.1 cm.; length: 22.7 cm.; width: 22.7 cm. • Tokyo National Museum

244. Iron kettle with "hailstone" surface and *tanzaku* (paper slips for writing poetry) designs • mid-sixteenth century • height: 19.7 cm.; mouth: 15.0 cm.; body: 25.8 cm.

245. Mounting of Mu-ch'i's *Evening of Snow* • A, D. purple silk with large peonies in gold foil; B. yellow-green silk with "Southeast Asian" pattern in silver brocade; C. white silk with small brocade peonies

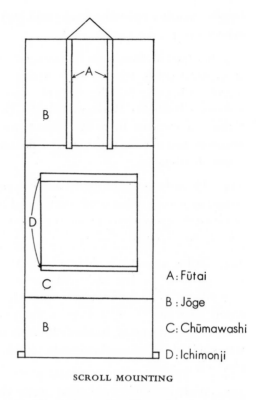

A: Fūtai
B: Jōge
C: Chūmawashi
D: Ichimonji

SCROLL MOUNTING

246. Mounting of calligraphy by Saigyō Hōshi • A, D. purple silk with floral pattern in gold foil

247. Mounting of calligraphy by Eisai Zenji • A, D. brown silk with floral pattern in gold foil; C. purple silk with floral pattern in gold foil

248. Mounting of calligraphy by Ikkyū • A, D. yellow-green silk with hare-and-flower pattern; C. purple silk with peony arabesques in gold foil

249. Mounting of calligraphy by Ikkyū • A, C. brown silk with large peony arabesques; D. light blue silk with large peonies in gold foil

259. Nō mask • Okina (Old Man) • height: 17.9 cm.

260. Nō mask • Magojirō (young woman) • height: 21.5 cm.

261. Nō mask • Hannya (jealous female ghost) • height: 24.6 cm.

262. Nō mask • Emmeikaja (young man) • height: 21.4 cm.

263. Nō mask • Akujō-beshimi (strong old man) • height: 25.7 cm.

264. Nō mask • Yaseotoko ("thin man"; a male ghost) • height: 24.1 cm.

265. Nō mask • Yorōboshi (blind youth) • height: 20.7 cm.

266. Nō mask • Ōbeshimi (strong old man) • height: 21.8 cm.

267. Nō costume • *tsujigahana* dyeing • *ca.* sixteenth century • Tokyo National Museum

268. Nō costume • *surihaku* (applied gold dust) design • sixteenth century • Tokyo National Museum

269. Nō costume • *kara-ori* brocade • seventeenth or eighteenth century

270. Nō costume • *kara-ori* brocade • seventeenth or eighteenth century

271–76. The Nō stage properties pictured are taken from the illustrations in the *Nōgaku Shinyō Daizen,* a mid-eighteenth-century treatise on Nō.

Fig. 1. Mu-ch'i • *Pa-Pa Birds in the Rain* (雨中叭々鳥) • Southern Sung (late thirteenth century) • 81.2 × 21.2 cm.

Fig. 2. Kao Jan-hui • *Flying Swallows and Landscape* (山水飛燕) • Yüan dynasty (fourteenth century) • 100.0 × 92.7 cm.

Fig. 3. artist unknown • *Amitābha Crossing the Mountain* (山越阿彌陀) • Kamakura period (thirteenth century) • color on silk • 101.2 × 83.3 cm. • Konkai Kōmyō-ji, Kyoto

Fig. 4. artist unknown • *Amitābha and Twenty-five Bodhisattvas* (阿彌陀二十五菩薩來迎) (detail) • Kamakura period (thirteenth century) • color on silk • 144.4 × 155.8 cm. Chion-in, Kyoto

Fig. 5. artist unknown • *Acala* (不動明王・赤不動) (known as the *Red Acala*) • Heian period (late ninth century) • color on silk • 165.9 × 95.8 cm. • Myōō-in, Mount Kōya, Wakayama Prefecture

Fig. 6. artist unknown • *Vajrayaksa* (金剛夜叉), one of the *Five Great Protectors* • Kamakura period (*ca.* thirteenth century) • color on silk • Daigo-ji, Kyoto

Fig. 8 (see Pl. 5)

Fig. 9 (see Pl. 16)

Fig. 10 (see Pl 18).

BIOGRAPHICAL NOTES

ASHIKAGA YOSHIMITSU (足利義滿; 1358–1408)
Yoshimitsu was the son of Ashikaga Yoshi-akira, and became the third Ashikaga shogun. In 1395 he entered the priesthood. Famous as the builder of the Rokuon-ji (Kinkaku-ji; the famous Golden Pavilion) in western Kyoto. He attempted to recreate the style of the Heian period nobility in his amusements, but at the same time possessed a deep artistic understanding and played an important part in introducing Chinese painting to Muromachi Japan. (Pl. 89)
1. 天山 (see Note, P. 397)

CHANG CHI-CHIH (Japanese: Chō Soku-shi) (張即之; 1186–1266)
Late Southern Sung period. A native of Ho-chou (present-day Anhui), he was born into a family of Confucians who had served as officials throughout the Sung dynasty. Calligraphy was his particular forte. He had long contact with Buddhist teaching through his more than thirty years' association with Wu-wen Tao-ts'an, and also seems to have been on familiar terms with such priests as Ta-hsieh and Hsi-yen Ch'an-shih of T'ien-t'ung, reaching a high level of attainment in Zen. (Pl. 124)
1. 樗寮 3.溫夫

CH'AN-YÜEH (Japanese: Zengetsu) (禪月; d. 913)
Entered the priesthood at age seven; excelled in poetry. In the T'ien-fu period (901–04) went to Szechwan. When the sovereign Wang Yen (854–925) was searching out worthy men in his western lands, he happened upon Ch'an-yüeh, brought him in for an audience, and awarded him a purple robe, after which he received]the name Ch'an-yüeh Ta-shih. He excelled in calligraphy and painting, and is known for his painting of *arhats*. He died at age eighty-one in Ch'eng-tu. (Pls. 29–32)
3. 德隱

CHIH-WENG (Japanese: Jikiō) (直翁; late thirteenth century)
Chih-weng is thought to be the name of a Zen priest who lived during the Southern Sung period, but nothing is known of his life. His paintings are considered outstanding among the works of Zen painter priests, and are noted for their dark and slender brushwork lines. For a long time he was known as Sotsuō, but restudy of the seals on the paintings has changed this reading to Jikiō. (Pl. 77)

CHUNG-FENG MING-P'EN (Japanese: Chūhō Myōhon (中峰明本; 1263–1323)

Late Sung, early Yüan period Zen monk. Born in Ch'ien-t'ang in Hang-chou. At Shih-tzu Yüan on Mount T'ien-mu he received the *dharma* from Kao-feng Yüan-miao, and after his master's death, succeeded him at the same site. Several times he refused invitations to become abbot of large temples. He hid his talents from the world, living in small hermitages in various places, each of which he named Huan-chu. His exercise of the Way was both masterful and lofty. The well-known Confucian Feng-tzu-chen and the famous painter and calligrapher Chao Meng-fu, to mention only two, are said to have come to him as disciples. He was awarded by imperial decree the title Fo-t'zu Yüan-chao Kuang-hui. (Pl. 125)

1. 幻住道 2. 孫氏 7. 智覺普應，法慧國師

DAITŌ KOKUSHI (大燈國師; 1282–1337)

Born in Issai, Harima Province. He received the *dharma* from Daiō Kokushi (Nanpo Jōmyō). In 1326, at the invitation of the Emperor Hanazono, he built the Daitoku-ji temple in Kyoto. During his lifetime, he was called Kōzen Daitō Kokushi. His eminent disciples included Tettō Gikō and Kanzan Egen. Daiō Kokushi, Daitō Kokushi and Kanzan are called "Ō-tō-kan," from the abbreviation of their names. (Pl. 131)

2. 紀氏 5. 妙超 7. 高照正燈，大慈雲匡真

DŌGEN ZENJI (道元禪師: 1200–53)

He was the son of a high government official named Kuga Michichika. He first studied Zen with Eisai Zenji, and in 1223 he left Japan for Sung China, where he received the *dharma* from the master Ju-ching of T'ien-t'ung. Dōgen thus became the transmitter to Japan of Sōtō Zen. He built the Kōshō-ji temple in Uji, later went to Echizen Province at the suggestion of his lay disciple Hatano Yoshishige, and there built the Daibutsu-ji (the present Eihei-ji). He stayed there for the remainder of his life. (Pl. 132)

1. 佛法房 5. 希玄 7. 佛性傳東國師，承陽大師

FURUTA ORIBE (古田織部; 1544–1615

A native of Mino Province. During the Tenshō era (1573–92) he gained the title Oribe no Shō. He studied Tea with Sen no Rikyū, and became one of Rikyū's "Disciples." He adapted Rikyū's taste to the military class and became Tea master to the shogunate. He developed many tea implements described as being of Oribe *konomi*, among which is the famous pottery style still bearing his name. The path he followed was continued by his successor Kobori Enshū. He is said to have had religious instruction from Shunoku Sōen. Committed suicide by order of the shogun. (Pl. 235)

6. 左介，重然

HAKUIN EKAKU (白隠慧鶴; 1685–11768)

Born in the village of Hara, Suruga Province. Hakuin was *dharma* successor to Shōju Rōjin Etan of Iiyama, Shinano Province. He returned as the head of the Shōin-ji, the temple of his native place. Thereafter, he rebuilt the Ryūtaku-ji, Izu. He received the posthumous titles Jinki Dokumyō and Shōsō Daishi. His disciples include Gasan Jitō (1727–97), Tōrei Enji (1721–92) and Suiō Genro (1716–89). His fame derives from his religious profundity, his success in spreading Zen to the general populace, his masterful calligraphy, Zen paintings, popular songs, books, etc. (Pls. 4, 6, 108–13, 136)

1. 鵠林，閡提翁，沙羅樹下老人 2. 杉山氏
5. 慧鶴

HASEGAWA TŌHAKU (長谷川等伯; 1539–1616)

Born in Noto Province. Tōhaku went to Kyoto and studied painting with the Kanō school. He also studied the painting of Sung and Yüan China, and eventually founded his own school. At different times he seems to have studied with Tōshun of the Sesshū line, Shōshō of the Soga school, and various masters of the Kanō school, but he revered Sesshū so much that he claimed himself to be the "fifth generation Sesshū." (Pls. 5, 98, 99; Fig. 9)

HON'AMI KŌETSU (本阿彌光悦；1558–1637)

Kōetsu's ancestors had been swordsmiths and appraisers, and he started his career in this field. His energies and wide interests were too strong, however, and he became both one of the most creative figures in the history of Japanese art and an artist of tremendously wide achievement—truly a Japanese "Renaissance man." At one point he studied under Furuta Oribe. In 1615 he was granted land at Takagamine in northern Kyoto, where he created a community of artists and craftsmen, whose work infused the entire Japanese art world with new vigor. (Pls. 18, 23, 207–09, 243, Fig. 10)
1. 自徳斎, 徳友斎, 大虚庵　6. 次郎三郎

HON'AMI KŪCHŪ (空中斎光甫；1601–82)

The grandson of Hon'ami Kōetsu. Besides continuing the Hon'ami family tradition of sword appraising. Kūchū was an excellent painter and calligrapher, potter, and Tea master belonging to the so-called Kōrin school. He left outstanding tea spoons signed with needle engraving, as well as excellent ceramic tea utensils. (Pls. 210, 234)
1. 空中齋　4. 光甫

HOSOKAWA SANSAI (細川三斎；1563–1645)

Azuchi-Momoyama, early Edo period. He served the three successive ruling houses of Oda, Toyotomi, and Tokugawa, and was given the fief of Kokura, Buzen. He studied Zen under Kokei and Gyokuho. He devoted himself to many arts, including the martial arts, and was particularly devoted to Tea, which he studied with his father Yūsai and with Sen no Rikyū. He is counted as one of the Tea masters known as the "Seven Disciples" of Rikyū. He is said to have labored to reestablish the Sen line after the death of Rikyū. (Pl. 237)
4. 忠興　6. 與一郎

HSIA KUEI (Japanese: Kakei) (夏珪；late thirteenth century)

From Ch'ien-tang. During the reign of Ning-tsung (1195–1224) he became the resident painter in the painting academy and was awarded the Golden Belt. Studied with Li T'ang and Mi Fu, and alongside Ma Yüan was considered an emminent artist of the Southern Sung Academy. In contrast to Ma Yuan's emphasis on powerful brushstrokes and orderly forms, Hsia valued ink tones and scenes of misty irregularity. Sesshū's brushwork and use of ink are said to be strongly influenced by Hsia Kuei. (Pl. 51)
3. 禹玉

HSÜ-T'ANG CHIH-YÜ (Japanese: Kidō Chigu) (虚堂智愚；1185–1269)

Zen monk of the late Northern Sung period; tenth generation in the Yang Ch'i line. The *dharma* teacher of Daiō Kokushi. He was a native of Hsiang-shan in Hsi-ming (Hui-chi, Chekiang). Received the *dharma* from Yün-an P'u-yen of T'ien-ning. In 1229 he joined the priesthood at Hsing-shen in Chia-ho, and subsequently served in the Pao-lin, Yü-wang, Pai-yen, Ching-t'zu, and Ching-shang temples. (Pl. 123)
1. 息耕　2. 陳氏

HUAI-SU (Japanese: Kaiso) (懐素；737–99?)

Middle T'ang. Born in Hunan. Left the secular world and joined the piesthood. He was a friend of Yen Cheh-ch'ing (709–85), a high government official and celebrated calligrapher. He was fond of calligraphy and drink, and when drunk could achieve perfect concentration in his grass style writing. He called himself the "Mad Monk." (Pl. 7)
2. 錢氏　3. 蔵真

HUANG T'ING-CHIEN (Japanese: Kō Teiken) (黄庭堅；1045–1105)

Famous Confucian of middle Northern Sung period. A native of Fen-ning in Hung-chou. Received his *chin* degree in 1066. A follower of Su Tung-po, both his poetry and calligraphy were excellent. He studied Zen

under the guidance of Hui-T'ang Tsu-hsin.
(Pl. 121)
1. 山谷道人　3. 魯直　7. 文節先生

IKKYŪ SŌJUN (一休宗純; 1394–1481)
A Zen priest of the Muromachi period and
the forty-seventh abbot of Daitoku-ji. His
mother is said to have been the consort of
the Emperor Gokomatsu. He received the
dharma from Kesō Shūdon of Katada, Gō-
shū. Entered Daitoku-ji in 1474 and there
built the Shinju-an subtemple. Later he
rebuilt Shūon-an in southern Kyoto, and
there lived the life of a recluse. He was
humorous and unconventional, and spent
his entire life as an *unsui,* or wandering
priest. Through poetry he sharply criticized
the religious and cultural life of the time.
(Pls. 135, 248, 249)
1. 狂雲子, 夢閨, etc.　5. 宗純

I-SHAN I-NING (Japanese: Issan Ichinei)
(一山一寧; 1247–1317)
The founder of the Issan branch of the Rinzai sect. From Chekiang Province. *Dharma*
successor to Wan-chi Hsing-mi of Ming-
chou, fourth generation after Mi-an Hsien-
chieh (1118–86). In 1299 came as an envoy
of the Yüan government to Dazaifu (Kyu-
shu), was temporarily confined there, but
afterwards summoned by Hōjō Sadatoki to
Kamakura, where he became the tenth head
of Kenchō-ji. Later he held positions as
head of Engaku-ji, Jōchi-ji, Nanzen-ji, etc.
(Pls. 8, 130)
2. 胡氏　7. 妙慈弘濟禪師

IWASA SHŌI (岩佐勝以; 1578–1650)
Painter of the early Edo period. Raised in
the Iwasa family of Echizen. In his later
years he was invited to Edo by the shogun.
He called his style an offshoot of the Tosa
school, but took pleasure in choosing subjects from the genre tradition. (Pls. 100,
101)
6. 又兵衛

JIH-KUAN (Japanese: Nikkan) (日観; late
thirteenth century)

Southern Sung. A Zen monk of the Mao-
nao-ssu temple in Hsi-hu. Jih-kuan liked to
drink, it is said, and enjoyed playing with
children when he was drunk. He painted
ink-wash pictures of grapes, and many of
these works were brought to Japan. One
such painting in the Inoue collection is
dated the tenth day of the seventh month,
1291; another, in the Nezu collection, was
painted in the eighth mouth of 1288. Thus
Jih-kuan seems to have been active during
the latter half of the thirteenth century.
(Pl. 76)
1. 日観, 知歸子　3. 仲言

JIUN ONKŌ (慈雲飲光; 1718–1804)
Founder of the Shingon *shōbō-ritsu* (precepts
of the true law) subsect. Born in Osaka.
From an early age visited many masters and
gained a wide knowledge of several sects of
exoteric and Esoteric Buddhism as well as
its meditative and disciplinary schools. He
became an accomplished scholar of Sanskrit and was well versed in Confucianism,
Shinto, Chinese classics, history and poetry.
He withdrew from the world into Kōki-ji
temple in Kawachi when he was fifty-eight.
(Pls. 137–141)
1. 百不知童子　2. 上月氏

JOSETSU (如拙; fifteenth century)
Little known of his life. He was a painter
priest recognized by the Shogun Ashikaga
Yoshimochi during the "Five Mountains"
period in Kyoto. His style shows a new
variation on the Sung and Yüan painting
that influenced him. A painting generally
attributed to Josetsu, *The Three Sages—*
Buddha, Lao-tzu, Confucius—in the Ryō-
soku-in of Kennin-ji, lists the death of the
artist as 1405. (Pls. 86, 87)

KAŌ (可翁; fourteenth century)
Personal history unknown, but once considered as one with Ryōzen. According to
a Japanese history of famous priests and an
Edo work on art (*Koga Bikō*), his name was
Sōnen; he was born in Chikuzen; he joined
the priesthood and about 1317 crossed to

Yüan China, where he stayed ten years. On his return, he became chief abbot of Sūfuku-ji temple in Chikuzen and later held the same post in several Kyoto temples. He died, by the same account, in 1345. Although the information here cannot be trusted, it is certain that Kaō, together with Mokuan, played a major role in building the foundations of Japanese ink painting. (Pl. 83)

KAO JAN-HUI (Japanese: Kōnenki) (高然暉; *ca.* fourteenth century)

In a major historical source for Chinese painting (*Kundaikan-sayū-chōki*; Muromachi period), the only thing noted is that he was of the Yüan period; there is nothing about him in Chinese records. His name may be a misreading of Kao Yen-ching (Kao K'o-kung), but this also is uncertain. His use of dots and line shows independence and a grasp of the unique features of Sung and Yüan painting, thus linking him with the Southern Sung style. (Pl. 50; Fig. 2)

KOBORI ENSHŪ (小堀遠州; 1579–1647)

Early Edo period. Served Toyotomi Hideyoshi and Tokugawa Ieyasu during the Keichō period (1596–1611). After studying Tea under Furuta Oribe, he became Tea master for the shogunate. All his tea utensils are imbued with *sabi*. During this time he studied Zen with Kōgetsu Sōgen (1574–1643). His tea rooms include the Mittan of Ryōkō-in (Daitoku-ji), the Bōsen of Kohō an, and the Hassō of Konji-in. He directed the Asahi, Zeze, and Takatori kilns along with the other "Seven Kilns of Enshū." (Pls. 21, 240)

1. 宗甫, 孤篷庵, 轉合, etc. 6. 作助

KU-LIN CH'ING-MAO (Japanese: Kurin Seimu) (古林清茂; 1262–1329)

Zen monk of late Sung-early Yüan. Eleventh generation from Yang-ch'i. Usually called Mao Ku-lin (Japanese: Mukurin). A native of Wen-chou. He received the *dharma* from Heng-ch'uang Hsing-kung of Neng-jen Temple in Yen-tang. He entered

the priesthood at Pai-yün-ssu temple in Chiang-chou, and later served as abbot of Kai-yüan, Hu-ch'iu, Yung-fu, and Pao-ning temples. His outstanding disciple was Liao-an Ch'ing-yü. Another disciple, Chu-hsien Fan-hsien, went to Japan. Getsurin Dōkyō and Sekishitsu Zenkyū were among his Japanese disciples. (Pl. 127)

1. 金剛憧, 休居叟 2. 林氏 7. 佛性禪師

LIANG K'AI (Japanese: Ryōkai) (梁楷; early thirteenth century)

Knowledge of Liang K'ai's life is found only in the *T'u-hui-pao-chien* ("Precious Mirror of Pictures"). He was skilled at painting figures, landscapes, Taoist and Buddhist subjects, demons and gods. During the Chia-t'ai period (1201–04) he was painter-in-attendance at the Imperial Painting Academy. Although awarded the Golden Belt, he did not keep it himself but hung it in the academy. He liked wine and drank often. Other painters of the academy were awed by his brushwork. The only extant works are very brief, in a style called "abbreviated brush." (Pls. 1, 37–46)

1. 梁風子

LIAO-AN CH'ING-YÜ (Japanese: Ryōan Seiyoku) (了庵清欲; 1288–1363)

Zen monk of the late Yüan period, twelfth generation in the Yang-ch'i line. He was a native of Lin-hai in T'ai-chou. He received the *dharma* from Ku-lin Ch'ing-mou. Entered the priesthood at K'ai-fu Temple in P'iao-shui and was later abbot of Pen-chüeh in Chia-hsing and Ling-yen in Su. (Pl. 122)

1. 南堂遺老 2. 朱氏 7. 慈雲普濟禪師

LING-SHAN TAO-YIN (Japanese: Reizan Dōin) (靈山道隱; 1255–1325)

Sung Dynasty. Patriarch of the Fo-hui line. Born in Hangchow. His family name is not known. He succeeded to the *dharma* of Hsüeh-yen Tsu-ch'in in the line of Wu-chun Shih-fan. His fellow disciple at the time was the Japanese Shōitsu Kokushi. In 1319 (or 1318) he went to Japan at the invitation of Hōjō Takatoki. He became the nineteenth abbot of Kenchō-ji, the twelfth abbot of Engaku-ji, and served in other famous temples. (Pl. 129)

LI T'ANG (Japanese: Ritō (李唐; early twelfth century)
From Meng, Honan Province, San-ch'eng, Ho-yang. He entered the Emperor Hui-tsung's art academy, but at the fall of Northern Sung he moved south to Ching-nan. With the reestablishment of the academy under the Southern Sung he once again became a member and in his old age became painter-in-attendance. He first studied painting under Li Ssu-hsün (1129), known for his "blue, green and gold outline" style. Then he adopted the northern landscape style of Li Ch'eng and Kuo Hsi, unifying the former's "ornamental subjectivism" with the latter's "objective realism," and developed his own new and independent style. There is a story that when Hui-tsung gave an examination on choosing a poem title, Li was the only successful candidate. (Pls. 35, 36)

MA LIN (Japanese: Marin) (馬麟; early thirteenth century)
Son of Ma Yüan. Served in the Sung Painting Academy under emperors Ling Tsung and Li Tsung. Received and carried on the traditional style of the Ma line, drawing landscapes in which mountains and streams are only partially stated. He specialized in painting plum trees. Painting histories claim he did not reach the heights his father achieved, but he seems nevertheless to have excelled in flowers, grasses, birds and animals. In any event, his art is representative of the Southern Sung Academy style. (Pls. 52, 54)
3. 欽山

MA YÜAN (Japanese: Baen) (馬遠; late twelfth century)
Active about the time of the Emperor Kuang Tsung (1190–94). Painter-in-attendance at the Sung Painting Academy. The outstanding talent among the six men over

five generations in the Ma line. Along with fellow member Hsia Kuei, he is an exemplary representative of the Southern Sung Academy's landscape style. Said to have studied painting under Li T'ang. In the dry ink brushwork of his trees, rocks and cliffs he used large, hatchetlike strokes. His compositions most often used the "one corner" style, and he was thus called "One-corner Ma." He exerted a great influence on later Chinese and Japanese painting. (Pl. 49)

MIYAMOTO NITEN (宮本二天; 1584–1645)
Real name: Musashi. Early Edo period. Son of Shinmen Munisai of Harima, but adopted into Miyamoto family. Reknowned as a swordsman. He is said to have studied with Kaihō Yūshō, but his preference for monochrome ink painting and his style suggest influences from the "abbreviated brush" style of Liang K'ai. He did many paintings of birds and of Taoist and Buddhist subjects. He showed a preference in the latter for fierce, quick depictions. (Pls. 102–07)

MOKUAN (黙庵; early fourteenth)
Mokuan Reien was once thought to have been a Yüan painter, but he was in fact a Japanese Zen monk who crossed to Yüan China and studied under famous teachers in various parts of the country. He died around 1345, without returning to Japan. Because most of his active life was spent in China, few of his works survive today. But he has long been a famous figure in Japanese ink painting. (Pl. 85)

MU-CH'I (Japanese: Mokkei) (牧谿; late thirteenth century)
Mu-ch'i is the style name of the priest Fa-ch'ang, a native of Szechwan. In Hang-chou he rebuilt the ruined monastery Lui t'ung-ssu on the shores of the Western Lake. He is thought to have been active in this region, but little has come to us about his painting career. He died between 1335 and 1340. He chose for his subjects dragons, tigers, monkeys, birds, landscapes, trees,

stones, human figures. He is considered the greatest of the ink-monochrome painters. (Pls. 2, 55–72; Figs. 1, 8)

MURATA SHUKŌ (村田珠光; 1421–1502)
Muromachi priest. The son of Murata Mokuichi, a blind court musician. Entered the priesthood at Shōmyō-ji in Nara. Later studied Zen under Ikkyū. Said to have built a hermitage in the Sanjō area of Kyoto and to have lived his life there in accordance with the Way of Tea. Served as Tea master for Ashikaga Yoshimasa. It is thought he studied painting and ikebana under Nōami, and also had enormous influence on later generations as the founder of *wabicha*. (Pl. 91)

MUSŌ SOSEKI (夢窓國師; 1275–1351)
Born in Ise. Received the *dharma* from Kōhō Kennichi. In 1325 he became chief priest of the Nanzen-ji temple by imperial decree of Emperor Godaigo. He next became chief priest of each of these temples in turn: Jōchi-ji, Engaku-ji, Erin-ji, Rinsen-ji, Saihō-ji. In 1339, by order of Ashikaga Takauji, he founded the Tenryū-ji temple. Among the many Zen-inspired gardens he built are the famous temple gardens at Tenryū-ji and Saihō-ji. (Pl. 134)
2. 藤原氏　3. 夢窓　5. 疎石　6. 七朝帝師
7. 夢窓正覺心宗普濟國師

NAN-CHÜAN (Japanese: Nansen) (南泉; 748–834)
Zen monk of the middle T'ang period, three generations from Nan-yüeh. Teacher of the famous Chao-chou Ts'ung-shen. Native of Cheng-chou in modern Honan. Received the *dharma* from Ma-tsu Tao-i, then went to live on Mount Nan-ch'üan in Ch'ih-chou (modern Anhui Province). He did not leave the mountain for thirty years, thus his name, Nan-ch'üan. (Pl. 116)
2. 王　5. 普願　6. 王老師

NONKŌ (のんこう; 1599–1659)
Potter of the early Edo period, the third generation and one of the more famous men

in the Raku line started by Chōjirō. He probably was inspired in his work by his relationships with Tea men such as Hon'ami Kōetsu and Sen Sōtan. He refused to pass on to his disciples certain of his methods for preparing and applying glazes. (Pls. 203–06)
1. 道入

OGATA KENZAN (尾形乾山; 1663–1743)
Middle Edo period. Native of Kyoto. Younger brother of Ogata Kōrin. While at the Jikishi-an in Saga, under the tutelage of the priest Dokushō, he devoted himself to painting, pottery, and other arts. Especially important is the instruction he received from the master potter Ninsei. In 1699 he built a kiln at Narutaki, in the Izumidani district of western Kyoto, and there produced the Kenzan pottery that boasts the fine designs of the Kōrin school. Later he moved to the Kantō area (which includes today's Tokyo) and made those pieces that are known (from the location of the kiln) as Sano Kenzan wares. (Pls. 211, 232)
1. 乾山, 深省, 陶隠, 尚古齋, 習静堂,　4. 惟允
6. 新三郎, 権平

RAKU CHŌJIRŌ (樂長次郎; 1516–92)
Azuchi-Momoyama period potter. Under Sen no Rikyū's direction he built kilns at Juraku-tei and there fired teabowls and other objects made with local clay. He is remembered especially for his Kyō, Ima and Juraku wares. As the earliest works to be designed from the outset for use in the Way of Tea, these have strongly influenced the pottery of later generations. His extant works include the well-known "Seven Bowls of Chōjirō." (Pls. 199–202)
1. 長祐　2. 田中, 樂

RYŌKAN (良寛; 1758–1831)
Edo period. Native of Echigo Province. Zen monk of the Sōtō sect. *Dharma* successor to Priest Kokusen of the Entsū-ji, Bitchū Province, who was twenty-five generations removed from the founder of the Sōtō Sect, Dōgen Kigen. Following the

death of his teacher in 1791, he lived in a hermitage called Gogō-an on Mt. Kugami in Niigata Prefecture. He mingled with villagers during his travels as a mendicant priest, and was known for his fondness for children. He left many *waka* and examples of his calligraphy. (Pls. 9, 142–44)

1. 大愚　2. 山本，3. 曲　4. 榮藏

SEN NO RIKYŪ (千利休; 1522–91)
Azuchi-Momoyama period. Native of Sakai. His real name was Tanaka Yoshirō, which he later changed to Sen Sōeki. Rikyū was his name as a Buddhist layman. He studied Tea with Kitamuki Dōchin and Takeno Jōō, and Zen from Shōrei Shūso and Kokei Sō-chin. He became the leading Tea master of the day, serving both Oda Nobunaga and Toyotomi Hideyoshi. Using the finest from the tradition of *wabi* Tea as it had evolved since Murata Shukō, he brought his rich creative powers to bear on the famous Kita-no tea meetings and on the synthesizing of a cultural system that made the traditions of the *roji* and *sōan* tea house a part of everyday life. His inspiration gave birth to Raku ware teabowls and his architectual preferences are seen in the Fushin-an and Myōki-an tea houses. He was ordered to commit suicide when he incurred the anger of Hideyoshi. (Pls. 238, 241)

SESSHŪ TŌYŌ (雪舟等揚; 1420–1506)
Born in Bitchū Province. Studied Zen as a youth at the Shōtoku-ji in Kyoto. Studied painting under Shūbun. In 1467 he traveled to Ming China. He painted some wall paintings in the Li-pu-yüan. After his return to Japan in 1469 he devoted himself to painting, spending most of his time in Yamaguchi Province. He died at age eighty-six. Many details of his life are still vague, particularly those about his youth. (Pls. 3, 92, 93)

SETA KAMON (瀬田掃部; 1548–95)
Azuchi-Momoyama period. Given an official position by Toyotomi Hideyoshi: chief of the Ōmi region. Studied Tea under Sen no Rikyū was and counted as one of his

teacher's "Seven Diciples." (Pl. 233)
4. 正忠，伊繁

SHIH-K'O (Japanese: Sekkaku (石恪; mid-tenth century)
Five Dynasties period. Born in Ch'eng-tu, capital of the Shu state (Szechwan). He served in the Sung capital as an official painter. Unsatisfied, he returned to Szech-wan. He was a humorous man given to joking, but he was also thoroughly versed in Confucianism. His painting style shows deep composure as well as wit. Many later painters learned from this combination of qualities. (Pls. 33, 34)

SHINBEI (新兵衛; sixteenth to seventeenth century)
Middle Edo period. Native of Kyoto. At first a trader in foreign goods. Studied Tea with Kobori Enshū. Also made tea caddies and bowls. He made and fired caddies at Kyoto, Mino, Bizen, Karatsu and Satsuma. Shinbei Shiga Raku is a generic term used for those works he produced from clay dug in the Shiga area. (Pl. 198)

2. 有來

SHUTOKU (珠徳; early sixteenth century)
Disciple of Murata Shukō. He was a craftsman of tea spoons (*chashaku*), at first making them from ivory and later from wood. These were known as the Shutoku style. Still later, it is said, he fashioned them from bamboo, in accord with Shukō's preferences. (Pl. 236)

SHŌITSU KOKUSHI (聖一國師; 1202–80)
Founder of the Tōfuku-ji temple in Kyoto. He was born in Suruga and went to Sung China in 1235. He joined Wu-chun Shih-fan on Mount Chia and received the *dharma* from him, carrying on the Zen of the Yang-ch'i line. He introduced to Japan the Neo-Confucianism of Chu-hsi and the literature of the Southern Sung. (Pl. 133)

1. 辨圓　2. 平氏　5. 圓爾　7. 聖一國師，寶鑑廣照，神光國師

SŌAMI (相阿彌; d. 1525)

Sōami is another name for Shinsō, son of Shingei, grandson of Shinnō. Nōami (Shinnō), Geiami (Shingei), and Sōami (Shinsō), the "three Amis," served the Ashikaga house for three generations. Sōami was the art advisor for the Shogun Yoshimasa. He was a skilled painter and wrote outstanding *renga* (linked verse) as well. He wrote the *Kundaikan-sōchōki*, a secret catalogue of the art works in the Ashikaga family collection. This is an extremely valuable document for judging the authenticity of paintings brought from China during that period. (Pls. 94–97)

SOGA DASOKU (曾我蛇足; d. 1483)

A friend of Ikkyū Shūjun, said to have learned painting from Shūbun. He did some of his work in the head priest's residence at Shinju-an, Daitoku-ji. As recorded at the Shinju-an, he died in 1483. (Pl. 90)

4. 宗譽

TA-HUI TSUNG-KAO (Japanese: Daie Sōkō) (大慧宗杲; 1089–1163)

Zen monk of the early Southern Sung period. Fifth generation in the Yang-ch'i line. Born in Hsüan-chou Ning-kuo (modern Anhui). Received the *dharma* from Yüan-wu K'o-ch'in at T'ien-ning-ssu temple in Tung-kung. At first he led a hermit's life in Ku Yün-men, Chiang-hsi. Later he spent time in Yü-wang and Ching-shan. He became involved in a political incident and was exiled for a time to Heng-chou and then to Mei-chou. (Pls. 118, 119)

1. 妙喜, 大慧　2. 系氏　3. 曇晦

7. 普覺禪師

TAKENO JŌŌ (武野紹鷗; 1502–55)

Late Muromachi period. A merchant from Sakai who dealt in leather for weapons and armor. He studied Tea under Shunkō and poetry under Sanjō Nishi Shōyuin Sanetaka. At forty-eight he studied Zen under Ōmori Sōtō and received the name Ikkan Koji. He built the Daikoku-an and there devoted himself to *wabi* Tea. (Pl. 239)

TAN'AN (單庵; active in sixteenth century)

According to the *Tōhaku Gasetsu* ("Tōhaku's Talks on Painting"), recorded by the priest Nittsū of the Honpō-ji temple, Tan'an was the son of a handicraft painter in Amagasaki. The painter Shinsō, impressed by his painting, asked the young man to study with him. Tan'an did become a pupil, but died at age twenty-five or twenty-six, leaving few works. It appears he studied the painting of Mu-ch'i and Yü Chien. His brushwork shows a delicate appreciation of ink gradations. (Pl. 88)

1. 單庵　4. 智傳

WU-AN P'U-NING (Japanese: Gottan Funei) (兀庵普寧; 1197–1276)

Second abbot of the Kenchō-ji temple in Kamakura. Founder of the Gottan branch of the Japanese Rinzai sect. He was originally from Hsi-shu. He stayed with Wu-chun Shih-fan at Yü-wang and Ching-shan and received the *dharma* from him. He built a small temple at Ling-yen on Mount Hsiang, but in 1260 he came to Japan at the invitation of Hōjō Tokiyori. He stayed for four years and then returned to China, where he lived, among other places, at Shung-lin in Wu-chou and Chiang-hsin in Wen-chou. (Pl. 120)

7. 宗覺禪師

WU-CHUN SHIH-FAN (Japanese: Bushun Shiban) (無準師範; 1177–1249)

Zen monk of the late Southern Sung; ninth generation in the Yang-ch'i line. He was born in Tsu-t'ung in the state of Shu (Mien-chou in Szechwan). He received the *dharma* from P'o-an Tsu-hsien of Ling-yin. Thereafter he lived at Hsüeh-tou in Ming-chou, at Yü-wang, Ching-shan in Hangchow, and elsewhere. He was awarded the title Fo-chien Ch'an-shih by Emperor Li-tsung. (Pl. 128)

1. 佛鑑禪師　2. 雍　3. 無準　5. 師範

7. 圓照

WU-HSÜEH TSU-YÜAN (Japanese: Mugaku Sogen) (無學祖元; 1226–86)

Founder of Engaku-ji in Kamakura. A native of Ming-chou. Received the *dharma* from Wu-chun Shih-fan of Ching-shan, and in 1278 he came to Japan by invitation of Hōjō Tokimune. His *dharma* successor was Kōhō Kennichi, who was the teacher of Musō Kokushi. (Pl. 126)

2. 許氏　3. 子元　7. 佛光國師, 円満常照國師

YIN-T'O-LO (Japanese: Indara (因陀羅; mid-fourteenth century)

Yüan Dynasty. Said to have been the head priest of the Ta-kuang-chiao-ch'an-ssu temple in Pien-liang, Honan. It has been suggested, judging from his name, that he was born in India and traveled to China later, but the details of his life are entirely unknown. (Pls. 78–82)

YÜAN-WU K'O-CH'IN (Japanese: Engo Kokugon) (圜悟克勤; 1063–1135)

Late Northern Sung period. Fourth generation Zen priest in the Yang-ch'i (Yogi) line of the Lin-chi school. Born in P'eng-chou (in modern Szechwan). He was a *dharma* successor to Wu-tsu Fa-yen (1024–1104). Called one of the "Three Buddhas," along with Fo-yen Ch'ing-yuan and Fo-chien Hui-ch'in. He was officially invited by Chang-shang-yü to live at the Ling-chü'an on Mount Chia in Li-chou (present Hunan). He later lived in Tao-lin, Chiang-shan, T'en-ning, Wan-shou, Chin-shan and else-where. In old age he returned to his old temple in C'heng-tu. (Pl. 117)

1. 佛果老人, 圜悟　2. 駱氏　3. 無著
7. 真覺禪師

YÜ CHI (Japanese: Gushū) (虞集; 1272–1348)

Well-known Confucian of the Yüan Dynasty. A native of Szechwan. In 1297 he served the Yüan government. During the reign of Emperor Wen Tsung he became a member of the Imperial Secretariat and was responsible for the formulation of administrative laws. He was an excellent poet, calligrapher and writer of prose. (Pl. 115)

1. 道園　3. 伯生　6. 雍公, 邵庵先生
7. 文靖

YÜ CHIEN (Japanese: Gyokukan) (玉澗; mid-thirteenth century)

There were three painter-priests of Sung times called Yü-chien. Among these the one whose real name was Jo-fen is believed to be the Yü-chien who, with Mu-ch'i, is judged one of the most distinguished painters of the golden age of ink painting. Jo-fen was from Wu-chou. He was a clerk at the Shang-t'ien-chu-ssu temple, but later returned to his native place and devoted himself to painting. His work is characterized by the free use of dark and light gradations of ink. (Pls. 73, 74)

3. 仲石

Note: The numbers and characters following each entry give names other than those used in the entry heading.

1. (号): style.
2. (俗姓): (a priest's) secular name.
3. (字): an extra name added to a family name, out of respect (in China) or at adulthood (in Japan). Not used by commoners unless famous.
4. (名): first name.
5. (諱): honorific title, conferred during life or after death.
6. (稱): nickname.
7. (諡): posthumous name.

INDEX